For Love, With Love, Through Love

For Love, With Love, Through Love

by Patricia "Patsy" Soto

Queenship

PUBLISHING COMPANY
P.O. Box 220 • Goleta, CA 93116
(800) 647-9882 • (805) 692-0043 • Fax: (805) 967-5843
http://www.queenship.org

To Whom it May Concern:

Patricia Soto is an active member of SS. Peter and Paul Parish in Wilmington. She is well known by her pastor as well as her Spiritual Director, Father Sean Cronin, a man of high repute and learning in our Archdiocese. While I have not personally heard her speak, I have the assurance from her Spiritual Directors that she is orthodox in her teaching and obedient to the magisterium of the Church. In addition, many fine priests of good standing who know her vouch for her honesty and goodwill. In the past she has spoken before many groups and has been well received.

I hope this will be helpful and will allow you to give Patricia Soto hospitality and welcome.

Very Sincerely Yours,
Most Reverend Joseph M. Sartoris
Auxiliary Bishop of Los Angeles
San Pedro Regional Bishop

Cover painting by Marge Thornberry. Used by permission.

Library of Congress Number # 00-132056

Published by:
    Queenship Publishing
    P.O. Box 220
    Goleta, CA 93116
    (800) 647-9882 • (805) 692-0043 • Fax: (805) 967-5843
    http://www.queenship.org

Printed in the United States of America

ISBN: 1-57918-129-5

Acknowledgments

I remember being told once by a very special spiritual teacher/ advisor, Mrs. Zelda Woeber, to be careful what you ask Jesus for; "He just might give it to you!" This advice came after I had already gone to Jesus and pleaded with Him, "Just save my husband and kids and I'll do anything you ask!" I didn't really expect Him to take me up on the last part of the sentence.

One day as I was returning a book about Our Lady appearing in Medjugorje to the library of St. Pius in Buena Park, I happened to see a sign about information being given that day in the church auditorium. So I went in to listen. When it was over, I went up to the people in charge asking for prayer for my daughter, who was in the hospital at the time. They offered to go to the hospital and pray with her, but I told them I didn't really think she wanted that. They asked me to speak to her and see. Two days later, they went to visit and pray with her at the hospital and two weeks after the visit, my daughter was in Medjugorje. I have never had the opportunity to go to Medjugorje, but I always say, Our Lady brought Medjugorje to me.

Something very special began to happen to me during the time my daughter was away. I didn't call them experiences because that is not the right word, so I'll call it a "journey."

This journey began in 1986, and in the past ten years Jesus has placed many special spiritual teachers/advisors to make sure someone was always there to watch over me.

Since this really isn't "my" book, as I was only Jesus' secretary, I asked Jesus if it was OK to dedicate this book. He said "yes" and even placed on my heart whom I should dedicate it to and thank.

First, my husband Art; to my children Jimmy, Ryan, Traci and Staci; to my parents Frank and Cecilia, all who have given me love and support. My spiritual directors over the years: Fr. Richard Hoynes, Fr. Paul Caporali, Fr. John Neiman, Fr. John Hughes and Fr. José Vettiyankal.

Finally to Fr. Luke Zimmer, my first spiritual director, who was there with me from almost the beginning. He now is at home with Jesus, and probably telling Jesus, "tell her not to be so impatient, all in His time."

Most important, I thank you, Jesus, for loving us all so much, giving us your teachings in the word, that we may know you; dying for us that we may have eternal life; the Sacraments, the Sacrament of Reconciliation, where we seek your forgiveness in order to prepare ourselves to receive the greatest miracle; you alive in the Sacrament of Holy Eucharist. And as You wait for us to visit you in the Tabernacles all over the world and love us even when we fail You, may we all surrender to your Holy Will, so that we may someday be with you in heaven.

— Patricia Soto

Foreword

This book follows others previously published, and it brings messages from the realm of the divine where the Father, the Lord Jesus and His Spirit have their abode. Mary speaks also to Patricia as in the past, and what they say is neither new nor different. It is obvious that the Gospel message comes through at its warmest and most loving level.

The ring of the mother's earnest concern for her children is easy to detect. The persistent question, however, still remains. Is this really Jesus and Mary, or some of the saints speaking? Unless the Church formally passes judgment, we will never know. Yet, if, reading through these expressions, we receive exhortation to a deeper, more faithful, prayerful Christian life, could we attribute these messages to anyone else but the Spirit of God? Saints and mystics reassure us that anything which enhances our devotion and draws us closer to God cannot come from the evil one.

I would like to remember, at this point, the episode in the Gospel where the Apostles were complaining that others were doing good works in the name of Jesus. Jesus simply said: "Let them. Whoever is not against us is for us." (Mk. 9, 40).

Another hallmark of authenticity is the obedience of the Christian soul to the prompting of the Spirit. These messages were humbly submitted, apparently by the request of the giver, to the scrutiny of a priest, for theological content. And they were approved. So, whether the messages were directly spoken by the Lord and His Mother or through other media, the content is helpful and sound. To read them with a spirit of criticism, or worse, cynicism, would destroy the possibility of any good receivable through them.

May God's blessing reach and stay with all those who accept these messages and follow the prompting of the Spirit through them.

Rev. Paul M. Caporali, S.D.B.
March 3, 2000

Introduction

The human heart finds little comfort in today's society. The overdrive of hype in business, politics, sports and entertainment imposes a grave distortion of reality upon all of us. We find ourselves swept along as in a tidal wave or cast aside, should we resist or question value or purpose. We often feel confused, helpless and isolated. "My flock is straying this way and that on mountains and on high hills ... no one bothers about them and no one looks for them." (Ezekiel 34:6).

Sacred Scripture addresses our needs down through the ages, but the noise of the world puts so many distractions in our way, diverting us from the true path of life. "The Lord is the strength of His people, the saving refuge of His anointed." (Ps. 28:8).

Christian people in many countries are hearing messages in their hearts which have a distinct quality of compassion for the helpless as well as inspiration for the humble and faithful. They are impelled to share their hearts with others, but are often repelled by blind minds and the deaf ear. "Reflect on the injunctions of the Lord, busy yourselves at all times with His commandments. He will strengthen your mind and the wisdom you desire will be granted you." (Sirach 6:37).

We all need help to listen carefully to the caring love and liberating mercy of Our Lord Jesus while Mary whispers her encouragement to her children. Jesus and Mary are totally devoted to our welfare, in loving detail. The Spirit of Divine Love shines upon the openhearted, seeking to embrace and animate us with new life.

Patricia Soto is chosen by God, guided by her spiritual advisors and encouraged by her love of souls to help us listen to the whispers of understanding shared with her by Jesus and Mary. We are blessed by such sharings and impelled to respond with whispered prayers of hope, love, faith and courage, to follow the way of life set out for us. We need to ponder the call of God to Elijah on Mt. Horeb. After mighty wind, earthquake and fire, God empowered Elijah by a gentle breeze, (1 Kings 19:8-18) and he obeyed God's call to anoint the new King for His people.

Inspired by the Sacred Heart of Jesus on the cross and the intense love of Mary's Immaculate Heart at the foot of the cross, we are persuaded to a new love. We must turn from darkness and selfishness to love of God and neighbor. We need to see, in a new way, those hurts and needs of one another. We need to listen carefully as God's loving whisper echoes in our hearts. It is then that sincere prayerfulness happens and we can come alive with the Spirit of God. We can sense Mary's motherly love and compassion. "My soul magnifies the Lord and my spirit rejoices in God my Savior." (Lk. 1:46).

As though welcoming you into a new neighborhood, may the reader feel welcomed into these pages which open before you. May you feel invited to pause and chat with Jesus and Mary as their words touch your heart. Try to open more freely and promptly to the touch of God's Spirit. Embrace a renewed spirit of life — more complete and profound than the many changes of our material life-styles. Let all speak their "yes" along with Jesus and Mary, "that they may have life … to the full." (John 10:10).

We need to savor our prayerful response, take our time with Jesus and Mary and smile with God's peaceful presence — in our Father, Our Lord Jesus and Our Holy Spirit, now and always.

— Fr. John C. Hughes, M.S.
Feast of the Epiphany — January 2, 2000

Mystical Mass Prayer

Father Luke Zimmer, SS.CC.

Eternal Father, we offer to You,
through the Immaculate and Sorrowful Heart of Mary
and the Just Heart of Joseph, in the Holy Spirit,
the Body, Blood, Soul and Divinity of our Lord Jesus Christ,
in union with each Mass celebrated today
and every day until the end of time.
With Mother Mary, St. Joseph,
each Angel and Saint in heaven, each soul in Purgatory, each
person in the Body of Christ and the family of God,
we offer each act of love, adoration, praise and worship.
We offer each act of thanksgiving
for blessings, graces and gifts received.
We offer each act of reparation for sins that have been, are
being and will be committed until the end of time.
And we offer each act of intercessory prayer.
We offer all of these prayers in union with Jesus in each Mass
celebrated throughout the world throughout all time.
We stand before You, Triune God,
like the Prodigal Son asking to be accepted,
like the Publican asking for mercy and forgiveness,
like the Paralytic asking for healing and strength,
and like the good Thief asking for salvation.
We consecrate ourselves and all of creation to You.
Eternal Father, we ask You in the Name of Jesus, through
the power of His Precious Blood, through His death on the
Cross, through His Resurrection and Ascension, to send forth
the Holy Spirit upon all mankind.
Holy Spirit, we ask for an outpouring of Your graces,
blessings and gifts;
upon those who do not believe that they may believe;
upon those who are doubtful or confused, that they may
understand; upon those who are lukewarm or indifferent,
that they may be transformed; upon those who are constantly
living in a state of sin, that they may be converted;
upon those who are weak, that they may be strengthened;
upon those who are holy, that they may persevere.
We ask You to bless our Holy Father. Give him strength and

health in mind, body, soul and spirit. Bless his ministry and
make it fruitful. Protect him from his enemies. Bless each
cardinal, bishop, priest, brother, sister and all aspiring to the
religious life, especially ... and grant many the gift of
a vocation to the priesthood and religious life.
Bless each member of our families,
relatives and friends, especially...
Bless the poor, the sick, the underprivileged,
the dying and all of those in need...
Bless those who have died and are in a state of purification,
that they may be taken to heaven...
We offer and consecrate ourselves and all of creation to you,
Heart of Jesus, Mary and Joseph.
We ask you, Mary and Joseph, to take us
with all of our hopes and desires.
Please offer them with Jesus in the Holy Spirit
to our Heavenly Father,
in union with each Mass offered throughout all time.
We consecrate ourselves to Archangels Michael, Gabriel and
Raphael, and each Angel, especially our Guardian Angel. We ask in
the Name of Jesus, through our Mother Mary,
Queen of all Angels, that You, O Heavenly Father,
send forth legions of Angels to minister to us:
Archangel Michael with his legions to ward off the attacks
of the world, the flesh and the devil;
Archangel Gabriel with his legions to teach us
that we may know and do Your will,
and that they may help us to catechize and evangelize;
Archangel Raphael with his legions to heal our woundedness,
supply for our limitations, strengthen us in our weakness, to
overcome demonic depression, to give us joy in the spirit,
to protect us in our travels and to supply for all of our needs.
Finally, we ask for the gift of unconditional love,
that we can live the love-life which was reflected in the
Holy Family at Nazareth, thus bringing about
justice and peace throughout the world.
Amen

Nihil Obstat: Very Rev. Richard Danyluk, SS.CC. Provincial
Imprimatur: Most Rev. Archbishop Roger Mahony, D.D.
Archbishop of Los Angeles, CA, U.S.A.
January 7, 1986

Book I

May 18, 1991
St. Paul of the Cross, 7:50 A.M. Message from Jesus

Little one, listen with your heart for I, your King, Son of the Father, speak this to you: "Unless you become as small children, you shall not enter into the kingdom of my Father."

My Holy Mother goes to many of my children pleading for prayer. She has asked many of my children to plead for my mercy.

Little one, if you will continue to visit me and pray with me daily, I say to you, "Walk the holy way of my cross; you shall see many changes — you will feel my precious love."

My Holy Mother has given my children many tools to fight the evil one — the daily rosary. Now my precious one, I also reveal to you the holy way. Walk with me daily this journey to the cross and you shall be sustained to do my Holy Will.

Oh my precious one, how I yearn for all of my children to listen to my Holy Mother's plea for prayer. I do not want to bring chastisement to any of my children, but this evil must be stopped! **I am the way! I am the light!**

Thank you, my littlest, for doing as my Holy Mother requested. I leave my Little Theresa to guide you. Seek her intercession and my Holy Will shall be done.

Prostrate yourself before me and beg my forgiveness and mercy for all my children.

May 30, 1991
10:45 P.M. Message of Our Lady

My Holy blessed Son has asked that you open your heart to learn intercessory prayer through my daughter, Little Therese.

My daughter, you do not feel at ease taking this message: there is much you do not understand, child.

Pray for understanding through the Holy Spirit.

May 31, 1991
9:35 A.M. Message of Our Lady

Dearest Patricia, do not be afraid but listen with your heart.

I, your Heavenly Mother, come to you this morning to continue my message which you were unable to continue.

Child, why do you not think my Son would allow Little Therese to speak to you? My daughter, if you will accept, my Son's Holy Will shall be done.

Little Therese will teach you the desires of my Son.

Intercessory prayer is prayer which deepens one's faith and exercises the mind and will into total obedience to my merciful Son.

Child, my daughter Therese is a great example of this, and that is why she has been chosen for you. Listen with your heart to my little Therese and you will learn much.

No, my child, you will continue to receive my messages, but they will not continue daily.

The messages now will be of instruction through my daughter Therese.

I ask, my daughter, that you continue in the daily method of prayer that you have been using, especially the Most Holy Sacrifice of Mass and receiving of the Blessed and Holy Sacrament of the Eucharist. This, my child, is spiritual nourishment in its greatest form.

You are saddened, my daughter, but do not be, for I am not leaving you, my child. As I have told you, the messages will continue, but not daily. Will you accept my Holy Son's request even though you do not understand?

As you finish evening prayer tonight, my daughter Therese will begin teaching you, little one.

May 31, 1991 Friday
Instruction from St. Therese

My dearest Patricia, I come to you this evening as requested by my Heavenly King and Father.

Dearest one, I have been asked to give you instruction on intercessory prayer. As we begin, let us pray together for my King's blessing. [We knelt and prayed the Our Father].

Little one, ask the Holy Spirit to fill your heart and mind with sincere contrition. [St. Therese asked that I do this now].

Now child, you remain very silent — the stillness should come from the depth of your soul. You must surrender mind, body and soul unto the Holy Spirit. Welcome the Holy Spirit with total submission to His Will.

You must realize the Holy Spirit lives within you; you are His temple. As you remain in the state of grace the Holy Spirit is alive within this temple.

Right now you are learning faith. You listen to this voice in your heart. Your mind tells you it is yourself speaking, but the Holy Spirit gives you this faith to know it is Our King, Our Heavenly Queen and Mother, or myself speaking to you.

It is the Holy Spirit that gives you this warm feeling right now as I speak.

This, little one, is enough for today. I ask that as you pray tonight, begin to open your heart to the Holy Spirit for His direction in prayer. Begin by first asking forgiveness as I told you in the beginning. We shall now kneel and ask Our King for His blessing. Remember humility and piety is walking in the steps of Our Beautiful King and Almighty Father.

June 1, 1991
11:47 P.M. Instruction from St. Therese

My dearest Patricia, Thank you for remaining obedient to Our King's wishes.

Child, this evening you will learn that, as you begin to internally meditate in your mind, prostrate yourself before Our Heavenly Father, asking forgiveness for all past actions which have offended Him. Now, still seeing yourself prostrated before Him, ask His divine mercy be given to you and all of mankind.

A willing soul can be used mightily, because a willing soul is a loving soul wishing to be used for Almighty God's glory.

You must learn to draw your strength for spiritual bonding to Almighty God from the Holy Spirit.

When you come to distraction during prayer you should immediately call upon the Holy Spirit. [It is at this time St. Therese gave me her prayer to the Holy Spirit].

Prayer of St. Therese To The Holy Spirit

Begin each morning by asking Jesus:
"Take not thy Holy Spirit from me."

Most Divine Holy Spirit, come to my aid.
You are my strength. Make my desire a total
commitment to my King's Almighty Will.

I place my complete trust in your guidance and direction and
I beg that you place your divine graces in every cell of my
being, body, soul and mind.
Amen.

You must always remember you are our Savior's vessel and
must constantly remind yourself you are nothing without our Savior
Jesus Christ Almighty.

"Little" must be your most ardent desire in order to remain
"little" for Our King's Almighty Reign.

My precious Patricia, release your will totally to the Holy Will
of Our Divine Savior.

Now child, let us kneel and pray the Prayer for Divine Mercy.

I will meet with you tomorrow evening after evening prayer.

June 2, 1991
11:45 P.M. Message of Our Lady; Feast of Corpus Christi

My precious daughter Patricia, thank you for listening with
your heart. Child, you are very tired, but I ask that you listen
carefully.

Little Therese has given you a prayer to the Holy Spirit, which
is to be published.

The world is in time of tribulation and great suffering. My Holy
Son wishes to bring peace. Through prayer, sacrifice and devotion
to the Holy Spirit this can be accomplished.

Kneel, my child, for my blessing. You will now receive instruction from my daughter, Little Therese.

June 3, 1991
12:15 A.M. Instruction from St. Therese

Dearest Patricia, it is time for me to speak to you of discernment.

Discernment is one of the gifts of the Holy Spirit and is used during intercessory prayer. It is by the grace of the Holy Spirit that you are warned of that which is evil.

It is through intercessory prayer that one dispels evil. It is not the person praying, but the Holy Spirit inside the person praying.

Little one, you are finding this lesson difficult. I ask that you pray to our Heavenly King for His mercy and to the Holy Spirit for the graces to allow you to open your heart to this instruction. I will continue this lesson in the morning.

June 3, 1991
8:55 A.M. Instruction from St. Therese
(continued from evening before)

Little one, through intercessory prayer you are calling upon our King and Savior, through the graces of the Holy Spirit, to accept your meek and humble prayer.

It is through intercessory prayer that a lost soul will be brought back to our Almighty King.

I spoke of discernment which is used to distinguish right from wrong and good from evil. Discernment through Intercessory Prayer allows one the ability to acknowledge truth from deceit. There are many times the evil one will try to deceive one into thinking he is doing our King's work, when in fact it is the evil one trying to defile one's soul.

June 3, 1991
11:45 P.M. Instruction from St. Therese

Dearest Patricia, this evening I will speak to you about faith.

The gifts of the Holy Spirit are all used during intercessory prayer, but faith is the most important.

As you release your will freely to our Savior through the Holy Spirit then you allow the work of our King to begin.

Remain *"little"* Patricia — it is through "littleness" that you become truly Our Savior's vessel.

Remember, little one, faith is a gift. Receive these gifts with Love and cherish these gifts by honoring our King through love.

Let us kneel and pray the Divine Mercy Prayer.

June 5, 1991
Instruction from St. Therese

Dearest Patricia, the gifts of the Holy Spirit are given to all at the time of Baptism. As one grows and matures, they should be taught about these gifts.

They should begin to realize the Holy Spirit is alive inside of oneself as long as they remain in the state of grace.

One should begin to understand these teachings to know how to pray.

A person comes to know the reality of the Holy Spirit as they come closer to a true commitment of their faith.

Child, it is through these teachings that one comes to the understanding of all prayer.

Child, you must begin to use what I have given you through instruction. Read it over and ask the Holy Spirit to keep this instruction implemented in your heart and mind through the mercy of our Divine Savior.

September 12, 1991
St. Paul of the Cross, 7:50 A.M. Message from Jesus

[I asked the Holy Spirit to direct me in Bible reading. I opened the Bible to Luke, Chapter 10: The Mission of the Seventy-Two]

I bring you, little one, to the ascension of this mountain. Be not afraid, for I will always be with you. It is to the cross, my precious, we will ascend. I invite you, little one, to now walk with me. Listen to your heart, little one, for I am the God of Everlasting Love.

My children do not realize that I am alive. They call me a myth, a figment of the imagination. [Jesus, how can you call them your children then, if they don't even acknowledge you?] Because, little one, I died for all — I love all my children. It is not necessary for them to love me to receivemy love, for I give it to all willingly. But it is necessary for them to know me so that they can begin to love me.

[I don't understand.] Little one, when children are conceived and brought into this world, I have already loved them through the Crucifixion for all humanity. But they have not known me yet for they have just entered the world. Now they should begin to learn about me, but many do not. It is not their fault, but whose fault little one?

[The parents?] No, child — humanity's! [How can it be humanity's fault?] They crucified me and continue to crucify me daily through their sin! [But what does that have to do with knowing and loving You?] How can they know me and love me if they continue in sin? So how can those little ones entering the world of sin know who I am? [Oh Jesus, I truly do not understand!] Then you must pray more for this direction from the Holy Spirit and as you read this over again you will begin to understand.

Do you remember in the song of love ... the forest? [Yes, my Jesus.] Well, you cannot ascend up the mountain until you clear the forest. [What is the forest; will I see it?] You are seeing it now, through the question you have asked me. [You mean understanding what you have told me this morning?] Yes, my little one.

Listen with your heart, my little one. Do not doubt, but trust me, love Me and surrender totally to me all of you, for as you surrender mind, body, soul and will, then I will transform you. You are my creation from the beginning. I am the Supreme Being and can do all. Nothing is an impossibility with me. But I will never take away anyone's free will. This must be your gift of love to me.

[I feel like it's going to take so long for me to learn and understand all of this.] Little one, did I not just finish telling you nothing is an impossibility with me? Time is nothing to me, little one, for my time is not like your time. Do not worry about these things — did I not just finish telling you to trust me? It is not you who will make you understand all of this; it is all done through me. Continue to open your heart to me, little one. Love me ... just love me!

September 13, 1991
St. Paul of the Cross, 8:30 A.M. Message from Jesus

Come, my little one, we shall again begin our journey in the song of love.

Do not be overwhelmed by the intensity of my profound love. Why do you expect less? [Jesus, I guess it is still hard to believe this is really happening!] Oh my little one, such lack of faith, like my Thomas — but I have given you my fruits of love, have I not? [Oh yes, Jesus!]

It is by faith, my little one, that you will overcome the obstacles placed before you as you make this journey with me. It is my presence within you that clears the obstacles in your path. Have you not understood what my Little Theresa gave you in the instruction of faith? Have you not continued daily to request I take not the Divine Holy Spirit from you? [Yes, my Jesus.]

Little one, desiring the Gifts of the Holy Spirit is the beginning of accepting my Holy Will and also a release to my all merciful love. It is this love that transpires the beginning of My Holy Union with you as one. This is enough for today, my little one.

September 14, 1991,
St. Maria Goretti, 7:30 A.M. Message from Jesus

Now, my little one, let us ascend to my triumphant cross.

This journey ... why are you afraid little one? [Because I don't know what to expect.]

My Joy, my precious! The sacrifice of my Body and Blood that was given to all! But so many do not partake of this, my food of spiritual nourishment. As each one partakes of my holy spiritual nourishment they receive the greatest miracle and are not even aware of this treasure!

You have come to realize my Holy Presence in this my spiritual food of nourishment. For you little one, it is still not knowing what or when. Is it not enough that my children gather with you in the prayer and Sacrifice of the Holy Mass? [Yes, my Jesus but I don't understand all of this. Where is it all leading?]

It is all leading to me, little one! Trust me, my little one! Do not look behind, for that part of your life is gone. Do not look ahead for that time is not here. But be with me now for *I am always* here within! Follow with Trust and Faith. Allow my presence within to soothe your wounds.

Do you see, my child, this forest which contains uncertainties? trust me and I will lead you through! Look at my gifts of love, little one. Receive my peace and receive these gifts to comfort you!

September 15, 1991
St. Pius V, 7:45 P.M. Message from Jesus

Little one, ascend with me to the triumphant cross. Are you willing, my daughter, to carry my cross?

You have heard in today's Gospel how my children were unwilling to accept my teaching and denied that I was teacher and Prophet — especially those of my townspeople who knew I was the son of a carpenter.

Many will mock you because of me. Many will doubt and bring doubt to your mind, but you must have faith and trust. Did you not begin to despair as you saw nothing but desert? But little one, I asked you to be not afraid and trust me and I brought you through the desert, did I not? [Yes, my Jesus, I was afraid and it was hard to trust, but after you brought us through I knew how faithless and untrusting I was … and I am sorry.]

I know, my little one. I continue to ask you to release yourself totally to me. Surrendering all will bring you strength through me. Do you feel the gentleness of my love? No other can give this to you, my little one! Through the trials and crosses of love I bring you this serenity as a gentle spring flowing through the wilderness. Continue, my lamb, to seek my love and it will flow abundantly through you!

September 16, 1991
St. Pius V, 7:50 A.M. Message from Jesus

Little one, once again we begin this journey.

Oh precious one, you have begun to realize the importance of calling upon the Holy Spirit. For it is His grace of direction and guidance which opens your heart to listen.

Yet many who have seen *still do not believe*! If my children would only come to me in faith and trust, their hearts could hardly sustain the magnitude of my love! Immerse yourself *totally* in me for I am the font of life! Deepen the unquenchable thirst for the fruits of the Divine Holy Spirit, for it is these fruits that will sustain you.

Walk in faith with me, little one, and you will be denied nothing. My people continues to deny the truth of my existence through their atrocities of sin. Those of my children willing to suffer the glory of my cross for humanity's sake will live within me and I within them.

Continue, my little one, to strive for my glory as you become one with me, for me, through me!

September 17, 1991
St. Paul of the Cross, 8:20 A.M. Message from Jesus

Let us begin this journey of dalvation, little one. Do you not know that I am salvation? [Yes, Jesus] Then why do my children deny me? [Because of sin?] Their sin? [No, not just their sin, but the sin of mankind.] Yes, my little one. You seemed perplexed when my beloved Paul spoke to you that even the sinners are part of my Mystical Body. [Yes, it would seem that if they're sinners they couldn't be part of your Mystical Body, but I just understood what you mean: we are all sinners!] Yes, my little one, all sin is serious, whether small or great!

[But if they don't want to belong to you and you say we have a free will, then how can they be your children?] Oh, my little one, whether they do not love me or want to belong to me does not take away my love from them. For I do not force them to love me or to want to belong to me; I only continue to love them. My love is never taken away from *any* child!

So you see, my little one, my love *even for those* children continues on! my love has never stopped, nor will it ever stop for any of my children.

September 26, 1991
St. Paul of the Cross, 8:35 Message from Jesus

Ah, my little one, such love you give me! You see, my little one, what my daughter Therese has told you in her teachings;

allowing the Holy Spirit to guide you in prayer, calling upon the Holy Spirit, begging My forgiveness. This, my little one, teaches you prayer from the heart — what my Holy Mother speaks of to all her children.

Now, precious one, let us begin our journey. There is still much doubt created by the evil one, but you begin to see his ploy. His temptations seem innocent, but oh, what lies! Through his maneuvering and tactics he's like the snake waiting to consume his prey so cautiously. But do not be deceived, for when he cannot encompass his victim, he becomes forceful and his measures become unruly.

But you have been taught and are protected by Michael, my powerful one, and you are not to fear. How many times I have told you: "Greater am I in you than he who walks this world."

You see, my little one, when temptation came upon man, he was not prepared, for he knew nothing of evil. My Father gave him innocence and purity in the beginning, but Satan was evil-consumed and in satanic arrogance Satan knew that man was given a free will. To deny this free will was not my Father's desire, so He allowed temptation. "For all is in accordance with my Will" says my Father.

As I spoke to you yesterday of original sin, you will understand my Father's just punishment at that time — which now brings us to Noah and the just punishment given then. Yet my Father said He would never again destroy all of humanity through the waters [floods].

My little one, consider Sodom and Gomorrah and my Father's just punishment through fire. Not all of humanity was punished. Do you recall Lot's wife being turned to salt for disobeying my Father's word?

[Dearest Jesus, I'm nothing before you! I don't want us destroyed, but I understand you have no choice because of this great evil. I don't really know what to say or how to feel right now... My Jesus, I only know I love you and want to please you!] Oh, my little one, you have been overwhelmed by today's lesson... It is a very difficult teaching, my little one!

Many chances have been given, but my children continue to sin and the *atrocities are unspeakable and unthinkable!* You feel very sad, my little one. You are feeling **only a very small fraction of my grief!** You could not withstand it if I allowed you to feel any more, so for now, my little one, your pain will remain constant. Oh, my little one, how special you truly are to me!

My little one, you will all go with my love and travel with my blessings and the protection of my holiest and mightiest of angels. Know I am with all of you! Kneel for your blessing...

September 27, 1991
St. Paul of the Cross, 8:25 A.M. Message from Jesus

Now, my little one, our journey continues.

In the depths of one's soul man can find his answer in truth, for the truth of my existence was placed in each man's soul. It is renewed in the receiving of my Holy Body and Blood — the greatest form of nourishment! Satan thinks that by destroying my temple — the soul of man — he can destroy my existence. But my Father will never allow this! For you see, my little one, I am the Resurrection! My Father is the Creator. Many will try to disclaim this, but it is truth unchangeable! my daughter, we must continue this lesson as you can return to me later today, for my Holy Mass has begun.

September 27, 1991
St. Pius V, 11:55 A.M. (continued)

Thank you, my little one, for returning.

Since man has free will to take the direction he desires, he does not realize that he is allowed to do so even though he chooses evil over me.

It is not a question of right or wrong, for I have told you that sin is sin. It is a question of whether man is willing to allow the loss of his soul for **all eternity!** His free will is never taken away. But the all-pure love and holiness of man's soul, placed there in the beginning, is now stained with the original sin of Adam.

Upon entering into this world, this sin must be removed by the Holy Sacrament of Baptism. I have spoken to you this: **free will** is *given* to man! As he comes to the age of understanding and reason, if he has allowed the re-entrance of sin then sin continues to encompass the soul if not freed by the Sacrament of Reconciliation. Man is taught through sin that prosperity is happiness and that man can and should do whatever it takes in order to continue his happiness. But man, once caught up in this error, becomes blinded to the truth of my Father;

What does man do for the **eternal** happiness of his *soul?*

September 28, 1991
St. Paul of the Cross, 8:45 A.M. Message from Jesus

As we ascend the mountain in the song of love, I speak to you, my little one, as I began — on the **importance** of reconciliation. In yesterday's teaching I spoke of sin, and understanding the stronghold Satan has once he manipulates his way into the soul of man through sin.

They become bonded to him through drugs, sex, lies, stealing, etc. All this they think is very innocent in the beginning, but the evil turns into distorted atrocities and killings. My daughter, it **must stop!**

Though you have committed these horrendous atrocities **I tell you now: Come back to me! I tell you now, humanity: Ask my forgiveness! hear my Holy Mother's plea.**

Man must comprehend what I speak of when I say the soul lives on forever. **Choose now, my people! I make this promise to those of my children who hear my words and act upon them through prayer, sacrifice and the spreading of my messages: I will save your families and those of you who take up my cross will live with me forever!**

September 29, 1991
St. Paul of the Cross, 8:45 A.M. Message from Jesus

My little one, let us ascend the mountain. Together we go forward!

Man has given himself honor in place of honoring my Father. Man has placed himself above the Creator, for man now has taken upon himself who is to live and who is to die!

Satan, fool as he is — since he ever desires living sacrifice, cannot implant his desires into the *soul* of man. The soul is judged and sent either to my Father's Kingdom or the pits of hell. But the soul will *always* belong to the Creator, my Father.

[Jesus, are you saying that Satan can never own the soul?] Yes, my precious little one! Satan has power to *rule over* the soul, but the soul will *always* belong to my Father-Creator. However, the suffering of the soul in the pits of hell is that it will **never** again be allowed the eternal joy of the Blessed Trinity.

Satan, at the end, will be returned forever to the pits of eternal hell to rule over himself.

October 2, 1991
St. Paul of the Cross, 8:15 A.M. Message from Jesus

My teachings, my precious, have thus far shown my Father's justice and all-consuming love for mankind — and the weakness of man to sin! Man closed his heart, mind, and soul to the Creator, my Father, just as Lucifer did with his bold attempt in the beginning to be greater than my Father, only to find his capabilities limited.

This, my little one, is the point man has reached. In the time of Lucifer, my Father banished Lucifer to the pits of hell, not destroying Lucifer and his band of evil conspirators.

You are in a time when there are continuous killings of my innocents; and I speak not only of abortion. There will be **no next generation** if man continuously destroys itself with the misconception that it has this right! Lucifer's plan is to destroy mankind. To take the entire universe with him to the pits of hell is his ploy. Man, blinded to truth, is allowing itself to be lead into his plan.

Now, my little one, through my Holy Mother's peace plan which has taken her all over the world to many victim souls, this offering of genuine love is restoring unification to my One True Church. But it shall take **more prayer and sacrifice**.

The love and offering of the Holy Mass in honor of the Feast of St. Therese was pure and holy in every sense of the word. There was a unity felt, as well as the presence of peace and love. My Holy Mother cries out to her children for this! This peace, love and unity can happen if my children will do as my Holy Mother requests, for nothing is an impossibility with me! My children must make their choice.

Come back to me, my people. Do not allow yourselves to remain blinded to my truths by Satan and his followers! Open your hearts, minds and souls to peace and unification through prayer, sacrifice and my Holy Mother's continuous pleas of reparation in this, her peace plan!

October 3, 1991
St. Paul of the Cross, Message from Jesus

Little one, as we ascend yet to a higher level on the mountain in the song of love, I ask that once again in your mind, you prostrate yourself before me, begging forgiveness for humanity's continuous sin.

Oh, my little one, man continues to deceive himself with the thinking that the world is fine the way it is. They fear nothing and though they see the world is in a real depression, they think the economy will clear itself and all will be back to normal. But they are very sadly mistaken, for the economy will drop to such a level as never before seen in the history of man! Even those who have always been well off will not be able to withstand such a change in their life style.

Man has continuously mocked me in his filthy portrayal of such horrendous nature in his movie making.

I understand your uneasiness at this message, but man must be made to understand that my Father **will not allow this horrendous desecration to continue!** It has come to a point that this desecration to the Blessed Trinity, the murderous contamination of His Creation and disassemblance and disarray in the Holy Mother Church will not be allowed to continue much longer!

I spoke yesterday of how the graces and gifts from me within *one* man could have stopped a schism. My little one, the **prayers, sacrifices** and **renunciation** pleaded for by my Holy Mother *must continue* by my beloved children!

If all my children would realize the power of the Blessed Sacrament of Penance and of the Holy Eucharist and understand the **importance** of truly seeing me in this Holy Eucharist, they would prepare themselves in order to receive the *limitless* Graces and blessings they are receiving. For they are receiving **all of me** in this blessed form! I ask all my children to become aware of my Holy Presence not only within the Holy Eucharist, but to realize my Presence in the **tabernacles** in all of my Churches. [**Come to me, my people, with reverence and love, for I have given all of me to you through my death on the cross and I come to you Resurrected in the blessed Eucharist!**]

October 8, 1991
St. Paul of the Cross, Message from Jesus

Little one, as we ascend the mountain we climb to yet another level in the song of love: your desire to love and please me.

You became overwhelmed when your heart was opened to the realization that I come to you, not only daily in the Blessed Eucharist, but now through my desire to show you my love in the offering of my Holy Mass at the Cenacle. If my children would allow my Presence within to reveal my love, they would desire never to leave my Presence.

A child learns love through example, but a child's love is pure and innocent. As he matures and develops, his love and trust in me should also mature and develop. But if the example and teachings discontinue, the child begins to seek his example and teaching in other areas. *The television becomes a child's constant companion and teacher!* Soon other youngsters become his teacher. Soon this child neither wants nor desires the example and teaching of the parents and the child never learns of my Presence in his life!

So how can this child see me within him, if he doesn't even know I exist?

My little one, I have never left them! I *must wait* until someone's prayers have reached this child's heart and then, as the child opens his heart to my desire, I allow my Presence within to be revealed.

October 10, 1991
St. Paul of the Cross, Message from Jesus

My little one, we begin again the ascension of the mountain in the song of love. This next plateau is the beginning road leading to the **foot of the cross.**

My little one, it is man's continuous sin which has never allowed my cross to be removed. It is this evil which has completely surrounded man on earth. If I were to allow the evil atrocities of man to continue, this darkness would consume the earth!

I have given my teaching so that man may once again return to my everlasting salvation.

From the beginning of time God, my Father, gave man a chance through His all-merciful Love. When man denied truth a second time, my Father's hand of justice came upon man. It has been so from the beginning and will be so to the end.

Man must realize he is being given another chance! My Mother began in Fatima and is continually returning to man through other apparitions, pleading always for man to return through Prayer, Sacrifice and Reparation. This has always been my Holy Mother's peace plan allowed by my Father; a chance for mankind to come back to truth.

Now I come through my teachings, asked by my Holy Mother and Queen to *renew* my children in heart, mind and soul. As I walked the earth and gave my children teaching.

Now I come again to give my word to you Oh my people! Will you offer a deaf ear or will you follow me as my children did in the days of old? You have been given *another chance* through the all-merciful love of my Father!

October 11, 1991
St. Pius V, 5:45 P.M. Message from Jesus

Little one, as we ascend the mountain in today's song of Love, you see the overwhelming obstacles and deliberate confusion caused by the evil one in order to dissuade you and the others from my holy mission.

But, as I have told you many times, you must *trust in me* for my Holy Will is to be done. This is the time my children are to call out to me! Pray for those of my children who continue with materialistic and irresponsible behavior. They are being led astray by sin!

[But Jesus, if they are not acknowledging You because of sin, how can they call on you?] My daughter, listen with your heart. I have told you many times that my children can desire me though they do not acknowledge my truth by their continuous acts of sin.

Do you see the power of prayer, sacrifice and renunciation? I am willing to receive my children *through even their slightest desire for* my love! For through even such slight desire, I will save any of my children from the fires of eternal damnation.

I have told you before; it is with **much sorrow** that a soul **through its own choice** enters the flame of justice! For I refuse *no* man if he asks my forgiveness or seeks my all-merciful love!

The evil one causes dissension and confusion. This is his way; my way is peace and love. Which do you think my children *should* want? [Your peace and love, my Jesus.] But they don't always choose my way, my daughter, because they do not know my way. But through prayer they can find my way , as by trust and faith, my little one, you will see my way.

October 12, 1991
Our Lady of Perpetual Help, 9:30 A.M. Message from Jesus

Little one, thank you for returning to receive my message.

My daughter, I place my children in your path so that I may speak through you to them. My presence is within you through the direction of the Holy Spirit. My daughter, surrender yourself totally to me, allowing my Holy Presence to be revealed through you to my children.

Understand, my daughter, the time upon earth is rapidly being consumed by the evil atrocities which I cannot permit to continue!

In the time of Moses, my children were released from bondage and led away. They were given my Father's all-consuming love and in the beginning, they were thankful. But once Moses left them alone, they were consumed by evil and allowed themselves to be led away from my Father. I have spoken to you of their punishment, my daughter. They were allowed to wander the desert for forty years!

My children of today commit such horrendous atrocities that the evil consumes them and they are *completely* lost in a barren desert. They don't even realize it!

I come now to bring them home! *How many will follow?* [I don't know, Jesus. I wish *all* of them!] Are you willing to suffer for my children to be led out of this desert?

[Yes, my Jesus! I'll suffer for you because I love you. I want to belong completely to you! But why do you keep asking me, Jesus — am I not *really* meaning "yes"?] Oh, my little one, I know you mean it! Come, my little one, come to my heart! Release yourself completely to me! [I'm trying, my Jesus! Help me!]

Remember, my people, my justice is upon you. Turn from the road of perdition and return to me! I wait, my children! Through the pleas of my Holy Mother, my justice is held back! Reflect on my words! *Heed* my words, oh tempestuous ones, for I have called you each by name!

October 13, 1991
St. Paul of the Cross, 5:47 P.M. Message from Jesus

My little one, you were allowed to see today what is to happen to my priests and churches **here** in these **free United States** if My children do not heed my words. In the secrets given at Fatima, My children were shown what you were shown today. The horror experienced by My children in Nicaragua and my beloved Romero was an example of what my beloved priests will suffer if there is not more prayer, sacrifice and renunciation offered in reparation for the evil atrocities being committed against my Sacred Heart.

I know, my daughter, how difficult it is for you to take this message.

Only through prayer, sacrifice and renunciation will my children withstand what is to be! Release yourself to me, my little one, for we continue on the path of Calvary. Do not fear, little one. As I promised, my Holy Mother will carry you through. I am always with you, my little one! **Do not fear!** But speak to my children of what I showed you, so that they may understand **why my Holy Mother cries for her children!**

October 14, 1991
St. Paul of the Cross, 7:30 A.M. Message from Our Lady

My children, I come again to plead with you for more prayer. My daughter has been given a vision which was given to my children at Fatima. I warned all my children then as I warn my children today:

the killings of my priests will come to your shores as it happens to my priests and my people in Yugoslavia and Croatia.

Pray, my children, pray.

Do not keep what I speak of to yourselves, but repeat my message to all. My children, if you cannot find someone to come to your cenacle, then begin alone and I and my little Therese will come to pray with you. Do not despair, my children, but plead in prayer to my all-merciful Son, for He has come through His messages of teaching to all my children.

He is listening; open your hearts to Him. Pour out your love to Him, my children, for He refuses His children **nothing**! You will feel my presence here for I am present amongst each of you. I love you, my children, and I bless each of you with special graces. Thank you, for responding to my call.

October 15, 1991
Feast of St. Theresa of Avila, St Pius V, 12:47 PM
Message from Jesus

Little one, come let us ascend to a higher level in this song of love.

You have been prepared, my little one, to receive my outward sign of love. Your desire is strong because it is my desire within you.

You, My daughter, have come before me stained and impure. But through my all-merciful Llove and forgiveness, I have cleansed you as fine, purified gold to receive me within. My light shall shine through you, my little one. But remain "little," my precious, and give all glory to me for my light shall be ever so bright that my radiance shall overshadow those remaining imperfections which I always continue to purify. If my children would allow my presence within to reveal my light, this light would penetrate the darkness of evil. Instead of darkness consuming all brilliance of light, the brilliance of my light will consume all darkness.

This period of purification which has begun will bring forth to my children of light an overwhelming reversal of evil from my all consuming love and purity of heart.

I bless each of you. My light, I give you through my all-merciful love to illuminate you with my brilliance.

October 16, 1991
Feast of St. Margaret Mary Alacoque,
St. Paul of the Cross. 8:11 A.M. Message from Jesus

Little one, let us ascend the mountain in the song of love. As we make our journey on through the path of Calvary, you see before you my cross. The weight of the cross bearing down upon My shoulders is created by man's continuous sin. Sin carried on by the children has brought this weight to an unbearable heaviness as I see them in despair lash out with revenge, anger and a resentment to authority.

The parents and authorities have resigned themselves to allowing what man has created. Man has created through his own depravation the way for continuous animalistic behavior among the youth.

Man continues to condone the killing of my innocents and wonders why the youth of today think nothing of killing another human being. Why should the youth consider killing an abnormal behavior when they see how society approves killings through abortion?

Oh, my little one, what man has brought upon himself through his cry for freedom! His desire to do what pleases him brings such destruction to this era of mankind that soon man's inhumanity to man will destroy all living matter!

So I come to gather my children through my all-merciful love and as I have spoken, this is now the time for my children to respond to my Holy Mother's call for prayer, sacrifice and renunciation!

October 19, 1991
Marian Peace Conference, Pueblo, Colorado,
Message from Our Lady

My little one, I, your heavenly Mother and Queen of the Americas, come to you as requested by my Holy Crucified Son. I request, my daughter, that this message be given here to my children who have come from many different parts of your country to be with me.

My children, my Holy Crucified Son and I thank you for your response to my call. All of you, my children, are here because I have chosen each of you. Many of you have heard my call in your hearts. I beg all my children — especially during this time — for more prayer, more sacrifice and more renunciation.

You hear through the news media very little of the atrocities being committed against my priests and children in Croatia. Please my children, I have repeatedly spoken that **if you do not heed my warnings these horrendous atrocities will soon come here to my children in this your land**! I do not come to so many of my children for more sacrifice and renunciation just for my children of Croatia!

No, my children, I come for you are not yet *comprehending* that Satan has *already* begun to infiltrate you with his vicious atrocities here! **I have promised that this senseless human sacrifice, these horrendous murders and mutilations being committed so freely through abortion will be stopped!**

You, my children, have been called and you have been shown *my weapon*! Lift your voices in prayer with my weapon in your hands, **my rosary**! I bless each of you with a special grace from my beloved Son to hear my call to you in this my holy peace plan!

October 21, 1991
5:50 P.M. Message from Jesus

My little one, as we ascend the holy mountain in the song of love, I ask you to embrace my being with the innermost of your soul, mind and heart. You have been seeking my heart and have been unable to feel my love.

Man cannot comprehend that I will never leave him and will honor and bless him for his simple trust and faith in my direction. For man, all must be seen, understood and done in *his* time. I have told you before, my little one, unless my children become as little children they cannot enter into the kingdom of my Father. Satan knows that by breaking man's faith through denial of my truth, he can corrupt the soul and will weaken man's comprehension of my Will.

All will be done in my time and through my direction. Man need not understand "when" or "why" if he truly trusts in me.

I do not stop loving nor do I chastise them for their unbelief. I do not refuse my children for their inability to partake in my holy work. It is their free will to accept or deny My request for I love them no less.

My little one, listen very carefully with your heart. My holy mission must continue on. You must not allow other's feelings to sway you from my direction. I never leave you, my little one — draw on my strength, close your mind to all that is around you. Follow me, my little one — I will never lead you astray. You have been given your direction; you only need to follow, my little one.

October 22, 1991
7:40 A.M. Message from Jesus

My little one, let us ascend this holy mountain together in this song of Love.

My children despair because they don't feel me, yet they don't feel me because they don't come to me here in love and trust. It is through seeking me that they will find, but they must seek me in all — not only in prayer. For all can be prayer if offered in love to me!

Many times my children come to a level in their relationship with me where they ponder if I am really alive in the Eucharist. And if I am alive, why can they not feel my Presence?

It is because they do not seek my Presence. Man occupies his daily needs with frivolous and materialistic values. They seek only what satisfies their needs and do not consider me as a need. They have become ritualistic in their spiritual duties — once a week attending a service and expecting to feel my Presence within a time limit. They do not come to me in love, but in duty. If they would attempt for a second to desire me, they would find me, but instead they are content with meeting their obligation and pursuing their needs of enjoyment and relaxation. It will not be until they are in a situation of drastic circumstance that they then expect my Presence to assure and strengthen them.

I do not leave any of my children, ever! I do not abandon them though they only seek me during crisis. On the contrary, it is at this time I open my heart and soothe their wounds and want only to give them my peace and joy. I wait for their return and never turn away or abandon in their search for me. If through *persistence in love* they seek me, they *shall* find me, *for I have never left them.*

October 24, 1991
St. Paul of the Cross, Message from Jesus

My little one, it is not my desire that my children continue on the road to perdition. I do not want to allow a chastisement to come upon My children, but they do not see the evil through the blindness they have allowed to affect them.

My death on the cross was for *all* my children, through the almighty and merciful love of my Father, who allowed His only begotten Son to be crucified for the sins of mankind.

But my children continue to allow themselves through their own **free will** to live in sin. They have been given the Sacrament of Penance which cleanses the soul. This contamination, which blinds man to sin, continually keeps man under the influence and manipulation of Satan.

My children, listen to me! Open your closed hearts to me! I do not plead for my sake, *but for yours!* Release yourself from the bondage of Satan! Return to my Sacraments; they were given *for your benefit* with the almighty and merciful love of my Father. Do not refuse me, my children, of loving you! I *died* for you my Children! Satan *destroys* you! But through me, your soul will have everlasting life!

October 27, 1991
St. Paul of the Cross, 7:35 A.M. Message from Jesus

My little one, as we begin the ascension up the mountain in the song of love, you find yourself near the top. It is at this level you shall remain with me for a period of time. My little one, this level is finding a trust that has been developing in you, but is not yet fully acceptable.

Do not be saddened, my daughter. My little Theresa remained at this level and was quite at peace until it was time to ascend my holy cross. You see, my little one, the purification and holiness I bestow upon each of my children is based on their *desire* to please me and on *releasing* all your being totally to Me. I can then completely mold and purify you into my saintliness. This was my Theresa's daily request as she sought my completeness within her.

You strive, My little one, and your love for Me does not allow you to sway from your quest of My Desires. For in releasing totally to Me, you have found an everlasting Peace — but also an unquenchable thirst for My Love.

Oh, my precious little one, you do not yet see the magnitude of complete oneness within you. Others are beginning to see it and soon all will know and see the purity and perfection of my love creating saintliness through the willingness of my vessel. You feel uneasy because you have heard about the " littleness" my Theresa continually speaks of, which you must strive for daily. Oh, my little one, through your desire to love me and seek my completeness, through releasing totally to me, you *will* remain little.

My completeness, my strength, can only come within you through *total release* to me! If all my children would do this they would know true peace and love in their lives; releasing in turn a peace and love that would unite all in oneness with me.

Seek me, my children, and you will **find** me.

Love me, my children, and you will **know** me.

Completely **release yourselves** to me, my children, and you will **see** the epitome of everlasting love and peace!

October 29, 1991
St. Pius V, 8:37 A.M. Message from Jesus

My little one, once again we are together in this song of love, resting at this level.

Do you see the beauty of my holy work? You see, my little one, my work is always done *in* love and *with* love. If my children would only open their hearts to me and allow me to remove the blinders Satan has continuously kept them in, they would see only love. They would feel my love in all they do as they offer all to me. It is a peace and love they can **only** find through me.

Satan's work consists in man pleasing only man's desires and whims. Man puts himself first and the happiness he feels is very shallow and fragile. He cannot understand why this happiness he feels leaves him with an emptiness. The pleasures he seeks do not satisfy him and so he continues in seeking more. He cannot find happiness and peace because what he seeks is not done through love and peace, it is done through deception and self-glory. This is Satan's way.

My Holy Mother's last message in Medjugorje was given in very brief but powerful words: "Pray! Pray! Pray!" Do my children *not comprehend* how desperate those pleas from my Holy Mother are? My children, *listen with your hearts* to those words given by my Holy Mother!

October 31, 1991
St. Dominic Savio, 7:00 A.M. Message from Jesus

My little one, we come to a level once again where we will rest together.

Oh my precious one, I have come to my children through my messages not to frighten with my words, but for them to prepare themselves! I have asked my children to return to the Sacraments. This world they live in has been so consumed in evil, with such atrocities, that **mankind *will* now be cleansed and purified!**

I have spoken to you of a beginning — not just for you, my little one — but for all those of my children who willingly and freely seek my all-merciful love. My children, **do not fear for yourselves and your families, but accept my Holy Will and seek my truths. You shall be protected under my Holy Mother's mantle of protection surrounding you and your families for your obedience and trust in me.**

Consecrate yourselves daily beginning **now** to my Most Sacred Heart and the Most Sacred Heart of my Holy Mother.

Do not pray against this cleansing and purification, but pray *for* it, my children, and seek the intercession of the Holiest Angels and Saints; they will intercede for you!

Know that I am with you! Know that I am the all-merciful, All Loving Jesus Christ, Saviour and King. Know I Am!

Do not fear me, but love me. Did I not die on the cross for you, my children? How could you not believe I would protect you, my children! But open your hearts to the holy words of my Blessed Mother and Queen: "Pray! Pray! Pray!"

November 1, 1991
St. Paul of the Cross, 7:37 A.M. Message from Jesus

My little one, let us now ascend upon my holy cross in this song of love.

You have been allowed to feel a great sadness which overcomes you, my little one. This is my sadness over the destruction of my children by sadistic and immoral atrocities. Satan destroys my children through such despicable means!

Oh, my little one, yes, my Heart breaks! For this continuation of destruction begins with my innocents in abortion, my youth in drugs and obscenities which lead to killings. No! It **must be stopped!** Pray, my children, Pray!

My Holy Mother cries for humanity and her heart is continually breaking and cannot be soothed.

Prepare yourselves, those of my children who hear these words! Heed them! **You have been warned!**

Pray, my children, Pray! Pray for the purification and cleansing of all my people. Do not pray against it, but pray for it so that these horrendous atrocities will be stopped! You are all under the protection of my Holy Mother if you consecrate yourselves daily to my Most Sacred Heart and the Most Sacred Heart of my Holy Mother. I bless each of you in the Almighty Name of my Father with the Precious Blood I shed for each of you, my children, and the grace for guidance and direction by the Holy Spirit.

November 6, 1991
St Pius V, 5:37 P.M. Message from Jesus

My little one, let us begin today in the song of love.

Once again we are at the foot of the cross. This ascension upon my holy cross is my gift to you, my little one, for not all my children are willing to carry my cross. Many have been called, but few open their hearts to listen to my desires.

If my children would allow themselves to walk my holy path, they would find true happiness. I come to my children to teach through my holy messages. My words are not different from when I walked the earth. As then, my children would listen to my teaching and know it was truth, so now my children hear and read these, my messages, and they will know it is my truth. They will know — as I taught my children before — that they must change their way and follow me.

Man cannot know my truth if he does not hear my word. If man is away from my church, he cannot hear my word. But through these messages, many will read my word, my teaching and they shall return to my church for they have been touched by me.

I love you, my children — come back to me! I *never* leave you, my children! I am here in the blessed tabernacle! I am the Blessed Host you receive during my Holy Mass! Have you prepared yourself to receive me? I have prepared your home *for you!* Come to me, my children ... do not stay away! I *love you, my children,* with my almighty and all-merciful love!

Do not fear me, my children, but know I am near always to love you!

November 8, 1991
St. Paul of the Cross, 7:40 A.M. Message from Jesus

My little one, let us ascend my holy mountain in the song of love.

My children, understand why my Holy Mother, your Queen, and I have brought you teachings and messages through many visionaries and locutionists. In my Bible, my teachings were given to all of humanity for them to understand *and obey* my Father's word — my word.

The time now upon you was foretold. Also, the many miracles and manifestations were foretold which would occur in the end times. But no-length of period or dates are ever given.

Have you prepared yourselves? **Are you ready**? Or do you think that I will not bring my Father's justice — my justice — upon you?

Oh my children, you will *soon* realize the reign of the Antichrist has begun! What my Mother has spoken to you of through her many apparitions and locutions is *now*!

Many of you who receive or hear this message will know my words are truth. Many of you will not want to believe and will close your hearts to it, *but that will not change what is!*

I am, my children! I love you, my children! Won't you listen to me **now**, my children! I am sending this message to reach **all** my children! **Be ready now!!** Ask my forgiveness **now!** I love you, my children!

— *Your Crucified Jesus*

December 23, 1991
St. Pius V, 8:42 A.M. Christmas Message from Jesus

My Christmas gift to each of you, my children, is to understand my eternal love given to each of you. During this time of Advent you have been taught that this is the hour of my birth, but do you realize, you not only celebrate the hour of my birth but also my death and my Resurrection.

You ask yourselves how can this be? Understand, my children, that at the time of my birth, I agreed to sacrifice so that through the Father Almighty I would allow myself to come in human form to this earth for the salvation of mankind. Knowing I was to die upon the cross, to be Resurrected on the third day, to sit at the right hand of my Father. Do you understand, my children, what I have allowed for the salvation of *all* your souls! I love you so much! My Father loves you so much, He gave His only divine Son to die on the cross for each of you! My love eternal to die for you! And now my Father gives you the eternal Holy Spirit, who comes to each of you as you call out for Our merciful love! Open your hearts to receive Us through Our everlasting gift to you in the Holy Eucharist, which brings to you each day, not only during Advent, Our love, Our peace, Our joy, Our desire to each of you all the days of your life.

My little one, this is my Christmas message to all of my children this Holy Christmas Year of 1991! Open your hearts to receive Us not only at Christmas but each day of the year! I love you.

April 21, 1992
St. Gregory the Great Church, 8:30 A.M.

Little one, I Who Am come to you to request these my teachings be given to my children.

It is not understood by my children the true meaning of my holy crucifixion.

I died for all of humanity. Not just for a chosen few, but for all!

Wisdom does not come to man, man gains wisdom through opening his intellect to my Father. Through my death an abundance of gifts are bestowed to all mankind.

Grace is a gift abundantly given to all of my children who are willing to accept these my gifts.

April 22, 1992
St. Gregory the Great Church, 7:30 P.M.

Little one, open your heart to receive my words. Do not forsake but remember I am always within a soul who desires me.

It is my desire to bring peace and pove to my children who seek my truths but I also want to bring peace and love to my children who do not believe in me.

I have told you before it is through sacrifice, prayer, fasting of my children that others will be saved.

I ask you, my little one, do not despair but pray, fast, sacrifice and offer all to me in reparation for the sins of mankind.

Live life in Me with Me and for Me!

Contemplate, meditate on my Holy Passion. For it is this my Holy Passion which has set man free from the bondage of sin.

April 23, 1992
St. Mary's Church, 7:30 P.M.

My little one, open your heart to receive Me.

I do not come to deceive but to deliver, for I am the all-merciful all loving Jesus Crucified.

My little one, I come in light to those of ‚y children who willingly abandon themselves totally to ‚e.

Remember, my children, the light which came upon this earth on the night of my birth!

I was born to remove the stain of original sin, which held My children in darkness.

It is my light of salvation which I bring you, my children.

Do not remain in the darkness of evil but allow my light to lead you.

Renew your baptismal vow in renouncing Satan and all his evil ways.

My gift to each of you through my unconditional love is my Holy Crucifixion.

Satan manipulates and deceives, I breathe the gift of light and life through my all-merciful and all forgiving love for each one of you.

Do not seek to judge, but seek to love!

April 24, 1992
St. Paul of the Cross Church, 7:00 A.M.

Little one, I Who Am, love all my children.

I am the all merciful all-loving Jesus Christ Crucified.

Do not place my all-merciful love in the shadows of the materialistic ways of the world.

I have told you many times you are in this world not of this world.

In order to hear my words you must place me before all.

It is not my way to love only those who love me but to love all even those who betray and offend me.

I ask for sacrifice and prayer but it must come with an ardent desire in wanting to love me and to seek my love!

Those of my children who ardently desire to love me must also love their neighbor.

You can not truly love me if you do not love your neighbor.

April 25, 1992
St. Pius V Church, 7:30 P.M.

My dearest little one, my holy desire is to give to all my children my all-merciful love.

It is within my power to save all my children but I do not go against their free will.

If man persists to deny my all-merciful love I cannot force it upon them.

Tomorrow, the first Sunday after Easter, is when I requested my beloved daughter, Sister Faustina, to honor this day as the Feast of My All-merciful love.

As you see in the picture the rays gush forth in never-ending all-merciful love. Those of my children who desire my mercy must only seek and these rays will penetrate their hearts.

Come forth, my beloved, in ardent desire. I will withhold nothing from the glory of my love.

April 27, 1992
St. Gregory the Great Church, 8:30 A.M.

Little one, as I spoke to you earlier, my children who are willing to open their hearts to me are like rosebuds in my garden.

I nurture them daily through my waters of life only enough so they may grow strong in me.

If my children would relinquish the ways of the world for me they would allow themselves the beauty of my kingdom in their hearts.

It is through forsaking all and trusting in me they shall see change.

I want to give all my children a new life, with the springs of grace that will abundantly flow in them if they will return to me.

April 28, 1992
St. Gregory the Great Church, 8:30 A.M.

Little one, come to the waters of my salvation through the mystery of my Body and Blood offered in the purest form.

I am the Bread of Life resurrected for the salvation of mankind.

It is, has been and will always be the greatest sacrifice offered in my churches all over the world.

This great miracle is relived in every Mass throughout the world.

My children, do you understand or believe this holy miracle, this my gift of humanity?

As you come to receive my Body and Blood do you know I Am!

Believe, my children, I come to each of you in the purest form. Do you come to me with the purest of heart, with the purest of intention, with the purest of soul?

I love you, my children, I will never abandon you! Will you abandon yourself? Will you abandon me?

May 11, 1992
St Pius V Church, 12:15 P.M.

My little one, know I am who comes to my people pleading for forgiveness of each other.

It is not my way for human life to be taken and destroyed with no feeling or concept of this destruction.

Forgiveness and love is not bought; it is my gift to all my people.

They must only open their hearts to me to receive these fruits of my Father's creation.

The evil runs rampant amongst this world and my children have blinded themselves to these gifts.

It is prayer and sacrifice that my children must offer in order for hearts to be opened to receive these gifts.

I have spoken to you of the great destruction which will soon take place in this land.

This is not my desire but will be allowed because the sin has contaminated man so severely that man thinks nothing of destroying human life.

Communication with me which I have given you can be for all who are willing to open their hearts to me, change their lifestyles, turn away from evil and partake of me.

As you have seen, my beloved, it is not easy to turn from the ways of the world, it is a continued struggle unless you are willing to turn all over to me!

May 12, 1992
St. Pius V Church, 12:15 P.M.

My little one, thank you for returning to receive my message.

Understand what the Holy Mass is! The consecration of the bread and wine.

It is re-enactment of my Crucifixion, my death upon the cross, in order that my children would have eternal life.

It is not only a re-enactment but a replenishment of each soul as they receive life.

My death on the cross is the life of the soul.

My children, my death was never in vain, for if but only one soul lives, my Father rejoices as this once-lost soul returns.

I am the Bread of Life, the unquenchless thirst of creation.

I will never forsake any who thirst for me!

May 16, 1992
St. Paul of the Cross, 8:00 A.M.

My little one, does man not understand that as he denies my truths he is accepting lies and horrendous misconceptions which only bring disarray and confusion?

All my children must remain obedient to the truth by obeying the Magisterium of my holy church in all its teachings.

My son, John Paul II, is the visible head of my church, all who deny and willfully disobey my Son's leadership denys and disobeys me!

This apostasy which has begun against the teachings of the Magisterium of my church has been brought by those from the bowels of hell loosed upon the world to once again split the authority of the church, but Satan will not reign over my one true church. Instead, what he has come to demolish will stand firm in me and I in them and what has been foretold in the word will now be upheld.

Do not forsake me, my children, but open your hearts to receive my truths, my all-merciful love. I have sent the Holy Spirit to place the flame of His everlasting light upon each of my children. Receive the breath of life which instills all truths of my redeeming grace.

May 18, 1992
St. Gregory the Great Church, 8:30 A.M.

My dearest little one, as one abstains from the holiness and graces received from my Sacraments he is led farther and farther away from me!

The Sacraments, as the rosary and other devotional means, are given for a purpose. These are tools to aid and be used against the sadistic and atrocious deceits used by Satan and his followers.

If my children could see the graces received for attending the holy sacrifice of the Mass they would be so overwhelmed.

Man becomes blinded. This darkness he is led into deadens all senses. He is unable to feel because of these atrocities he commits. Only evil will make him feel and only for a brief time, so he must endow himself with more evil.

Satan knows if man allows only a wisp of light through me, man will return to me, so Satan blinds him completely with more and more deception.

This is why my Holy Mother asks all my children for more prayer and sacrifice, for it is through others' prayers and sacrifice many of my children lost will be saved.

It is through the sacraments, prayer, sacrifice, that will unite all My children, illuminate and bring light to this darkness.

May 20, 1992
St. Gregory the Great Church, 8:30 A.M.

I am the Redeeming Savior of the world. I come to release my children from the bondage of sin, but my children are so overcome by evil, unless they release themselves totally to me they will remain in bondage.

I ask you, my children, hear my plea, hear the plea of my Holy Mother, offer more sacrifice, more prayer or my children's hearts will remain closed and under the bondage of sin.

I ask you, my daughter, pray and release yourself totally to me, trusting in me. I am the way, I will never lead you astray.

September 28, 1992
St. Gregory the Great, 8:30 A.M.

My little one, I, your heavenly Mother and Queen of the Americas, come to bring you peace.

I love each of you, my children. I ask, as you are my children, that you open and listen with your hearts to my urgent plea.

I do not come to speak to you of disasters or punishments. No my children, I come to plead with each of you for your souls.

Yes, the evil one is rampant with fury to dissuade you from my Holy Son. Throughout the ages, the evil one has continuously manipulated and caused such misery and evil atrocities, to gain the souls of many.

I come to plead with you for prayer and sacrifice and yes to carry my weapon upon you. The holy rosary is a great weapon and Satan mocks and seeks to destroy this weapon.

My children, you have been given your free will. The Almighty Father, my Holy Son and Holy Spirit have never taken this gift away. It is your decision, my children, how you will use this gift.

You alone make the decision to give your soul to the bowels of hell for all eternity or to turn from the evil perdition and receive the fruits of eternal salvation.

As your Mother, I come to teach you, love you and to lead you away from the evil.

It is up to you, my children, who you desire to follow.

I love you, my children. I am always with you.

January 9, 1993

My children, I have shown you the way. Through Prayer, sacrifice and surrendering totally to my Son, you shall know His Mercy.

It is my Son's desire to make known these requests of prayer, sacrifice and renunciation, through one's example.

Many of you have not continued with my requests. Your families souls and many souls will be lost if you do not heed my warnings.

Continue daily to surrender yourselves to the Blessed Trinity and strive to pray the fifteen decade rosary.

As I told my children in Medjugorje, if you can only pray one decade of the rosary do this, for special graces are bestowed upon you to help you until you succeed in reciting the fifteen decades.

Do not worry, my children, of disasters or chastisements, this is not the desire of my Son. Instead use your time wisely in prayer and daily duties. It is more important to use this time in prayer than in worrisome concern over what you are not able to control.

Remember, I am always with you in prayer and as you continue to strive to be examples of my Son's love, you will be the light in this darkened world of sin.

I thank you, my children, for responding to my call and I bless each of you with a special grace to continue to strive to be one with my Son.

January 11, 1993
St. Gregory the Great, 8:30 A.M.

I, your Heavenly Mother, come to lead you my children to my Son. Many have not understood when I ask you to pray from the heart, love from the heart.

It is not just with your heart, my children, but to unite with the Heart of Jesus. This is how you are to pray and to love.

It is by surrendering yourselves totally to the Blessed Trinity.

Prayer from the heart is uniting with Jesus in total surrender to Him your will.

One in being with the Father, Son and Holy Spirit is total surrender.

Understanding the will of the Father, Son and Holy Spirit comes through total surrender of your will. Learn to walk in the light of the Blessed Trinity, as opposed to walking in darkness through sin.

As you, my children, are willing to turn away from sin in obedience to the Father, Son and Holy Spirit, prayer from the heart begins to become a realization.

Book II

For Love, With Love, Through love

1995 July 31, Monday

Jesus said: "Little one, offer all to me, for it is in offering sacrifice that many children will be saved. I have given many messages and I understand your reluctance at writing, but my child, I thank you for your obedience to my call.

"My daughter, listen with your heart. I have given you my gifts abundantly, gifts that others would not consider gifts. My Mother asked if you were willing to accept the 'joy of the cross;' are you willing, my beloved? My daughter, it is because you are willing to offer all to me; this is what pleases me.

"Little one, did you not understand the parable of the loaves and fishes?"

(Earlier, Jesus asked me to read Matthew. I thought I heard Matthew 6, but I was wrong; I replied, "Jesus, you said Matthew 6!")

"I said Matthew 14 and 15, my daughter. In the parable of the loaves and fishes, did you not understand that miracles are given for those of my children who need signs to believe? For those of my children who believe by faith, a greater grace is given as they believe without signs. My graces given to those of my children in the parable of the loaves and fishes was not only the grace to see the multiplication of the fish and loaves, but that I Who Am came obedient to the will of my Father, as a man, who would speak to my children, teaching through my words, that which my Father had promised was. But, my children did not understand, because they would not listen with ears of the soul, nor would they see with the eyes of the soul, faith. The miracle of loaves and fishes was given so that I would feed them with the food of life.

"As I sat alone on the mountain, I already knew that I would be alone in the garden of Gethsemane, to suffer my agony alone, out of love and obedience to my Father.

"As the crowds began to gather to listen to my teachings, I wanted to prepare them to receive the gift of life, for my death was to be the gift of eternal life to all of mankind.

"As my disciples questioned, why should I not send these my children away? My answer to them is what I say to my children now, in these present times. I am who feeds those who hunger for eternal life, and as I bless this bread to fill your pangs of hunger, I also fill you with my love, for soon I will have to leave you in order that you may have life eternal. But they did not understand my words and they were most willing to turn against me, as they begged for my death upon the cross.

"Now I feed my people in the daily consecration of my Holy Mass and they still do not see me alive, willing to die for each again and again. As I told you this morning, my little one, they do not see with the eyes of their souls but with the eyes of the world, which blinds them to my truths.

"Open your eyes and ears of the soul, my children and you will be fed, you will see and hear my truths; you will see and hear me."

Approved by Rev. Sean Cronin

1996 February 23, Friday, 12:37
EUCHARISTIC ADORATION

Jesus said: "My precious little one, praise be to Jesus, for Jesus is Lord.

"I come, my little one, again as I have in the past, to give you my word. My teaching! Listen with your heart. As I spoke to you yesterday, open your heart to my children."

(Patsy: Jesus, this is very difficult.)

"It is because you are not trusting, my little one. Bring my little ones to me, my children. Teach them of me. For if you do not teach them, how are they to know me?

"As my Mother spoke of teaching the babies in the womb; speaking gentle loving words to them is written in books, why not speak to them of my word, and of my love?

"Teach these, my children, so they may know who I am. For I tell you now, if you continue to deny me, my Father in heaven will deny you. I, Who Am, will give life eternal. Only I can give life eternal; not man; nor he who speaks the lies of the red dragon."

(Patsy: Jesus, I don't understand.)

"My daughter, you will know that it is I Who Am, who speaks truths to you, my little one; for I will bring you peace. Know me, my daughter, through prayer and the Holy Eucharist; for he that comes in darkness cannot give peace."

(Patsy: Jesus, please help me to be firm in you, and not to fear.)

"My daughter, know that Michael my beloved warrior is always with you."

(Patsy: But why are you telling me this, Jesus? What is it you are telling me?)

"To know that I Am, who gives you my strength, my protection, my love, to carry my cross. Are you willing my daughter?

"Be at peace."

Approved by Rev. Sean Cronin, 1996

1996 March 13, Wednesday, 11:10
EUCHARISTIC ADORATION

Jesus said: "I come to you, my little one. Praise be to Jesus Christ, King, Redeemer and Saviour. Open your heart, my little one, for it is I Who Am, who comes to bring you light, holiness, purity, humility. For as you seek me, I come, so that you will know me.

"I Who Am, Saviour. I Who Am shed my holy blood for each of my children to give life eternal. Pierced by a crown of thorns, which I Who Am give you, my child, to wear because you have sought me.

"It is I, my beloved, whom you sought in prayer, and as you offered me your love, my little one, I give you in return my love incomparable; for it is only my love which can quench the thirst for that love which is not of this earth. My love can fill the emptiness of the brokenhearted.

"Listen my child, with the ears of the soul, for my words cannot be heard with the ears of the world.

"Place your trust completely in me, for I will not lead you astray. You have asked that I teach you of my body, blood, soul and divinity, ever present in the Holy Eucharist. It is the Bread of Life Eternal, my child. It is the greatest gift, which if received in love, can reach even the hardened of heart."

(Patsy: But Jesus, if the person is hardened of heart, how can this person receive you in love?)

Jesus said: "My daughter, if a person seeks my love through the Holy Eucharist, there *is* love in this person, hardened of heart, who has with the grace given in receiving me, sought me. I who am love, is within this soul; now love is given and received, for I am love. I am alive, my child, in the holy Sacrament of the Eucharist. So if I Who Am is received, I am within the soul who has received me. This, my child, is my love everlasting, given to each who desire my love, even if they don't realize they are desiring me, seeking me, when they receive the Sacrament of the Holy Eucharist. I within them, they within me, have become one.

This is enough for today, my child. I am with you. Thank you for responding to my call."

Approved by Rev. Sean Cronin

1996 May 02, Thursday, 14:45
EUCHARISTIC ADORATION

Of Divine Love

Jesus said: "Little one, thank you for opening your heart to my call. Praise be to Jesus, for Jesus is Lord, King, Saviour and Redeemer.

"My daughter, as we continue along this journey, I will teach you my word. My teachings are given for all, that they may know me. But unless they read my word daily, they will not understand nor receive the love I give to all in my word!

"My beloved John's teachings are truly written in the style and declaration of love. My love surpasses and abounds the essence of pure love. In John's teachings he describes in words the beauty of my love.

"Open to John 1."

THE GOSPEL ACCORDING TO JOHN
JOHN 1:

⁴ What came to be through him was life, and this life was the light of the human race.

Jesus said: "Did I not teach you I Who Am brings eternal life to all who eat my body and drink my blood, the purest and truest form of love? I am love, my little one."

John 1, cont'd:

⁶ **A man named John was sent from God.**
⁷ **He came for testimony to testify to the light, so that all might believe through him.**
⁸ **He was not the light, but came to testify to the light.**
⁹ **The true light, which enlightens everyone, was coming into the world.**

Jesus said: "You see, my daughter, I am the true light, and as each child who comes to me, desiring me, seeking me, I offer to all my body, my blood, my being, and they will see light, for I am the light which takes away all darkness. The darkness which the evil keeps my children in. The darkness which can only deaden the soul. But I Who Am will enlighten the mind, the soul, and permeate into the darkest crevices of these lost souls; and my light will shine forth and bring these, my children, out of the darkness.

"This is enough for now, my child. I bless you in the Almighty Name of the Father, Son and Holy Spirit."

Approved by Rev. Sean Cronin

1996 May 03, Friday, 21:15
EUCHARISTIC ADORATION

Jesus said: "My child, praise be to Jesus, for Jesus is Lord. Peace, my child.

"It is I Who Am, my beloved. I bring you my peace. The peace which is not of this world. Only the peace I can give. Listen with your heart, my daughter. I will again teach you of my word.

"Open to Matthew 6. It is a teaching on this peace I speak to you of."

THE GOSPEL ACCORDING TO MATTHEW
MATTHEW 6: Purity Of Intention

⁷ **In praying do not babble like pagans, who think that they will be heard because of their many words.**
⁸ **Do not be like them. Your Father knows what you need before you ask him. The Lord's Prayer.**

⁹ **This is how you pray: "Our Father in heaven, hallowed be your name, your kingdom come, your will be done on earth, as in heaven. Give us today our daily bread, and forgive us our debts as we forgive our debtors."**

Jesus said: "Peace, my peace, my child, can only come through forgiving one another. The person who will not forgive will always be unsettled in his ways. His mind will have no peace and his transgressions will seem unbearable. He will look for the things of this world to comfort him but he will not find comfort. Oh, my child, his justice will be as he has handed to the one he will not forgive. Peace and forgiveness are inseparable; you cannot have one without the other; and as we continue with the prayer of my Father, you will see, without peace and forgiveness, you are not doing the Will of my Father."

Matthew 6, cont'd:

¹³ **And do not subject us to the final test, but deliver us from the evil one.**

Jesus said: "You cannot be delivered from the evil one if you choose to stay in sin. Unforgiveness is a great offence not only against the Father but also against the Son and the Holy Spirit. Oh, my children, understand my words, do not let the sun set with anger on your lips, for if you truly desire to seek the forgiveness of the Father, you must forgive all the injustices committed against you, then you will truly have my peace.

"This is enough for today, my child. Shalom, my little one, and peace to your family. Thank you for responding to my call."

Approved by Rev. Sean Cronin,

June 06 1996 May 06, Monday, 11:15
EUCHARISTIC ADORATION

Jesus said: "Peace, my little one. Jesus is Lord, Redeemer, King and Saviour. Thank you for opening your heart once again for my teaching.

"My daughter, open to Isaiah 10. I will speak to you on chastisement."

THE BOOK OF ISAIAH
ISAIAH 10:Social Injustice

¹ **Woe to those who enact unjust statutes and who write oppressive decrees, depriving the needy of judgment and robbing my people's poor of their rights, making widows their plunder and orphans their prey, what will you do on the day of punishment?**

Jesus said: "My people do not listen to my word, my child. I have sent many messengers to my people. Do they think that my hand can be held back much longer. They continue in sin as if sin were life. This is what my children have chosen. Life in sin, with sin, life as sin."

³ **What will you do on the day of punishment when ruin comes from afar? To whom will you flee for help? Where will you leave your wealth, lest it sink beneath the captive or fall beneath the slain. For all this His wrath is not turned back, His hand is still outstretched.**

Jesus said: "My daughter, please do not fear. Those who should fear and tremble close their eyes and ears to my word. Pray, my daughter, pray. Continue to offer all to me. Know that I am with you."

Approved by Rev. Sean Cronin

1996 May 07, Tuesday, 13:20
EUCHARISTIC ADORATION

Jesus said: "My precious child, peace of the Father, Son and Holy Spirit be upon you. Praise be to Jesus, for Jesus is Lord, Saviour and Redeemer.

"My child, the ways of the world are not your ways; you are *in* this world, not *of* this world. It is necessary for all my children to pray, but because they remain worldly; they see no need for prayer.

"Open to Luke 7, my child."

THE GOSPEL ACCORDING TO LUKE
LUKE 7: The Healing Of The Centurion's Slave

¹ When he had finished all his words to the people, he entered Capernaum.

² A centurion there had a slave who was ill and about to die, and he was valuable to him.

³ When he heard about Jesus, he sent elders of the Jews to him, asking him to come and save the life of his slave.

⁴ They approached Jesus and strongly urged Him to come saying, "He deserves to have you do this for him.

⁵ For he loves our nation and he built the synagogues for us."

⁶ And Jesus went with them, but when He was only a short distance from the house, the centurion sent friends to tell him, "Lord, do not trouble yourself for I am not worthy to have you enter under my roof.

⁷ Therefore I did not consider myself worthy to come to you; but say the word and let my servant be healed.

⁸ For I too am a person subject to authority, with soldiers subject to me, and I say to one 'Go,' and he goes; and to another, 'Come here,' and he comes, and to my slave, 'Do this,' and he does it."

⁹ When Jesus heard this He was amazed at him, and turning, said to the crowd following him, "I tell you, not even in Israel have I found such faith."

Jesus said: "My child, my son *[the centurion],* though in this world and though he himself a leader, still knew who I was. His prayer brought the healing of his servant. My people wander in a barren desert, they have no time for prayer, but are overwrought with the distractions of this world. They find no pleasure in the simple things of this life. They are so preoccupied in themselves and they wonder why they cannot find happiness or peace. As my beloved son spoke of yesterday, on one hand the people have so much wealth they become greedy and want so much of the materialistic world. And then, there are the poor; they have not even a place to sleep or a warm meal to soften the pangs of hunger. Where is the justice? Where is the centurion who cared enough for his brother the servant, that he asked in prayer for his servant's healing?

"When my Father created the world, its beauty and overwhelming abundance of vegetation, fruits, the natural wonders, it was for all. But my children were not satisfied, beginning with my daughter Eve and her desire to seek more pleasures, more wisdom. So my Father exiled Adam and Eve to seek to care for themselves; and it continued on; man's desire to create his own destiny, never satisfied and putting God completely out of one's life. If one can turn away completely from the creator of all that is good, right and just, how can one care for another? In this world plagued with such contempt, distrust, and social injustice, where is that centurion, my child?

"Pray, my child, pray. Be at peace, my daughter. Thank you for responding to my call."

Approved by Rev. Sean Cronin

1996 May 08, Wednesday, 13:20
EUCHARISTIC ADORATION

Jesus said: "My daughter, thank you for opening your heart to me and for responding to my call. Praise be to Jesus, for Jesus is Lord, King, Redeemer, and Saviour.

"Little one, open to John 8. Today I will speak to you on fulfilling the commitment to one's state of life. For you see, my daughter, each one has been given a duty or mission in this life. Many are called but few chosen; not chosen because they have not responded to the grace given to them to help to fulfil their mission."

THE GOSPEL ACCORDING TO JOHN
JOHN 8: The Adultress

⁷ **But when they continued asking him, he straightened up and said to them, "Let the one among you who is without sin be the first to throw a stone at her."**

⁸ **Again, he bent down and wrote on the ground.**

⁹ **And in response, they went away, one by one, beginning with the elders.**

Jesus said: "Was it the mission of the elders to judge, my daughter?"

(Patsy: Jesus, I don't think any of us have a right to judge, wasn't it their mission to teach and pray?)

"Yes, my daughter, but they were not willing to accept the grace given to them by my Father to help them in their mission. Hypocrites! They babble their words. This is not prayer, my child. Prayer is offering. An offering of love, with words, actions. Instead they made themselves high priests; their knowledge of the word was interpreted to suit their own needs. This was not the mission given them by my Father, for if they had truly accepted their mission in life, they would have known me; and as they knew me, they would have known the Father and the Holy Spirit. Instead they chose to create their own mission. They became judge and overseer to fulfil their own desires and will. Not the desire nor the will of my Father.

"How could they bring the people to my Father when all they desired was to please themselves? You see, my daughter, the ways of the world, man's self-righteousness was even then. They desired to create their own destiny, and their desire was for their own profit. If my children would place the will of the Father first, and ask for the grace through prayer to help them in their state in life or mission in this life, they would abound in the richness and fulfilment in the state of life my Father has chosen for them; they would know the will of my Father.

"This is enough for today, my daughter. My peace be with you. Shalom, my child."

Approved by Rev. Sean Cronin

1996 May 09, Thursday, 08:35
EUCHARISTIC ADORATION

Jesus said: "My little one, praise be to Jesus, for Jesus is Lord, Saviour, Redeemer. As you come to me willingly and lovingly to seek me in all you do, I am with you.

"Open to Jeremiah 3."

THE BOOK OF JEREMIAH
JEREMIAH 3: The Infidelity of Israel

² **Lift your eyes to the height and see, where have men not lain with you? By the wayside you waited for them like an Arab in the desert, you defiled the land by your wicked harlotry.**
³ **Therefore the showers were withheld. The spring rain failed. But because you have a harlot's brow you refused to blush.**

Jesus said: "We spoke of chastisement, justice, my daughter. I know your displeasure to take these type of messages, but, my daughter, listen with your heart. Do not fear for my justice has been spoken of since the beginning of time. The harlotry of one's soul, my child, is the allowance of keeping one's soul in the state of sin. Allowing one's immortal soul to be lost to the clenches of the evil one. Go on, my daughter, to the next verse."

Jeremiah 3, cont'd:

⁴ **Even now do you not call me "my father," you who are the bridegroom of my youth.**

Jesus said: "Such bitterness! My children refuse my love; the pure love I, as the bridegroom, so willingly offer to all my children. I will always be the groom waiting anxiously for the return of all my children. To lie in wait in all the tabernacles in all the world."

Jeremiah 3, cont'd:

⁵ **Will he keep his wrath forever, will he hold his grudge to the end? This is what you say, yet you do all the evil you can.**

Jesus said: "The evil one holds on to one's soul bringing the soul deeper and deeper into his clutches. My children, I am the way. Release yourselves to me. I am the groom who can release you from the bondage of sin. Come to me in the Sacrament of Reconciliation; this your release from the bondage of sin. Once cleansed by the

Sacrament of Reconciliation, come to me in the Sacrament of the Holy Eucharist, where I await you. This is my love. This is my Body. I await you, my children. Do not stay in the harlotry of despair, but come to me. Prepare yourselves to meet your groom, who awaits to give you life eternal.

"This is enough for today. Be at peace, my little one. Shalom, my children."

Approved by Rev. Sean Cronin

1996 May 11, Saturday
EUCHARISTIC ADORATION

Jesus said: "Praise be to Jesus, for Jesus is Lord, Redeemer, King and Saviour. Thank you for opening your heart to my teaching. You will open to Matthew 5.

"In order for my people to know me, they must first be willing to give up the ways of the world. They must realize that being in this world is a gift, created by God the Father; and unless they realize the importance of putting the Creator, my Father, in their lives, they will not have eternal life. Their souls could perish in the flame of eternal fire."

THE GOSPEL ACCORDING TO MATTHEW
MATTHEW 5: The Beatitudes

² **He began to teach them saying "The Beatitudes."**
³ **Blessed are the poor in spirit, for theirs is the Kingdom of God.**

Jesus said: "Do you understand what 'poor in spirit' means?"
(continued in 1996 May 13)

Approved by Rev. Sean Cronin

1996 May 13, Monday
EUCHARISTIC ADORATION

Jesus said: "Praise be to Jesus, for Jesus is Lord, Redeemer, Saviour and King. Thank you, my child, for opening your heart to receive my teachings. Let us return to Matthew 5, v2.

"'Poor in Spirit' is referring to those willing to seek me and to surrender completely to me their free will. These, my precious children, understand that in surrendering completely to me they are willing to become non-existent to the ways of the world. To refrain from all offences being committed against my most wounded Sacred Heart.

"My child the 'poor in spirit' are willing to go against the ways of the world, remembering always they are *in* this world, not *of* this world. Pride is forgotten, and remembering humility is always necessary to be examples of the 'poor in spirit.' Truly releasing the essential focus of one's spiritual life to God the Father, God the Son, and God the Holy Spirit. Willing to die unto one's self that we may live in them. This, my daughter, is 'poor in spirit.' Blessed are the poor in spirit for theirs is the Kingdom of Heaven."

THE GOSPEL ACCORDING TO MATTHEW
MATTHEW 5: The Beatitudes

4 Blessed are they who mourn for they shall be comforted.

Jesus said: "My child, for these my children, who are willing to stand up for their faith at all cost, yes my child, these are called martyrs; this is the ultimate act of love, and this is actually happening now where my children in Africa, Bosnia, China, San Salvador, Russia, many of my children are dying for their faith, and they are giving the ultimate sacrifice, offering life to have life eternal."

Matthew 5, cont'd;

5 Blessed are the meek for they shall inherit the land.

Jesus said: "These gentle of heart, my daughter, can be called the centurions of today. Caring for their brothers and sisters in need through prayer and sacrifice. These children are responding to my call for their brother's spiritual needs. Take heed my children, when it is time for you to answer in the final judgement, were you examples of true commitment to my Father in all aspects of your daily walk of life in faith, in the Sacraments, in your obedience to the commandments?

"This is enough for today, my daughter. I bless you in the Almighty Name of the Father, Son and Holy Spirit. Peace to you, my child. Shalom, my children."

Approved by Rev. Sean Cronin

1996 May 14, Tuesday, 08:00
EUCHARISTIC ADORATION

Jesus said: "Praise be to Jesus, for Jesus is Lord, Redeemer, King and Saviour.

"My little one, thank you for opening your heart for my teaching. Open to Matthew 5, my daughter. We will continue on the Beatitudes, given for all my children that they may enter into the kingdom of my Father.

"So many of my children do not even know what the Beatitudes are. My children, open your hearts to my teachings. They were given for your benefit. Teach your children my word. How will they learn about me, if you yourselves are not willing to teach them? You are their example."

THE GOSPEL ACCORDING TO MATTHEW
MATTHEW 5: The Beatitudes

⁵ **Blessed are the meek for they shall inherit the land.**

Jesus said: "What land, my child?"
(Patsy: "Is it heaven, Jesus?")
"No, my child. Do you remember the forest?"
(Patsy: "Yes, Jesus, that's where we were talking about spiritual growth; we have to clear the forest before we can climb up the mountain.")
"Yes, my child. Those who are meek, my daughter, have walked through the forest, up the mountain now in a spiritual clearing, where the clarity of one's spiritual walk with me is contemplative and serene. They have reached a height in the mystical realm of holiness."
(Patsy: "Oh, my Jesus, how do you do this?")
"Understand the words my child, 'Blessed are the meek.' These precious souls have surrendered completely to the will of my Father

and have allowed the Holy Spirit to direct them. They have seeked to know me and my love through prayer. My child, my gifts are given abundantly as a Father who desires only the best for his children. I Who Am, have given, but my children are not open to receiving my gifts.

"This is enough for today my daughter. I love you my little one. Peace of the Almighty Father, Son and Holy Spirit, to you and your family. Shalom, my little one."

Approved by Rev. Sean Cronin

1996 May 15, Wednesday, 09:05
EUCHARISTIC ADORATION

Jesus said: "Praise be to Jesus, for Jesus is Lord, Saviour and Redeemer. Thank you for opening your heart to my teaching. I will continue, my little one, on the Beatitudes.

"Open, my child, to Matthew 5: v6."

THE GOSPEL ACCORDING TO MATTHEW
MATTHEW 5: The Beatitudes

⁵ **Blessed are they who hunger and thirst for righteousness for they will be satisfied.**

Jesus said: "My daughter, a righteous person in the worldly sense does not have the desire to seek through prayer a closer union with the Father, Son, and Holy Spirit. Righteousness in the spiritual life is uniting in prayer with the Father, Son, and Holy Spirit.

"As I have taught you, if you offer to me your daily duties in this life, asking to unite your offering with the offering of my crucifixion, this is prayer. Anything offered to me in love is considered prayer. A righteous person then seeking to please the Blessed Trinity in their spiritual life, will consider all he does before he does it, and will unite his offering with the offering of my love as the crucified Son to the Almighty Father, Son, and Holy Spirit. The offering becomes purified through my blood, shed on the cross for all of mankind. Do you see the splendor of magnificence in the unity of one's offering of love with the offering of love of the Father, Son, and Holy Spirit? The righteousness of one's spiritual life as one continues to seek the Father, Son, and Holy Spirit in holiness and purity in their offering of prayer.

"This is enough for today, my little one.

"I give a special blessing in the name of the Almighty Father, Son and Holy Spirit. Shalom, my little one."

Approved by Rev. Sean Cronin

1996 May 17, Friday, 09:05
EUCHARISTIC ADORATION

Jesus said: "Praise be to Jesus, for Jesus is Lord, Redeemer, Saviour. Thank you, my little one, for returning for my teaching. Receive my peace, my daughter. Open to Matthew 5. We will continue with the Beatitudes."

THE GOSPEL ACCORDING TO MATTHEW
MATTHEW 5: The Beatitudes

⁵ Blessed are the merciful for they will be shown mercy.

Jesus said: "My mercy, my little one, is not as the world sees mercy. A child taken from its mother's womb through the hands of an abortionist because the child is somehow a problem for the mother, this is not mercy, my little one. This is murder.

"My lost innocents are at the mercy of the murderers!

"When they come before my Father, what will their excuse be? Where was the mercy they showed my lost innocents as they were in such torment shredded to pieces, like paper in a paper shredder. Where is the mercy as they make these decisions to wipe out millions of my lost innocents?"

(Patsy: "This message, my Jesus, is hard to take." But Jesus asked me to go on.)

Jesus said: "This mercy we speak of, my daughter, is as the world sees mercy. In the Beatitudes, I referred to the mercy, justice, and love, which has been given to all from the Creator, my Father. In this world, where men have chosen to deny God, to close their hearts and mind to the Will of my Father, where chance after chance has been given for mankind to return to my Father; have I not shown mercy. Now it is time for my justice. The merciful will be shown mercy for justice's sake. For my children will see now that mercy and justice must go hand in hand, through their own misguided conception of mercy."

Approved by Rev. Sean Cronin

1996 May 19, Sunday, 19:35
EUCHARISTIC ADORATION

Jesus said: "My daughter, praise be to Jesus for Jesus is Lord, Redeemer, Saviour and King. Thank you, my daughter, for opening your heart to receive my teaching."

THE GOSPEL ACCORDING TO MATTHEW
MATTHEW 5: The Beatitudes

8 Blessed are the clean of heart for they shall see God.

Jesus said: "The clean of heart, my little one, have but one focus in their lives, to always place God the Father, God the Son, and God the Holy Spirit in every aspect of their lives. Knowing that by doing this, they are surrendering completely to the Will of the Father. They realize that putting the Blessed Trinity in all they do is offering continuous prayer in their life to the Blessed Trinity. For you see, my daughter, prayer is a grace given to all, and if one is open to the Holy Will of the Father, they allow the Holy Spirit to give them direction in all they do. Child, it is through a continuous prayer life that one comes to know the Holy Spirit. The Holy Spirit will live within one's soul, the temple of the Holy Spirit, if the soul is free from sin.

"One can be baptized in the Holy Spirit, which happens when one asks for an anointing of the Holy Spirit in prayer. In the Sacrament of Confirmation, the confirmed is making a recommitment to purity in thought, word, and example to the teaching of the church.

"This is enough for today, my little one. Peace, my beloved. Shalom, my children."

(Looking up the question "What is Confirmation?" in the pamphlet published by The Regina Press, the answer is as follows: "Through the Sacrament of Confirmation, Jesus confers on Christians the Seal of the Holy Spirit, empowering and obligating them to be his witnesses.")

Approved by Rev. Sean Cronin

1996 May 21, Tuesday, 20:19
EUCHARISTIC ADORATION

Jesus said: "My dearest little one, peace unto you. Thank you for opening your heart for my teaching. I Am, my little one. Praise be to Jesus, for Jesus is Lord, Redeemer, Saviour and King. I, Who Am, come to give you my word to teach all, my daughter, that these teachings may be given to all my children, that they open their hearts to my word. As I taught my children by the Sea of Galilee, I once again come to teach my children my word.

"Let us return to Matthew 5, v8."

THE GOSPEL ACCORDING TO MATTHEW
MATTHEW 5: The Beatitudes

8 Blessed are the clean of heart for they shall see God.

Jesus said: "It is by the grace of the Father that my children who have opened their hearts, minds and souls to His Will, shall see the Father, Son, and Holy Spirit. Pure of heart, my daughter, as I spoke to you of earlier, is just that. Opening the heart, mind and soul in obedience to the Will of the Father, Son, and Holy Spirit."

(Patsy: "This should be easy, Jesus.")

"Oh, my child, nothing in this world is easy. For you see, my child, as I have told you many times, my children must remember they are only *in* this world, not *of* this world. The obstacles that are in this world surround my children, especially with materialistic values, which entice children to become worldly. I have said before, it is easier for a camel to pass through the eye of a needle, than for one who is rich to enter into the Kingdom of God. For you see my little one, as one becomes worldly, he fills himself with what he considers the riches of the world, the pleasures of the world; the blind leading the blind, my child; they do not see the true richness and fullness that could be eternal. Only the richness and fullness of the foolhardy, and when they seek more pleasures because they are not satisfied, they fall into deeper darkness of the soul and mind, looking for more gratification; but they will never appease this hunger, for they will never find true happiness, joy and fulfilment without the Father! You see, my daughter, only the pure of heart shall see the face of the Father, and as they see the Father they shall see the Son, and the Holy Spirit.

"It is time to rest my beloved. Rest in my peace, my little one. I love you, my daughter. Shalom, my children."

Approved by Rev. Sean Cronin

1996 May 22, Wednesday, 08:24
EUCHARISTIC ADORATION

Jesus said: "My little one, praise be to Jesus, for Jesus is Lord, Redeemer and Saviour.

"Open to Matthew 5, v9."

THE GOSPEL ACCORDING TO MATTHEW
MATTHEW 5: The Beatitudes

⁹ **Blessed are the peacemakers for they shall be called children of God.**

Jesus said: "My daughter, a peacemaker is one who not only lives in peace, but also brings peace to all those around him. His actions are always done in peace. One who is in a continuous prayer life will always be at peace.

"You see, my child, my peace comes from within, and as my children are willing to seek the Holy Will of the Father, Son, and Holy Spirit through their prayer life, they receive our gifts abundantly.

"My children, unite your prayers with the Father, Son, and Holy Spirit. Pray, my children, pray.

"I bless you in the Almighty Name of the Father, Son, and Holy Spirit. Shalom, my children."

Approved by Rev. Sean Cronin

1996 May 23, Thursday, 15:55
EUCHARISTIC ADORATION

Jesus said: "Praise be to Jesus, for Jesus is Lord, Redeemer, Saviour and King. Thank you, my daughter, for opening your heart once again to my teaching.

"Open, my daughter, to Matthew 5, v9 and we will continue."

THE GOSPEL ACCORDING TO MATTHEW
MATTHEW 5: The Beatitudes

⁹ Blessed are the peacemakers for they shall be called children of God.

Jesus said: "The peacemakers, my child, they will be called children of God. How difficult it is in this world today to be at peace with one another. There is so much conflict that conflict seems now to be normal. Why, my children, do you take my words so lightly? Do you not see where your ways are leading you? Oh, my children, I know how difficult it is to turn the other cheek. To pray for one another instead of causing more pain and anger to one another.

"Do you not realize, as I wept so bitterly in the Garden of Gethsemane, that those tears were being shed for each one of you? Oh, my children, in this world torn by such evil do you not see that I am the light? I am the way? I am the truth? Must you continue to destroy and torment each other in bitter conflict because you are not willing to turn to God who created you with His supreme love? I Who Am have never forgotten you. I Who Am wait unceasingly for your return. Be known as peacemakers, children of God.

"Pray, my children, pray. Seek me in all you do, and offer to me your daily work. Come to me in prayer. I have never left you. I await your return. I love you."

Approved by Rev. Sean Cronin and Rev. Richard Hoynes

1996 May 29, Wednesday
EUCHARISTIC ADORATION

Jesus said: "Praise be to Jesus for Jesus is Lord, King, Redeemer and Saviour. My little one, thank you for opening your heart to receive my teaching.

"We will continue with the Beatitudes my child."

THE GOSPEL ACCORDING TO MATTHEW
MATTHEW 5: The Beatitudes

⁹ **Blessed are the peacemakers for they shall be called children of God.**

Jesus said: "I spoke to you earlier on a righteous person in the worldly sense, my little one, and the difference of a righteous person committing himself to the Will of the Father, Son, and Holy Spirit.

"Such a difference, my daughter, and there are repercussions in this world for one, who because they are surrendering to the Will of the Father and turn away from their worldly ways, many times they are outcast by those even closest to them. How sad! My children are willing to laugh and ridicule one for their religious beliefs because they themselves have forgotten what truth, peace and joy are.

"They remain blinded by the evil and darkness they have chosen to surround themselves with.

"Righteousness in the worldly sense becomes dishonour and maliciousness, corrupting themselves and those who choose to follow the worldly ways, becoming more indignant and unresponsive to the truth, light and love of the Father, Son, and Holy Spirit."

Approved by Rev. Sean Cronin and Rev. Richard Hoynes

1996 May 30, Thursday
EUCHARISTIC ADORATION

Jesus said: "Peace be unto you, my little one. Praise to the Father, Son, and Holy Spirit, for Jesus is Lord, Saviour, Redeemer and King. Thank you, my child, for opening your heart for my teaching.

"As I have given you teachings on the Beatitudes, I wish to continue with righteousness now in the spiritual sense. It is difficult for my children to release themselves totally to me. For you see, my child, surrendering means dying unto one's self. All my children have been given a free will, and with this free will many choices are made. Sadly, my child, many wrong choices. My children seek the many pleasures of this world, not wanting to prepare themselves for the eternal life of one's soul. They choose to close their eyes to the fact that one's soul lives on forever.

"To become righteous for spiritual gain, my little one, means surrendering to the Will of the Father in all that one does. To put God the Father, God the Son, and God the Holy Spirit, first in their lives. But this would be very difficult for those unwilling to surrender completely to God the Father's plan. Instead they choose the ways of the world, seeking only to please themselves.

"This unwillingness to be open to the promptings of the Holy Spirit leads them astray, only to deaden their senses, taking them further away from the Blessed Trinity.

"A righteous person seeking God and not the pleasures of man surrenders unconditionally to the Will of the Father, therefore pleasing the Father, Son, and Holy Spirit, and receiving the grace to stand firm against all that is not of the Father; bringing one closer in union with the Father, Son, and Holy Spirit. As this holy righteousness empowers the gifts of the Holy Spirit, this, my child, brings forth a union of this Holy Soul with the Father, Son, and Holy Spirit, and the righteous will have the kingdom of heaven as the righteous have inherited the land for the sake of the righteous; for He that is Almighty speaks only truth.

"I love you, my children. Shalom, my little one."

Approved by Rev. Sean Cronin and Rev. Richard Hoynes,

1996 June 01, Saturday
MESSAGE FROM OUR LOVING MOTHER

Our Loving Mother said: "Little one, praise be to Jesus, for Jesus is Lord. Thank you, my little one, for responding to our call.

"My child, these teachings, as the many messages that have been sent to my childreren, have been allowed; for these are the times spoken of, where, through the Will of God the Father, Satan was allowed to roam free, slithering on his belly as a predator lying in wait to destroy the souls of those permeating in the wrath of sin, enticing all who willingly refuse the love of the Father, Son, and Holy Spirit.

"Time is short, my little one. Time, not as man knows it, but as the Almighty Father wills it."

Approved by Rev. Sean Cronin and Rev. Richard Hoynes

1996 June 01, Saturday, 13:13
EUCHARISTIC ADORATION

Jesus said: "My child, praise be to Jesus, for Jesus is Lord, Redeemer, King and Saviour. Yes, my child, I embrace my children as they sing praise and exultations to me. For I as the Father, Son and Holy Spirit embrace and enkindle the love of my children.

"Open to Ezekiel 7."

THE BOOK OF EZEKIEL
EZEKIEL 7: The End Has Come

¹⁹ They shall fling their silver unto the streets and their gold shall be considered refuse. Their silver and gold cannot save them on the day of the Lord's wrath.

Jesus said: "Why, my children, do you not listen to my word? Do you think my word was given just for the sake of giving testimony? No, my children, learn from my word, read my word and take to heart, for I do not plead for my sake, but for yours my children.

"I have spoken on the Beatitudes. These teachings are given for your benefit. Change your ways, my children; listen to my word. My teachings are for each one of you. For time is of the essence, and consequently, your souls are in jeopardy of being spewed to the abyss. For I tell you now, my children, turn from your evil ways, or you shall not know the Father, Son, and Holy Spirit. For to dwell in the house of the Lord you must be cleansed and purified. You have a free will, my children, but will your free will be your downfall?

"I love you, my children. Come to me, my children. I bless you, my children.

"In the beginning, my child, God created man that man might have life eternal. And God said, *'My children shall know me and I shall know mine, that my children shall not perish in the eternal fires.'*

"Pray, my child, pray. My peace be unto you. Thank you, my little one, for opening your heart to my teaching. I know how difficult this is for you. I thank you for responding to my call. Listen with your heart, my daughter, for I leave you with my Mother."

Approved by Rev. Sean Cronin and Rev. Richard Hoynes

1996 June 03, Monday, 11:29
MESSAGE FROM OUR LOVING MOTHER

Our Loving Mother said: "My little one, praise to the Holy Father, Son, and Holy Spirit. Thank you, my daughter, for responding to my call.

"My children, have you not undestood the words my Son brings you in His teachings?

"Do not surround yourselves with the things of this world which draw you away from the love of my Son. What does it matter if you have materialistic wealth and lose your soul to the predator, seeking only to take you with him to the perils of everlasting fire?

"Oh, my children, I have pleaded with you to turn from the ways of the world and to turn to prayer, but to my dismay, many of you do not listen.

"I, as your Mother, will not turn away from you, but I will continue to pray for each of you.

"Pray, my children, pray. Unite your prayers with mine and I will offer them as tokens of my love, to the Father, Son, and Holy Spirit. Become the branches of love that my Son speaks of to each of you, and know that I, as your mother, will entwine each branch with the splendor of my Son's love, protecting you from the predator of evil.

"I love you, my children.

"Pray, my little one pray, and know I am with you."

Approved by Rev. Sean Cronin & Rev. Richard Hoynes

1996 June 03, Monday, 11:29
EUCHARISTIC ADORATION

Jesus said: "Praise be to Jesus, for Jesus is Lord, King, Redeemer and Saviour. Peace unto you my daughter. Thank you for opening your heart to listen to my teaching.

"My little one, open to John 15, v3, and they shall know the Father as the Son and the Holy Spirit.

THE GOSPEL ACCORDING TO JOHN
JOHN 15: The Vine And The Branches

³ You are already pruned because of the word that I spoke to you.

Jesus said: "I Who Am, my little one, I am the word; and the word is the Father, Son, and Holy Spirit; and as you know the word, you know me.

"Suffer not, my little children, through your own desires for pleasures of the world; but know that as you do the Will of the Father, the pleasures of this world will mean less and less to you; for you will know truth, and the truth is my word.

"Love one another as I have loved you; and know that as I am the vine, you are my branches, and your love shall bring forth new branches, as you testify in my name.

"The vine cannot be intertwined with that which is not of me; nor can that which is of the world grow in love, but shall wither and die, for it is not of the Father; nor can it be of the Son; nor can it be of the Holy Spirit. For if it is not of the Blessed Trinity, then it is of the world.

"Many times I have told you, you are *in* this world not *of* this world. Know my word and you shall know me! Love as I have loved you, that branches may flourish and spring forth new branches to carry forth my teachings; and in the end, as you have done as my Father has willed, then shall you have life everlasting.

"Be at peace, my children! Live in my peace.

"I bless each of you in the Almighty Name of the Blessed Trinity, the Father, Son, and Holy Spirit.

"Thank you for opening your heart to my word. I love you, my little one."

Approved by Rev. Sean Cronin and Rev. Richard Hoynes

1996 June 04, Tuesday, 09:15
EUCHARISTIC ADORATION

Jesus said: "My dearest little one, praise be to the Father, Son, and Holy Spirit, for Jesus is Lord, Redeemer, King and Saviour. I bless you with my peace, my little one.

"Open to Jeremiah 16."

THE BOOK OF JEREMIAH
JEREMIAH 16: Jeremiah's Life a Warning

¹¹ You shall answer them; it is because your fathers have forsaken me, says the Lord, and followed strange gods, which they served and worshipped; but me they have forsaken and my law they have not observed.

Jesus said: "My daughter, pray for my people. Do my people not understand my justice must come to this land, for if I allow these atrocities to go on much longer, many more souls shall perish to the pits of eternal fire."

Jeremiah 16 cont'd

¹³ I will cast you out of this land into a land that neither you nor your fathers have known. There you can serve strange gods day and night, because I will not grant you my mercy.

Jesus said: "Change your ways, my children; return to prayer; stay strong in me. Surround yourselves in the holiness of my presence through prayer, and you shall be comforted. I do not come to punish, I come to teach you my way; to love you; to bring order and peace back into your lives; but this can only be done through prayer.

"That you may know me and my love, seek me in all you do. I await your return to me.

"My daughter, thank you for responding to my call."
Approved by Rev. Sean Cronin and Rev. John Neiman

1996 June 05, Wednesday, 08:00
EUCHARISTIC ADORATION

Jesus said: "Praise be to Jesus, for Jesus is Lord, Redeemer, Saviour and King. Peace unto you my children.
"My little one, open to Corinthians 1."

THE FIRST EPISTLE OF PAUL TO THE CORINTHIANS
CORINTHIANS 1: Greeting to the Church

² **Send greetings to the church of God which is in Corinth; to you who have been consecrated in Christ Jesus and called to be a holy people, as to all those who, wherever they may be, call on the name of our Lord Jesus Christ, their Lord and ours.**
³ **Grace and peace from God our Father and the Lord Jesus Christ.**

Jesus said: "My little one, all are called to be holy, that they may enter into the Kingdom of God. Holiness is prayer and prayer is love; and where there is love, there I am, my child, for I am love.

"My children, each of you are called to be ambassadors of my love. This is not difficult. If you seek to love me, you seek to love the Father as the Son and the Holy Spirit. Our love is everlasting.

"As you seek to know me, you seek my love; and as I have loved you, so you shall love one another; and where there is love, there is peace. But this love and peace comes through prayer. I am love and life eternal."

Corinthians 1, cont'd:

Thanksgiving

⁵ **That in him you were enriched in every way, with all discourse and all knowledge.**

⁶ As the testimony to Christ was confirmed among you

⁷ so that you are not lacking in any spiritual gift as you wait for the revelation of our Lord Jesus Christ

⁹ God is faithful, and by Him you were called to fellowship with His Son, Jesus Christ, Our Lord.

Jesus said: "My little one, my children speak of fellowship in the churches. Do they truly understand this term? This was given by the Father, as he gave his only begotten Son to die, crucified, so that all may have life eternal. I gave my life for each of you, my children, I ask you for holiness. Is this such a terrible exchange?

"As I looked up to the Father, I asked my Father to 'forgive them, for they know not what they are doing!' Now can I ask my Father, once again, 'Father, forgive them for they know not what they are doing?'

"Open your eyes, my children, do you not see my love?

"I bless each of you in the Almighty Name of the Father, Son, and Holy Spirit.

"Shalom, my little one."

Approved by Rev. Sean Cronin and Rev. Richard Hoynes

1996 June 06, Thursday, 10:04
EUCHARISTIC ADORATION

Jesus said: "My daughter, my peace unto you. Praise be to Jesus, for Jesus is Lord, Redeemer, Saviour and Messiah.

"I have come to bring you my word, for I am the word, the Messiah; and I bring through my word, my peace, my love, my joy, to all those willing to receive me. In my truth and splendour, I come, my little one, to bring my teachings. Thank you for responding to my call. Bring yourself into my presence through prayer, my daughter. Open to Galatians 3: v2."

THE EPISTLE OF PAUL TO THE GALATIONS
GALATIONS 3: Justification Through Faith

² I want to learn only this from you; did you receive the spirit from works of the law, or from faith in what you heard?

³ Are you so stupid? After beginning with the spirit, are you now ending with the flesh?

⁴ Did you experience so many things in vain — if indeed it was in vain.

⁵ Does, then, the one who supplies the spirit to you and works mighty deeds among you do so from works of the law or from faith in what you heard?

⁶ Thus Abraham believed God, and it was credited to him as righteousness.

Jesus said: "Righteousness, my daughter, as I have spoken of before in the spiritual sense, can then be considered a virtue needed to bring forth a conviction of one's primary existence on this earth. Holiness is needed to bring one closer to unity with the Father, Son, and the Holy Spirit.

"Righteousness in the worldly sense brings forth vanity and takes away the presence of holiness.

"You see, my daughter, how much a difference the same word can have?

"My Father created man unto the image and likeness of God the Creator; Satan destroys the inner beauty of man's soul, for Satan can only destroy.

"As you open your hearts, my children, to my word, you will know truth; but if you stay focused on the materialistic values and worldly endeavors, your heart will not be open to my truths, for through your own free will, the righteousness of the world will lead you to the false god of lies and creator of evil."

Galatians 3, cont'd:

⁷ Realize then that it is those who have faith, who are children of Abraham.

⁸ Scripture, which saw in advance that God would justify the Gentiles by faith, foretold the good news to Abraham saying, "Through you shall all the nations be blessed."

⁹ Consequently, those who have faith are blessed along with Abraham who had faith.

¹⁰ **For all who depend on works of the law are under a curse. For it is written, "Cursed be everyone who does not persevere in doing all the things written in the book of law."**
¹¹ **And that no one is justified before God by the law is clear, for "The one who is righteous by faith will live."**

Jesus said: "Righteous by faith, my daughter, not righteous by the esteemed. Live in my word, by my word, for I Am Word.

"I love you, my children. Shalom, my little one."
(Patsy: I looked up the word "esteem" in the dictionary: "To esteem oneself, lucky, to have a high opinion of.")
Approved by Rev. Sean Cronin and Rev. Richard Hoynes

1996 June 07, Friday
EUCHARISTIC ADORATION

Jesus said: "Praise be to Jesus, for Jesus is Lord, Redeemer, Saviour and King. Thank you for responding to my call. Open my daughter, to Jeremiah 1.

"In the time of Moses, my daughter, my children were released from the bondage of slavery, that they would serve God the Father with their whole being, might and soul. They were given all they needed to live in peace and love with the Father. But as Moses came down from the mountain he found them worshipping idols and living in sin. They had turned from my Father as the children of today have turned from my Father."

THE BOOK OF JEREMIAH
JEREMIAH 1: Oracles in the Days of Josiah

¹ **The words of Jeremiah, son of Hilkiah, of a priestly family in Anathoth, in the land of Benjamin.**
² **The word of the Lord first came to him in the days of Josiah, son of Amon, king of Judah, in the thirteenth year of his reign,**
³ **and continued through the reign of Jehoiakim, son of Josiah, king of Judah, and until the downfall and exile of**

Jerusalem in the fifth month of the eleventh year of Zedekiah, son of Josiah, king of Judah."

Jeremiah 1, cont'd:

⁴ **The word of the Lord came to me thus:**
⁵ **before I formed you in the womb I knew you.**

Jesus said: "Oh, my little one, I Who Am, as I spoke to you yesterday, am the word; do you understand this, my little one?"

(Patsy: "No, Jesus, not really!")

Jesus said: "The word spoken of, my daughter, is God the Father, God the Son, and God the Holy Spirit. My love is everlasting, and as I am the beginning and the end, I shall not have other gods before me. As I have given you life, the soul shall have life eternal; but if my children choose their idols over me, then the soul shall perish in the flames eternal. As these souls perish in the flames eternal they will call out to me, but I will not hear them, for as they are most willing to put their idols before me, they whom I have formed and knew before they were born. I dedicated them, now I must release them; for they have chosen through their own free will, as the children did in the time of Moses, chose their idols to betray me. Oh, my children, why do you continue in the abyss, when you can have life everlasting? Know the word and you shall know me and as you know me, shall you know the Father and the Holy Spirit.

"Thank you, my little one for responding to my call. Shalom, my daughter."

Approved by Rev. Sean Cronin and Rev. Richard Hoynes

1996 June 11, Tuesday, 14:45
EUCHARISTIC ADORATION

Jesus said: "Praise be to Jesus, for Jesus is Lord, Redeemer, Saviour, Messiah.

"Reach out to me, my children, you who have such little faith; know that I am the Messiah, the deliverer, as John spoke to my people, renouncing them for their sins, so I speak to you. You shall know my mercy was then as it is now, for I gave you life eternal, that your sins be cleansed through the waters of Baptism. I give the Sacrament of Reconciliation, so your sins may be forgiven, through my holy ones' anointed hands, to offer the Sacrifice of the Holy Mass, a reenactment of my death upon the cross, that you may have life eternal.

"Open, my little one, to Matthew 3."

THE GOSPEL ACCORDING TO MATTHEW
MATTHEW 3: John the Baptizer

⁴ John wore clothing made of camel's hair and had a leather belt around his waist. His food was locusts and wild honey.
⁵ At that time Jerusalem, all Judea, and the whole region around the Jordan were going out to him.
⁶ They were being baptized by him in Jordan river as they acknowledged their sins.

Jesus said: "You see, my little one, the love of my Father, as He sent my beloved John to give teachings in His Almighty Name. And the Baptisms of the waters that their sins might be forgiven. Has my Father not shown his mercy as He gave His only begotten Son to die, that my children may have life everlasting?"

Matthew 3, cont'd:

⁷ When he saw many of the Pharisees and Sadducees coming to his baptism, he said to them, "You brood of vipers! Who warned you to flee from the coming wrath?
⁸ Produce good fruit as evidence of your repentance,
⁹ and do not presume to say to yourselves, "We have Abraham as our father," for I tell you, God can raise up children to Abraham from these stones.
¹⁰ Even now the axe lies at the root of the trees. Therefore, every tree that does not bear good fruit will be cut down and thrown into the fire.
¹¹ I am baptizing you with water for repentance, but the one who is coming after me is mightier than I. I am not worthy to carry his sandals. He will baptize you with the holy spirit and fire.

Jesus said: "My daughter, on the Feast of Pentecost, as my apostles, disciples, and my Holy Mother were in prayer, upon them came 'tongues of fire,' the anointing of the Holy Spirit. And I said to them, 'Go forth in my name and preach my word that they may know for their sins I have died; and you shall forgive in my name that their souls shall not perish in the flame of everlasting fire.' As I gave them the Holy Spirit, to live on forever in the soul, the temple of the Holy Spirit, the soul must be free of sin, that the Holy Spirit may abide in the soul cleansed, free of sin, by the Sacrament of Reconciliation.

"Now, my sons, with the anointed hands, must go forth and teach as my apostles taught, and forgive as my apostles forgave, and offer the Holy Sacrifice of the Mass as if it were their only Mass, and their last Mass; for I am the Only Begotten Son.

"I gave my life that all my children may have life eternal. I am the Bread of Life, and as they consecrate the bread and wine, they are bringing me, body, blood, soul and divinity in the form of a wafer and wine to give life everlasting.

"I love you, my children. Shalom, my little one."

Approved by Rev. Sean Cronin & Rev. Richard Hoynes

1996 June 12, Wednesday, 07:45
EUCHARISTIC ADORATION

Jesus said: "Praise be to Jesus, for Jesus is Lord, Redeemer, Messiah.

"Welcome, my little one. I thank you and your husband for coming to be with me. I bless you in the almighty name of the Father, Son, and Holy Spirit. Remain in my presence, my little one. Do not worry about the others around you.

"As my little Therese spoke of to you, it is in remaining little, allowing the Holy Spirit to lead you in all you do. Surrendering totally and completely to the Holy Will of the Father, Son, and Holy Spirit; this is the little way, my child.

"Now, I shall prepare you to surrender completely to the Will of the Father through prayer. It is necessary to make a commitment to prayer, and as I have told you before, prayer can be also offering your daily work to me with love. But, I also ask that a time is set aside where you place yourself in my presence and offer prayers, vocalizing in your heart, which is contemplative prayer, or simply just sitting and allowing the Holy Spirit to lead you in silence.

"Now open to Luke 1."

THE GOSPEL ACCORDING TO LUKE
LUKE 1: The Announcement of the Birth of John

⁵ In the days of Herod, king of Judea, there was a priest named Zechariah of the priestly division of Abjah. His wife was from the daughters of Aaron, and her name was Elizabeth.

⁶ Both were righteous in the eyes of God, observing all the commandments and ordinances of the Lord blamelessly;

⁷ but they had not child because Elizabeth was barren, and both were advanced in years.

⁸ Once when he was serving as priest in his division's turn before God

⁹ according to the practice of the priestly service, he was chosen by lot to enter the sanctuary of the Lord to burn incense.

¹⁰ Then, when the whole assembly of the people was praying outside at the hour of the incense offering,

¹¹ the angel appeared to him, standing at the right of the altar of incense.

¹² Zechariah was troubled by what he saw and fear came upon him.

¹³ But the angel said to him, "Do not be afraid, Zechariah, because your prayer has been heard. Your wife Elizabeth will bear you a son, and you shall name him John.

¹⁴ And you will have joy and gladness, and many will rejoice at his birth,

¹⁵ for he will be great in the sight of the Lord, he will drink neither wine nor strong drink. He will be filled with the Holy Spirit even from his mother's womb,

¹⁶ and he will turn many of the children of Israel to the Lord their God."

Jesus said: "Do you see, my little one, how, because of the commitment of prayer, my Father rewarded Zechariah and Elizabeth? It is not the rewards that should draw one to prayer but the love of the Almighty, who, because of his perfect love, created man in his own image. Do you also see how one is drawn closer to God the Father, God the Son, and God the Holy Spirit, through prayer?

"It was in prayer that John was able to go forth and draw others to the Father. It was also through prayer that John, while in the womb, was filled with the Holy Spirit. How many Johns have been aborted, my child, because there was no prayer?

"Oh, my little one, yes, you feel my sadness. My children do not see that because they have stopped praying, many in their families are living in sin, many are losing their souls, because they do not know what prayer is.

"My Mother weeps for the loss of these children's souls. She weeps for the loss of innocence through abortion. Only if my children would listen and return to me. Speak to me, my children, I await you. I am listening.

"Thank you for responding to my call, my little one, Shalom."
Approved by Rev. Sean Cronin and Rev. Richard Hoynes

1996 June 17, Monday, 14:15
EUCHARISTIC ADORATION

Jesus said: "Welcome, my little one, I thank you and your husband for coming to spend time with me.

"Praise be to Jesus, for Jesus is Lord, Redeemer, Saviour, King and Messiah. Thank you for opening your heart to receive my teaching. Open to Leviticus 1, for I am he who is light, and I bring my peace, my holiness unto all who are willing to come to me. I am the Alpha and the Omega — the Beginning and the End, and to all who read my word, they shall have my truths, for I am truth undeniable. I am the word and the word is eternal."

THE BOOK OF LEVITICUS
LEVITICUS 1: Ritual of Sacrifices

¹ **The Lord called Moses, and from the meeting tent gave him this message:**

² speak to the Israelites and tell them when anyone of you wishes to bring an animal offering to the Lord, such an offering must be from the herd or from the flock.

³ If his holocaust offering is from the herd it must be a male without blemish. To find favour with the lord, he shall bring it to the entrance of the meeting tent

⁴ and there lay his hand on the head of the holocaust, so that it may be acceptable to make atonement for him.

Jesus said: "My daughter, atonement in the time of Moses is no different than in these present times. Atonement is asking forgiveness of the Father, Son, and Holy Spirit, for any and all offenses being committed against the Blessed Trinity; for I have told you sin is sin, no matter how small or large the offence. It is the act of desiring to be forgiven, which brings forgiveness because of my merciful love; but it is also necessary that a change is made within this person, with a true desire not to commit the sin again. In acknowledging one's offence against the Blessed Trinity, one also acknowledges a true desire to remain in union with the Blessed Trinity through prayer and example for one another, remembering that belonging to the Blessed Trinity as the Father Abba King, Son, Redeemer, Messiah, and Holy Spirit, Paraclete, Spouse, are Three in One, and the holy soul receiving the Blessed Eucharist then becomes one with the Father, Son, and Holy Spirit. The Blessed Trinity as one with the Mystical Body united; this, my daughter, should be the desire of all my children; for all my children are within the Mystical Body of Unity.

"Prayer offered by one soul reflects on all souls of the Mystical Body. If one child offers prayer to the Blessed Trinity, it is offered from all souls; yet if one denies my truth, not all souls are condemned for that one soul; that is my mercy; but my justice must come forth, and this will cause abandonment from the Mystical Body to the souls denying my truths.

"Pray, my little one, pray. I ask all my children to pray and surrender completely to me, for upon surrendering completely to me, you shall have life eternal.

"Thank you, my daughter, for responding to my call."

Approved by Rev. Sean Cronin and Rev. Richard Hoynes

1996 June 19, Wednesday, 13:20
EUCHARISTIC ADORATION

Jesus said: "Praise be to Jesus, for Jesus is Lord, Redeemer, King, Savior and Deliverer.

"My child, open your heart and receive my peace. Do not allow the ploys of the evil one to distract your peace.

"My daughter, pray during these distractions, calling out my name, instead of becoming angry. Return to me as you are able, and I will continue with the teachings.

"I love you, my little one. Shalom; my peace take with you."
Approved by Rev. Sean Cronin and Rev. Richard Hoynes

1996 June 20, Thursday, 02:13
EUCHARISTIC ADORATION

Jesus said: "Praise be to Jesus, for Jesus is Lord, Saviour, Redeemer and Deliverer. Open your heart, my little one, for my teaching. Thank you for preparing yourself through prayer, to place yourself in my presence.

"Open to Jeremiah chapter 15, my daughter; read from chapter 15 to chapter 31."

THE BOOK OF JEREMIAH
JEREMIAH 31: The New Covenant

[31] **"The days are coming," says the Lord, "when I will make a new covenant with the house of Israel and the house of Judah.**

[32] **It will not be like the covenant I made with their fathers the day I took them by the hand to lead them forth from the land of Egypt; for they broke my covenant, and I had to show myself their master," says the Lord.**

[33] **"But this is the covenant which I will make with the house of Israel after those days, says the Lord. I will place my Law within them, and write it upon their hearts; I will be their God, and they shall be my people.**

[34] **No longer will they have need to teach their friends and kinsmen how to know the Lord. All from least to the**

greatest, shall know me," says the Lord, "for I will forgive their evil doing and remember their sin no more."

Jesus said: "In Jeremiah's teaching, you will see that the focus of the lessons are so that my children learn from their mistakes, and that it is necessary to turn from sin in order that my peace and my love are brought back into one's life. The state of the soul must be that sin be avoided in order that the Holy Spirit may abide in the temple of the Holy Spirit, one's soul."

Approved by Rev. Sean Cronin and Rev. Richard Hoynes

1996 June 24, Monday, 09:00
The Feast of St. John the Baptist
EUCHARISTIC ADORATION

Jesus said: "Praise be to Jesus, for Jesus is Lord, Redeemer, Saviour and Deliverer. Thank you for opening your heart for my teaching, my daughter.

"Who is Immanuel my Daughter?"

(Patsy: "Jesus, you.")

"Yes, my little one, I am Immanuel, the deliverer!"

THE BOOK OF ISAIAH
ISAIAH 11: The Rule of Immanuel

¹ But a shoot shall sprout from the stump of Jesse and from his roots a bud shall blossom:

² The spirit of the Lord shall rest upon him; a spirit of wisdom and of understanding, a spirit of counsel and of strength, knowledge and of fear of the Lord,

³ and his delight shall be the fear of the Lord. Not by appearance shall he judge, nor by hearsay shall he decide;

⁴ but he shall judge the poor with justice and decide aright for the land's afflicted. He shall strike the ruthless with the rod of his mouth and with the breath of his lips he shall slay the wicked.

⁵ Justice shall be the band around his waist, and faithfulness a belt upon his hips.

Jesus said: "My child, be at peace, conform your ways to uphold my direction. It is, as has been written; I came so that my people should be set free. Am I not he that came from the Father through the Holy Spirit and I give to mine the wisdom the Father has given me? And as the Holy Spirit shall lead you, so shall it be as my Father has willed it. Do you remember, my little one, the parable of the vineyard? In the parable of the vineyard, the labourers questioned the landowner as to why some labourers who worked less hours were paid the same as the others. Do my children have a right to question my judgments?"

(Patsy: "Jesus, I don't understand.")

Jesus said: "God the Father has given equally to all his children from the beginning of time; for all men were created in his image and likeness. He gave His only begotten Son, that all may have life eternal. He chose my Mother to bring forth the Deliverer. My Father has given faithfully to his children and he asks very little in return. But as the landowner was questioned and the workers displeased, "When from the root of the tree of Jesse came forth the Son of God, Satan in his arrogance questioned and renouncing the Father's word, resolving that he was to reign king; but fool as Satan is, brought forth the wrath of God upon himself and his followers; and Satan continues to prey upon my people, continually seeking to destroy man's soul.

"My children, do not stay in the darkness of the evil predator, but return to the light which my Father placed within you. Do not question as the labourers in the vineyard questioned but surrender to the Will of the Father, as the bud which blossomed forth from the stump of Jesse.

"Thank you, my daughter, for responding to my call. Shalom, my people."

Approved by Rev. Sean Cronin and Rev. Richard Hoynes

1996 June 25, Tuesday
EUCHARISTIC ADORATION

Jesus said: "My peace come unto you, my beloved. Praise be to Jesus Christ, for Jesus is Lord, Saviour, Redeemer, Messiah. I, Who Am, come to you my, daughter, once again to bring you teachings of my word.

"As Ephesians 6 states, 'Put on the armour of God,' the armour, my daughter, against the evil predator of souls, is prayer; and Satan fears especially the greatest of all prayers and supplication, my Holy Mass and receiving the Holy Eucharist. For he knows truth and my truth he fears. For it is I who come alive to the souls of mankind, body, blood, soul and divinity. The evil one knows that as I am received, I am giving life eternal to the soul who receives me. The evil predator seeks to empower one's soul before I am within this soul; for once I am received, he no longer can enslave his victim."

THE EPISTLE OF PAUL TO THE EPHESIANS
EPHESIANS 6: The Battle Against Evil

[10] **Finally draw your strength from the Lord and from his mighty power.**
[11] **Put on the armour of God so that you may be able to stand firm against the tactics of the devil.**
[12] **For our struggle is not with flesh and blood but with the principalities, with the powers, with the world rulers of this present darkness, with the evil spirits in the heavens.**
[13] **Therefore put on the armour of God, that you may be able to resist on the evil day, and having done everything to hold your ground.**
[14] **So stand fast with your loins girded in truth, clothed with righteousness as a breastplate.**
[15] **And your feet shod in readiness for the gospel of peace.**
[16] **In all circumstances hold faith as a shield, to quench all the flaming arrows of the evil one.**
[17] **And take the helmet of salvation and the sword of the spirit, which is the word of God!**

Jesus said: "Do you see, my little one, how I emphasize the 'word of God'? I told you earlier in my teaching, "I am word and the word is the Father, Son and Holy Spirit. Learn, my children, my word. As you read my word, I will fill you with the grace to know my word. And as you know the word you will know me.

"It is all done through prayer, my children. And what is prayer? It is the offering of your love to me. Come to me, my little ones. I invite you to the springs of everlasting grace which will consume you with my eternal love.

"Thank you, my little one, for surrendering to my will and responding to my call.

"I love you. Shalom."

Approved by Rev. Sean Cronin & Rev. Richard Hoynes

1996 July 26, Friday, 07:30
Feast of St. Joachim and St. Anne
EUCHARISTIC ADORATION

Jesus said: "Praise be to Jesus, for Jesus is Lord, Saviour, Redeemer and Messiah Deliverer. Thank you for coming to be with me today, my little one and for coming to receive my teaching.

"Today is a very special day, my little one, as it is the feast of my holy grandparents; a sign of holiness and true example of the meaning of a holy family united with the Almighty Father, Son and Holy Spirit.

"My daughter, trust in me. I am your strength. It is through me, my little one, that all is accomplished. I only ask that you trust in me. Allow my mercy to flow, for it is in surrendering completely to me which allows you to be used to receive my teaching.

"Open to Sirach 1."

THE BOOK OF SIRACH
SIRACH 1: Praise of Wisdom

¹ **All wisdom comes from the Lord and with him it remains forever.**

Jesus said: "My children open your heart to receive my wisdom; but this wisdom can only be given to you if you remain in unity with my Holy Will.

"How, you ask, is this done?

"Through prayer, my children, and through keeping my commandments; in surrendering your will completely to the Father, Son, and Holy Spirit. I understand it is not easy to surrender your free will. You must first come to me in prayer with a daily commitment in the dialogue of love; then you receive my grace to help you to desire and accomplish a surrender of your free will.

"My beloved grandparents, Joachim and Anne, surrendered to the Will of the Father, as they gave their only child to be used mightily to the Will of the Father. And this holy innocence in surrendering her free will through the power of the Holy Spirit, the Son of the Father, was brought forth to set all humanity free. I surrendered to the Will of the Father when I died on the holy cross of salvation for all my children.

"Do you see the beauty of surrendering to the Will of the Father, Son and Holy Spirit? Do you see the magnitude of love evolved in the surrender of one's free will?

"I love you, my children. Shalom, my little one."

Approved by Rev. Sean Cronin

1996 June 27, Thursday, 07:00
EUCHARISTIC ADORATION

Jesus said: "Praise be to Jesus, for Jesus is Lord, Saviour, Redeemer, Messiah, Deliverer. My peace unto you my beloved. Thank you for coming to receive my teaching.

"And in the days of Herod, my daughter, man worshipped idols. They lived to fulfil themselves in the worldly pleasures. When it came time to renounce their idols, for they *also* had been given a chance to return to God the Almighty Father. They chose to betray him, and his wrath was brought upon them.

"Now open to Sirach 7."

THE BOOK OF SIRACH
SIRACH 7: Conduct in Public Life

1 **Do no evil and evil will not overtake you;**
2 **avoid wickedness and it will turn aside from you!**
3 **Sow not in the furrows of injustice, lest you harvest it sevenfold.**
4 **Seek not from the Lord authority, nor from the king a place of honour.**
5 **Parade not your justice before the Lord, and before the king flaunt not your wisdom.**

6 Seek not to become a judge if you have not strength to root out crime, or you will show favour to the ruler and mar your integrity.

7 Be guilty of no evil before the city's populace, nor disgrace yourself before the assembly.

8 Do not plot to repeat a sin; not even for one will you go unpunished.

Jesus said: "As in the time of Herod, my daughter, my people of today place their idols before God, and they have been given warning, that my justice shall come in the flames of fury. They offered holocausts to their gods, their idols; but there is only one God, and I shall bring forth my justice with a vengeance.

"Now in these present times they offer human sacrifice. Do they think my lost innocents will be forgotten? They desire to use my precious unborn for experimental testing. These my precious innocents have souls. And their souls call out to me for justice. Not even in Herod's time, with the slaughter of so many innocents, does it compare to the atrocities of today's mutilations!

"I warn you my people, you have slithered in the realm of evil discourse far too long. Repent and stop this evil holocaust or suffer as you have chosen to make my lost innocents suffer."

Sirach 7 cont'd:

16 Do not esteem yourself better than your fellows; remember his wrath will not delay.

17 More and more, humble your pride; what awaits man is worms.

"I am with you, my beloved."

Approved by Rev. Sean Cronin,
Rev. Richard Hoynes and Rev. John Neiman

1996 June 28, Friday, 06:55
Feast of St. Iraneus
EUCHARISTIC ADORATION

Jesus said: "Praise be to Jesus, for Jesus is Lord, Saviour and Messiah. My peace unto you, my little one. Thank you for coming to receive my teaching. Open to Jeremiah 4, v11, for we shall continue. As I have given my warning and my people have not seemed willing to listen.

"Has my Mother not come to many seeking prayer and change of heart? Change from the evil destruction upon my Innocents."

THE BOOK OF JEREMIAH
JEREMIAH 4: The Invasion From The North

[11] At that time it will be said of this people and of Jerusalem, "From the glaring heights through the desert a wind comes toward the daughter of my people not to win now; not to cleanse,

[12] does this wind from the heights come at my bidding, and I myself now pronounce sentence upon them."

[13] See! Like storm clouds he advances, like a hurricane his chariots; swifter than eagles are his steeds: "Woe to us! we are ruined."

[14] Cleanse your heart of evil, O Jerusalem, that you may be saved. How long must your pernicious thoughts lodge within you?

[15] Listen! They proclaim it from Dan, from Mount Ephraim they announce destruction:

[16] "Make this known to the nations; announce it to Jerusalem: the besiegers are coming from the distant land, shouting their war cry against the cities of Judah."

[17] Like watchmen of the fields they surround her, for she has rebelled against me, says the Lord.

[18] Your conduct, your misdeeds, have done this to you; how bitter is this disaster of yours, how it reaches to your very heart!

Jesus said: "My daughter, remain in my presence; do not worry about others around you, for you are here to be with me, my little one. This continuous destruction of my unborn innocents must stop. The mutilations in the name of science is an abomination which will draw disaster from every corner of the earth. Continue on this deathwatch and see the furious wrath of destruction you have called upon yourselves. Pray, my daughter, pray. Cry out, my people, in my name, that this contamination of evil is stopped before more of my innocents are mutilated. Woe unto you if you continue on this destructive path.

"Pray, my little one, pray.

"If all families would gather in my name, family unity could be restored; this destruction of innocents would stop. Peace would be brought back into this world.

"Seek me, my children. Return to me, my children. Pray, my children."

Approved by Rev. Sean Cronin and Rev. Richard Hoynes

1996 July 01, Monday, 14:45
Feast of Blessed Father Serra
EUCHARISTIC ADORATION

Jesus said: "Praise be to Jesus, for Jesus is Lord, Saviour, Redeemer, Deliverer. Thank you, my little one, for coming to be with me. Open to Isaiah 10. Remember, my children, I have chosen each of you. You are my branches, I am the vine. I come to give you life eternal, not to destroy. I am He Who comes in the Almighty Name of the Father, Son, and Holy Spirit. I am the breath of life!"

ISAIAH 10: Sennacherib's Invasion

30 Cry and shriek, O daughter of Gallim! Hearken, Laishah! Answer her Anathoth!
31 Madmenah is in flight, the inhabitants of Gebim seek refuge.
32 Even today he will halt at Nob, he will shake his fist at the mount of daughter Zion, the hill of Jerusalem!
33 Behold, the Lord, the Lord of hosts, lops off the boughs with terrible violence; the tall of stature are felled, and the lofty ones brought low;
34 the forest thickets are felled with the axe, and Lebanon in its slpendor falls.

Jesus said: "My little one, as I come now to teach my people, I do not turn from them because they do not want to listen. I, as my

Mother, have never stopped loving all my children; but I cannot and will not allow them to continue on this path of destruction.

"I have pleaded with mankind since the beginning of time to withdraw from worldly pleasures seeking to destroy man's soul. A free will has been given to each man, and man must choose the path he is to take. If one desires to continually reject the chances I have placed before them, then my justice must be brought forth.

"Man has taken it upon himself to deny the rights of the unborn innocents. It is God the Father, the Creator, not man, who superimposes this decree of life and death. It will be done according to the will of the Father, not according to the will of man."

THE BOOK OF ISAIAH
ISAIAH 10: Social Injustice

[33] Behold, the Lord, the Lord of hosts, lops off the boughs with terrible violence; the tall of stature are felled, and the lofty ones brought low.

Jesus said: "My child, God created man, and only God has the right to take life. The soul lives on forever. Whether it lives eternally with the Father, or in the flame of everlasting fire, is of man's choosing, because man has the gift of a free will."

Approved by Rev. Sean Cronin and Rev. Richard Hoynes

1996 July 02, Tuesday, 07:45
EUCHARISTIC ADORATION

Jesus said: "Praise be to Jesus, for Jesus is Lord, Saviour, Messiah and Deliverer. Come, my children, come back to me. For I Am, and I bring you to life everlasting through my body, my blood, my soul, my divinity.

"My child, thank you for opening your heart once again for my teaching.

"Truly, I say to you child, my Mother is referred to as the 'rose,' and I am the 'bud,' as I am the Rose of Sharon. I am the beginning and the end, as I am word.

"Now, my little one, open to Psalm 21, v9."

THE BOOK OF PSALMS
PSALM 21: Thanksgiving and Prayers for the King

⁹ **Your hand will reach all your enemies, your right hand will reach your foes!**
¹⁰ **At the time of your coming you will drive them into a furnace.**

Jesus said: "My little one, as they have continued on this path of evil destruction, they shall suffer more than the sufferings of my lost innocents."

Psalm 21,v10 cont'd:

Then the lord's anger will consume them, devour them with fire.
¹¹ **Even their descendants you will wipe out from the earth, their offspring from the human race.**

Jesus said: "As they have mutilated millions of my lost innocents, my daughter, they now, in what they call medical breakthrough and scientific experimentation on my precious innocents, have taken them from their mother's womb alive, and then to be dissected in the name of science.

"My daughter, as in the Psalm of David, Psalm 22, my lost innocent souls call out to me."

PSALM 22: Passion and Triumph of the Messiah

² **My God, my God, why have you abandoned me? Why so far from my call for help, from my cries of anguish?**

Jesus said: "Pray, my children, pray.

"I am with you, my little one. Thank you for responding to my call."

Approved by Rev. Sean Cronin and Rev. Richard Hoynes

1996 July 04, Thursday, 08:20
EUCHARISTIC ADORATION

Jesus said: "Praise be to Jesus, for Jesus is Lord, Saviour, Redeemer, Messiah. Thank you, my little one, for coming to be with me.

"Prayer, my daughter, is a dialogue of love with commitment to God the Father, Son, and Holy Spirit. If this enactment desiring to belong to the Blessed Trinity is faithfully done, the person will come to develop a greater desire to commitment in this holy dialogue with the Blessed Trinity. As one begins to seek me in this commitment of love, the desire to unite one's love with my love then becomes a constant desire to seek me in all they do. They will realize there is no love as mine, for you see, my daughter, I am the pure essence of love, and to reach this only takes a commitment to one's dialogue of love to me.

"Open, my daughter, to Psalm 33."

THE BOOK OF PSALMS
PSALM 33: Praise of the Lord's Power and Providence

¹ **Rejoice you just, in the Lord; praise from the upright is fitting.**
² **Give thanks to the Lord on the harp; on the ten-stringed lyre offer praise. Sing to God a new song;**
³ **skillfully play with joyful chant.**
⁴ **For the Lord's word is true; all his works are trustworthy.**
⁵ **The Lord loves justice and right and fills the earth with goodness.**

Jesus said: "Oh, my little one, do you see the beauty of my love? My love is for all. I do not love one less than another, but for those who seek my love, they will know me. For those who do not, they will not be able to know my love. I can fill all the desire of true love because I am love; and if one will begin to read my word, they will know me, for I am word. It is through the word they will find love.

"This is enough for today, my little one. Thank you for responding to my call. As you come to receive me in the Holy Eucharist, I open the doors to the springs of life eternal. Draw from those springs daily to refresh your desire for me.

"Shalom, my little one."

Approved by Rev. Sean Cronin,
Rev. John Neiman and Rev. Richard Hoynes

1996 July 05, Friday, 07:45
EUCHARISTIC ADORATION

Jesus said: "Praise be to Jesus, for Jesus is Lord, Saviour, Redeemer, and Messiah.

"Welcome my little one, thank you for coming to be with me. I am the font of mercy, and all who come to me shall be refreshed from the springs of unboundless graces. For my mercy will be given to those of my children who seek me in all they do. Be refreshed, my children, come to the font of mercy, receive my love, my children; surrender completely to me."

"Open to Matthew 10."

THE GOSPEL ACCORDING TO MATTHEW
MATTHEW 10: Mission of the Twelve

1 **Then he summoned his twelve disciples and gave them authority over unclean spirits to drive them out and to cure every disease and every illness.**
2 **The names of the twelve apostles are these: first Simon called Peter, and his brother Andrew; James, the son of Zebedee, and his brother John;**
3 **Philip and Bartholomew, Thomas and Matthew the tax collector; James, the son of Alphaeus, and Thaddeus;**
4 **Simon the Cananean, and Judas Iscariot who betrayed him.**

Matthew 10 cont'd:

16 **Behold, I am sending you like sheep in the midst of wolves, so be shrewd as serpents and simple as doves.**
17 **But beware of people, for they will hand you over to courts and scourge you in their synagogues.**

[18] **And you will be led before governors and kings for my sake as a witness before them and the pagans.**

Jesus said: "My daughter, I have sent many of these my messengers out to my people asking for prayer. Many of these my messengers are ridiculed, but I give you all the grace to continue to deliver my messages, my teachings to my people; for if even just one of my children is saved, then all of heaven rejoices."

Matthew 10 cont'd:

[19] **When they hand you over, do not worry about how you are to speak or what you are to say. You will be given at that moment what you are to say.**
[20] **For it will not be you who speaks but the Spirit of Our Father speaking through you.**

Jesus said: "For I tell you now, my little one, if they allow the Holy Spirit to speak through these my messengers, truth shall be heard, and they will know my truths if they open to my word."

Matthew 10 cont'd:

[21] **Brother will hand over brother to death, and the father, his child; children will rise up against parents and have them put to death.**

Jesus said: "My little one, are these things not happening now in these present times? Do they not see that which was prophesized so long? The warnings that have been given so that my children will fall to their knees in prayer. Open your hearts, my children, to my word. For I say to you now, you must turn to me, seek me in all you do or suffer my just wrath for the sins in which you continue to wallow."

Matthew 10 cont'd:

[22] **You will be hated by all because of my name, but whoever endures to the end will be saved.**

Jesus said: "You see my children, you who have willingly opened your heart to my messages. As in the time of my apostles, they also feared the ridicule and the repercussions for testifying in my name. But I was with them as I am with each one of you; and I am your strength.

"Come follow me, my children, and I will lead you home.

"Pray, my children, pray. Know that I am with each one of you.

"Shalom, my little one."

Approved by Rev. Sean Cronin,
Rev. John Neiman & Rev. Richard Hoynes

1996 July 06, Saturday
EUCHARISTIC ADORATION

Jesus said: "Praise be to Jesus, my child, for Jesus is Lord, Redeemer, Saviour, King and Deliverer. Peace unto you, my children.

"It is through prayer that you open the hearts of men. I have given my teaching on the dialogue of love, which is your praise in prayer to God the Father, Son, and Holy Spirit.

"Prayer can also be a plea from the heart in time of sorrow and need. Prayer is all communication with the Father, Son, and Holy Spirit.

"Open to Lamentations 1."

THE BOOK OF LAMENTATIONS
LAMENTATIONS 1: Jerusalem Abandoned and Disgraced

¹ **How lonely she is now, the once crowded city! Widowed is she who was mistress over nations; the princess among the provinces has been made a toiling slave.**

Jesus said: "This verse, my child, speaks of a nation, which because they turned away from God, was left to stand alone. This is where *your* country is at. A place alone, consumed by evil; because this is what my people have chosen."

Lamentations 1 cont'd:

² **Bitterly she weeps at night, tears upon her cheeks, with not one to console her of all her dear ones; her friends have all betrayed her and become her enemies.**

Jesus said: "My daughter, your country stands alone, and soon all will see how; as they have taken God out of their schools, and killed the innocent in the name of justice; opened the door to death with dignity in the name of freedom and the right of choice; allowed explicit sex, violence in the form of entertainment. How much lower into the abyss is there to go and my people wonder why their country stands alone?"

Lamentations 1 cont'd:

³ **Judah has fled into exile from oppression and cruel slavery; yet where she lives among the nation she finds no place to rest; all her persecutors come upon her, where she is narrowly confined.**

Jesus said: "How many times must I tell you? Open your eyes, my children, and see the misery that you yourselves are bringing down upon yourselves."

Lamentations 1 cont'd:

¹² **Come, all you who pass by the way, look and see, whether there is suffering like my suffering, which has been dealt me, when the lord afflicted me on the day of his blazing wrath.**

Jesus said: "Do not stay in this epitome of darkness any longer, but come to the light and I will give you life eternal.

"Pray, my children, pray. Surrender completely to me.

"Thank you for responding to my call, my little one. Shalom, my children."

Approved by Rev. Sean Cronin,
Rev. John Neiman and Rev. Richard Hoynes

1996 July 09, Tuesday, 07:05
EUCHARISTIC ADORATION

Jesus said: "Welcome, my little one, thank you for coming to be with me and for opening your heart to receive my teaching. I, Who Am, bless you, your family, and all those who come to be here with me.

"Now, my little one, open to Isaiah 3."

THE BOOK OF ISAIAH
ISAIAH 3: Judgement of Judah and Jerusalem

¹ **The Lord, the Lord of hosts, shall take away from Jerusalem and from Judah support and prop (i.e., all supplies of bread and water).**

² **Hero and warrior, judge and prophet, fortune teller and elder,**

³ **the captain of fifty and the nobleman, counsellor, skilled magician, and expert charmer.**

⁴ **I will make striplings their princes; the fickle shall govern them,**

⁵ **and the people shall oppress one another, yes every man his neighbour. The child shall be bold toward the elder, and the base toward the honourable.**

⁶ **When a man seizes his brother in his father's house saying, "You have clothes! be our ruler, and take in hand this ruin!"**

⁷ **Then shall he answer in that day "I will not undertake to cure this, when in my own house there is no bread or clothing! You shall not make me ruler of the people."**

⁸ **Jersualem is crumbling, Judah is falling, for their speech and their deeds are before the lord, a provocation in the sight of his majesty.**

Jesus said: "My daughter, again we speak of my justice. I understand your reluctance to take this teaching. Jesus is Lord, Saviour, Redeemer, Deliverer, and it is precisely that because I *am* the Deliverer, that my teaching must be on my Justice. My children are not opening their hearts to me, nor to my word."

(Patsy, "But Jesus, I just started writing your teachings.")

Jesus replied: "But my daughter, these teaching's have always been. My people have turned away from the Mother Church and have turned away from me."

(Patsy, "But what about the ones who remain faithful to you?")

Jesus replied: "I remain faithful to them."

(Patsy, "Then why do we go over the teachings on your justice? Please forgive me, Jesus, for asking these questions, but I don't understand.")

Jesus replied: "My daughter, if just one child receives this message and turns from evil, I have told you all of heaven rejoices. Just as the shepherd who loses one of his sheep, he doesn't stop and think, "Do I go look for the missing lamb?" He knows his sheep, and knows they are unable to care for themselves, so he goes and looks for this lost lamb. As with me, my little one, I continue to look for my lost sheep, even just one I look for.

"Listen, my children, open your hearts to my teachings. I do not come to teach that you might fear, but if this fear brings you back to me, then know it is I who will comfort you.

"Pray, my children, pray.

"Thank you, my beloved, for responding to my call, for I *do* know how difficult this is for you.

"Shalom, my little one."

Approved by Rev. Sean Cronin and Rev. John Neiman

1996 July 10, Wednesday
EUCHARISTIC ADORATION

Jesus said: "Welcome, my little one. Thank you for coming to be with me and for bringing your son to the Holy Sacrifice of the Mass.

"My child, open your heart to receive my teaching; for it is I who come so that my children may refresh their hearts from the tree of knowledge.

"Open to Jeremiah 15."

THE BOOK OF JEREMIAH
JEREMIAH 15: The Great Drought

¹ **The Lord said to me: even if Moses and Samuel stood before me, my heart would not turn toward this people. Send them away from me.**

Jesus said: "If my children do not turn away from this path of evil destruction upon my lost innocents, then as my Father has decreed, then shall I send those who have mutilated and tortured my lost innocents, I shall send them away, and then my mercy shall be removed away from them, because I have pleaded for mercy for my lost innocents, and they have turned away from me.
"Now open to Ezekiel 3."

THE BOOK OF EZEKIEL
EZEKIEL 3: Eating of the Scroll

¹ **He said to me: Son of man eat what is before you; eat this scroll, then go, speak to the house of Israel.**
² **So I opened my mouth and he gave me the scroll to eat.**
³ **Son of man, he then said to me, feed your belly and fill your stomach with this scroll I am giving you. I ate it, and it was as sweet as honey in my mouth. He said,**
⁴ **Son of man, go now to the house of Israel, and speak my words to them.**

Jesus said: "And I say to you my children, open to my word, for if you do not know my word you cannot know me. How will you be able to set examples to your children if you do not understand what I am asking you; and how can you understand what I am asking you if you do not read my word?"

Ezekiel 3 cont'd: The Prophet as Watchman

¹⁷ **Thus the word of the Lord came to me; son of man: I have appointed you a watchman for the house of Israel. When you hear a word from my mouth, you shall warn them for me.**

Jesus said: "I have given my warning, my children, and with my warning I have taken from my word that you may see that which was spoken of before has come to pass and is to be; but unless you open your hearts to my word, you will remain in the blindness which keeps you from my truths.

"Thank you, my little one, for responding to my call. I am with you.

"Now open the eyes of your soul that you may see. Describe what you see, my daughter."

(Patsy: "I see a desert and there are little children walking. They seem lost, some are sad, some are crying.")

Jesus replied: "My daughter, these are the many children who do not know me. They do not even know for whom or what they are looking for. They only know and feel this loss and sadness.

"Are these yourselves, my children, or are they *your* children? Do you feel this sadness; this loss? Then come to me. I will take you out of this desert."

Ezekiel 3 cont'd: Ezekiel's Dumbness

²² The hand of the Lord came upon me and he said to me; get up and go out into the plain, where I will speak with you.

²³ So I got up and went out into the plain, and I saw that the glory of the Lord was in that place, like the glory I had seen by the river Chebar. I fell prone,

²⁴ but then spirit entered into me and set me on my feet, and he spoke with me.

Jesus said: "I love you, my children. Shalom my little one."

Approved by Rev. Sean Cronin,
Rev. John Neiman and Rev. Richard Hoynes

1996 July 11, Thursday, 07:45
EUCHARISTIC ADORATION

Jesus said: "Welcome, my little one. Praise be to Jesus, for Jesus is Lord, Saviour, Redeemer and Messiah. Thank you for coming to receive my teaching.

"Open to Thessalonians 1."

THE FIRST EPISTLE OF PAUL TO THE THESSALONIANS
THESSALONIANS 1: A Model for Believers

⁷ **So that you became a model for all the believers in Macedonia and in Achaia.**

⁸ **For from you the word of the Lord has sounded forth not only in Macedonia and in Achaia, but in every place your faith in God has gone forth, so that we have no need to say anything.**

Jesus said: "As in my previous teachings, my daughter, if one allows the Holy Spirit to come forth, the grace is given for the person to be used as our vessel. Faith and trust, my little one, comes through prayer and in allowing the prompting of the Holy Spirit; this vessel shall be used.

"Close your eyes my little one. What do you see?"

(Patsy: "I see people kneeling and a flame over their head.")

Jesus said: "These are my children who have opened their hearts to me, asking and desiring to do my Holy Will. The many messengers, like yourself, my little one, who are willing to be used as my vessels."

1 THESSALONIANS 2: Paul's Sincerity

¹ **For you yourselves know, brothers, that our reception among you was not without effect.**

² **Rather, after we had suffered and been insolently treated, as you know, in Philippi, we drew courage through our God to speak to you the Gospel of God with much struggle.**

Jesus said: "You see, my little one, why you must prepare yourself to place yourself in my presence to receive my teaching. Yet even when you find it difficult to receive my teaching, you continue on; you try. This is my strength and your willingness to try through the grace I give you, my daughter."

1 Thessalonians 2 cont'd:

⁴ **But as we were judged worthy by God to be entrusted with the Gospel, that is how we speak, not as trying to please human beings, but rather God, who judges our hearts.**

Jesus said: "What do you see now, my little one?"
(Patsy: "I see a large heart consuming a small heart.")
Jesus said: "As you continually seek to please me in all that you do, your desire and willingness to be used as my vessel, I gently consume and transform your heart uniting it with mine, that we are one."

1 THESSALONIANS 5: The Need For Preparartion

⁸ **But since all are of the day, let us be sober, putting on the breastplate of faith and love and the helmet that is hope for salvation.**
⁹ **For God did not destine us for wrath, but to gain salvation through our Lord Jesus Christ,**
¹⁰ **Who died for us, so that whether we are awake or asleep we may live together with Him.**
¹¹ **Therefore encourage one another and build one another up, as indeed you do.**

Jesus said: "I am with you, my children. Pray, my children, pray.
"Shalom, my little one."

1996 July 12, Friday, 14:45
EUCHARISTIC ADORATION

Jesus said: "Thank you my daughter for coming to be with me and for bringing my children to come and visit with me. I bless each in the Almighty Name of the Father, Son and Holy Spirit. Praise be to Jesus, for Jesus is Lord, Saviour, Messiah and Deliverer.

"I come that my nations may find peace, but it will only be if they open their hearts to prayer. It was not I that separated the children in their religions, for I love all my children equally. This was done through man's own deception of truth. For there is only one God, that is God the Father, God the Son and God the Holy Spirit. As there is only one God, there is but one true faith, and it is led by my chosen one, my beloved John Paul II, who is a true shepherd and will lead my flock through the many attacks which besiege my one true, holy, catholic, and apostolic faith, the Mother Church."

THE BOOK OF ISAIAH
ISAIAH 2: Zion, the Messianic Capital

² **In the days to come, the mountain of the Lord's house shall be established as the highest mountain and raised above the hills. All nations shall stream toward it;**
³ **many peoples shall come and say: "Come, let us climb the Lord's mountain to the house of the God of Jacob, that he may instruct us in his ways, and we may walk in his paths." For from Zion shall go forth instruction, and the word of the Lord from Jerusalem.**
⁴ **He shall judge between the nations and impose terms on many peoples.**

Jesus said: "My daughter, my children must stand together as one with the Mother Church. Yes, as it has been written, there shall come the time where division is plotted against my Holy One, but my house shall not fall, but rise. I shall consume the unjust which have plotted against and brought forth division, but the rock on which I founded my church will remain strong, firmly planted. The foundation I will hold upright."

THE BOOK OF EZEKIEL
EZEKIEL 17: Crimes of Jerusalem

²² **Therefore thus says the Lord God: I, too, will take from the crest of the cedar, from its topmost branches tear off a tender shoot, and plant it on a high and lofty mountain;**
²³ **on the mountain heights of Israel I will plant it. It shall put forth branches and bear fruit, and become a majestic cedar.**

Birds of every kind shall dwell beneath it, every winged thing in the shade of its boughs.

²⁴ And all the trees of the field shall know that I, the Lord, bring low the high tree, lift high the lowly tree, wither up the green tree, and make the withered tree bloom.

Jesus said: "As I, the Lord have spoken, so will I do. For you see, my daughter, even for all those who come against me, with all that they wish to destroy, against my one, true, holy, catholic, apostolic church, it is I they come against, and it is I that will meet them at the temple door. Then my wrath shall consume them.

"I love you, my little one. Be at peace, my daughter. Shalom my people."

Approved by Rev. Sean Cronin,
Rev. John Neiman, and Rev. Richard Hoynes

1996 July 15, Monday, 11:40
EUCHARISTIC ADORATION

Jesus said: "Welcome, my children. Thank you, my little one, for coming to receive my teaching. Praise be to Jesus, for Jesus is Lord, Redeemer, Saviour and King.

"My teaching today will be on John 18."

THE GOSPEL ACCORDING TO JOHN
JOHN 18: Jesus Arrested

²⁷ **Again, Peter denied it, and immediately the cock crowed.**

"You see, my child, how even my beloved Peter denied me. Yet he became the rock on which my church was built. My love, my precious, is all forgiving and all loving. It can not be measured. I only ask my children to return this love. My teachings now are to be given to all, for it is these times spoken of in the Bible, where the evil is overwhelming my children with an obsession of materialism, sex and violence.

"Open, my daughter, to Zechariah 7."

THE BOOK OF ZECHARIAH
ZECHARIAH 7: True Fasting

⁸ This word of the Lord came to Zechariah:

⁹ Thus says the Lord of hosts: render true judgment and show kindness and compassion toward each other.

¹⁰ Do not oppress the widow or the orphan, the alien or the poor; do not plot evil against one another in your hearts.

¹¹ But they refused to listen; they stubbornly turned their backs and stopped their ears so as not to hear.

¹² And they made their hearts diamond-hard so as not to hear the teaching and the message that the Lord of hosts had sent by his spirit through the former prophets.

¹³ Then the Lord of hosts in his great anger said that, as they had not listened when he called, so he would not listen when they called.

Jesus said: "Just as with Peter, my little one, I do not turn away from my children. Instead, I come to give them my love through these teachings. As in the day of teachings to Zechariah, I am, I have always been, I will always be, then as is now I am word and the word is love, and the word is God the Father, God the Son, and God the Holy Spirit.

"Deceive yourselves not, my children. Listen to my word, and you listen to me. Know my word and you know me.

"Pray, my children, pray.

"I bless you, my daughter, and your precious son, in the Almighty Name of the Father, Son and Holy Spirit.

"Come to me my children. I am here in the blessed tabernacle. I await you to come back to me. I love you, my children."

Approved by Rev. Sean Cronin,
Rev. John Neiman and Rev. Richard Hoynes

1996 July 16, Tuesday
EUCHARISTIC ADORATION

(Patsy: On this day I was asked by one of my spiritual advisors to ask Jesus to please clarify the message of July 6, 1996, where Jesus spoke of "the country left to stand alone.")

Jesus said: "My daughter, the country that has turned away from God, has no desire to seek God nor to place the Blessed Trinity within their hearts. It is they who have turned away from me, not I from them. They have desired to withdraw from me; not I from them. So I, in my Justice, must allow them to wallow in their own decisive destruction.

"My son, *[Spiritual Advisor],* has spoken of the free will given to mankind, this is the free will of mankind, to take God out of your country. This is the decision man has chosen through his own free will. This, my daughter, is what I meant when I said, 'the country is left to stand alone.' Man has chosen this through his own misguided conception of free will."

Approved by Rev. Sean Cronin,
Rev. John Neiman & Rev. Richard Hoynes

1996 July 18, Thursday, 07:15
EUCHARISTIC ADORATION

Jesus said: "Praise be to Jesus, for Jesus is Lord, Saviour, Redeemer. Thank you for coming for my teaching my daughter. I bless you in the Almighty Name of the Father, Son and Holy Spirit.
"Open to EzekieL 3."

THE BOOK OF EZEKIEL
EZEKIEL 3:

⁷ **But the house of Israel will refuse to listen to you, since they will not listen to me. For the whole house of Israel is stubborn of brow, and obstinate of heart.**

"My children, do not be like my children from the house of Israel. I tell you I am a just God, and my justice shall come like the swiftness of an arrow. You shall seek my mercy, but unless you change from your evil ways you shall not find my mercy.
"Open, my daughter, to John 15."

THE GOSPEL ACCORDING TO JOHN
JOHN 15: The Vine and the Branches

¹ **I am the true vine, and my Father is the vinegrower.**
² **He takes away every branch in me that does not bear fruit, and everyone that does, he prunes so that it bears more fruit.**

Jesus said: "My children, you as the branches must bear good fruit through example and prayer, for there are many in your families who need much prayer. Do not allow your branch to wither and die but drink from the spring of everlasting grace that you may be refreshed. As you come to me, the font of mercy, I shall not turn away, I shall fill you with my love, my peace, my strength to go forth and bear good fruit.

"I love you, my children. Shalom, my little one."

Approved by Rev. Sean Cronin,
Rev. John Neiman and Rev. Richard Hoynes

1996 July 19, Friday, 15:30
EUCHARISTIC ADORATION

Jesus said: "Praise be to Jesus for Jesus is Lord, Saviour, Redeemer. Welcome my children. Thank you my daughter for coming to receive my teaching.

"Open, my daughter, to Colossians, for I am he who comes in the Almighty Name of the Father, Son and Holy Spirit, to bring to you, my children, my teachings, my way, my light. Come into my presence, my children, and remain in me, for I am the way.

"I open the gates to eternal love through the waters of everlasting grace. I come to each of you body, soul and divinity, that you may have life eternal. Unless you eat my body and drink my blood, you shall not have life everlasting. Take from the font of my mercy, for you cannot withstand the arrows of temptation; for my mercy is your shield. My strength, your strength; but only through surrendering totally to me shall you reap from my unboundless grace."

THE EPISTLE OF PAUL TO THE COLOSSIANS:
II The Preeminence of Christ: Fullness and Reconciliation

¹⁵ He is the image of the invincible God, the first born of all creatures.

¹⁶ In him were all things in heaven and on earth, the visible and the invisible, whether thrones or dominions or principalities or powers; all things were created through him and for him.

¹⁷ He is before all things, and in him all things hold together.

¹⁸ He is the head of the body, the church; he is the beginning, the first born from the dead, that in all things he himself might be preeminent.

¹⁹ For in him all the fullness was pleased to dwell,

²⁰ and through him to reconcile all things for him, making peace by the blood of his cross (through him), whether those on earth or those in heaven.

²¹ And you who once were alienated and hostile in mind because of evil deeds."

Jesus said: "Now, my children listen, to my word. Change is what I ask. Change from evil deeds."

Paul, cont'd:

²² He has now reconciled in his fleshy body through his death.

Jesus said: "When you eat my body and drink my blood, you shall have life everlasting. In the Sacrament of the Holy Eucharist I am alive. I will give you new life. New life in me."

Paul, cont'd:

²³ Provided that you persevere in the faith, firmly grounded, stable and not shifting from the hope of the gospel you heard.

"My word, my children, I give you. Teachings to know, to

understand. Listen to my word. Read my word, and you shall know me."

Paul 23 cont'd:

Which has been preached to every creature under heaven, of which I, Paul, am a minister.

"As I spoke to Paul, as I taught Paul, I teach you now. Will you not open your hearts to my teachings?

"I love you, my children. Shalom, my little one, I am with you."

Approved by Rev. Sean Cronin,
Rev. John Neiman and Rev. Richard Hoynes

1996 July 22, Monday, 15:30
EUCHARISTIC ADORATION

Jesus said: "Praise be to Jesus, my child, for Jesus is Lord, Saviour, Redeemer, Messiah.

"Come to me, my children; come to the springs of everlasting grace, the font of mercy. For I shall give you life eternal.

"I shall soothe your wounded hearts. Will you soothe mine? Open to my word and receive from the tree of knowledge, that you may rest in the realm of everlasting glory; but only if you are willing to surrender completely and totally to me.

"Open, my daughter, to Ruth 2."

THE BOOK OF RUTH
RUTH 2: The Meeting

¹¹ **Boaz answered her: "I have a complete account of what you have done for your mother-in-law after your husband's death; you have left your father and your mother and the land of your birth, and have come to a people you did not know previously.**
¹² **May the Lord reward what you have done! May you receive a full reward from the Lord the God of Israel, under whose wings you have come for refuge.**

Jesus said: "As with my daughter Ruth, those of my children willing to surrender completely to the will of the Father, Son and Holy Spirit, I do not abandon them especially in the time of their need. It may not be the answer they are looking for, but it is done according to my will; and as I have said, I will soothe their wounds.

"This teaching is part of my ancestry, my child. My Father created man unto his likeness, and he gave His only begotten Son that man may not perish in the flames of eternal fire. He gave His only begotten Son a tree of ancestors, that his children would see the loving nature of the Father.

"The family is a very important part of a Sacrament, my child; united one with the Father, Son and Holy Spirit. Do not make a mockery of the family, my children. Pray for the unity of the family. Pray, my children, pray.

"I am with you, my little one. Shalom, my children."

Approved by Rev. Sean Cronin,
Rev. John Neiman and Rev. Richard Hoynes

1996 July 23, Tuesday
Feast of St. Bridgit
EUCHARISTIC ADORATION

Jesus said: "Praise be to Jesus for Jesus is Lord, Saviour, Redeemer and Messiah. I welcome you, my daughter. Thank you for coming to spend this time with me and for opening your heart to receive my teaching.

"Oh, my child, how my heart yearns for my people to change their ways from this evil path of destruction on which they see no error in their sinful lives.

"The evil one has truly closed their eyes and hearts to the goodness and holiness of which man was created for. It will take a great deal of prayer, my child. Prayer for all my children. A commitment to prayer daily; this is what I ask, my child; and as I have said, prayer from the heart is a dialogue of love with the Father, Son and Holy Spirit.

"Do not get confused, my children. All that you offer to me in prayer, is considered prayer; but you must also set a time daily to be in communion of prayer with me through my word; through formal prayers you have been taught; through the rosary, and the greatest prayer of all my child, the Holy Sacrifice of the Mass.

"Now open to Psalm 51."

THE BOOK OF PSALMS
PSALM 51: The Miserere: Prayer of Repentance

1. A Psalm of David.
2. When Nathan the prophet came to him after his affair with Bathsheba.
3. Have mercy on me, God in your goodness; in your abundant compassion blot out my offense.
4. Wash away all my guilt; from my sin cleanse me.
5. For I know my offense; my sin is always before me.
6. Against you alone have I sinned; I have done such evil in your sight that you are just in your sentence, blameless when you condemn.
7. True, I was born guilty, a sinner even as my mother conceived me.
8. Still, you insist on sincerity of heart; in my inmost being, teach me wisdom.
9. Cleanse me with hyssop, that I may be pure; wash me, make me whiter than snow.
10. Let me hear sounds of joy and gladness; let the bones you have crushed rejoice.
11. Turn away your face from my sins; blot out all my guilt.
12. A clean heart create for me, God; renew in me a steadfast spirit.
13. Do not drive me from your presence, nor take from me your Holy Spirit.
14. Restore my joy in your salvation; sustain in me a willing spirit.
15. I will teach the wicked your ways, that sinners may return to you.
16. Rescue me from death, God, my saving God, that my tongue may praise your healing power.
17. Lord, open my lips; my mouth will proclaim your praise.
18. For you do not desire sacrifice; a burnt offering you would not accept.

¹⁹ **My sacrifice, God, is a broken spirit; God, do not spurn a broken, humbled heart.**

²⁰ **Make Zion prosper in your good pleasure; rebuild the walls of Jerusalem.**

²¹ **Then you will be pleased with proper sacrifice, burnt offerings and holocausts; then bullocks will be offered on your altar.**

Jesus said: "This, my child, is a prayer, which if one prays with love and sincerity of the heart, opens the gates of my mercy upon them.

"Pray, my child, pray; do not let my mercy go uncalled upon. For my mercy is greater than the sins of the world. There is no end to my mercy, and it is my mercy which shall set you free.

"I love you, my children.

"Thank you my little one for taking this time to be with me. I understand the hardships you face but know that I am with you. My peace unto you, my beloved, and unto your family.

"Shalom, my children."

Approved by Rev. Sean Cronin,
Rev. John Neiman and Rev. Richard Hoynes

1996 July 25, Thursday, 07:30
EUCHARISTIC ADORATION

Jesus said: "Praise be to Jesus, for Jesus is Lord, Saviour, Messiah and Teacher, my beloved. For I come to teach you my way, my child, and the way to draw from the springs of everlasting grace, the font of mercy.

"I am, my daughter, he who comes in the Almighty Name of the Father, Son and Holy Spirit. Shine forth through me, my little one, that they only see an example of my love, for in my truths shall you walk, and all glory and honour shall be unto the Father, Son, and the Holy Spirit.

"Open, my daughter, to Romans 1."

THE EPISTLE OF PAUL TO THE ROMANS
ROMANS 1: Greetings

¹ **Greetings from Paul, a servant of Christ Jesus, called to be an apostle and set apart to proclaim the Gospel of God.**

Jesus said: "I call each of you, my children, to be my apostles, to walk only in truth, my truths, my children. For it is only if you walk in the light of my truths that you shall be set free. It is only through my light; and you can only receive my light through the Sacrament of the Holy Eucharist. It is this light that leads you out of darkness."

Romans 1, cont'd:

² **Which he promised previously through his prophets as the holy scriptures record.**

Jesus said: "My word, my children. It is my word that will set you free, for I am word; and the word is the Father, Son and Holy Spirit."

Romans 1, cont'd:

³ **The gospel about his Son, descended from David according to the flesh.**

Jesus said: "And you shall eat my flesh and drink my blood, and have life everlasting. All taught in my word, my children. But unless you open to my word, how can you know my word? How can you know my teachings or my truths? For it is the truths from my word that shall set you free."

Romans 1, cont'd:

⁴ **But established as Son of God in power according to the spirit of holiness through resurrection from the dead, Jesus Christ Our Lord.**

Jesus said: "Oh, my children, do you not see how my Father gave His only begotten Son that I would shed my blood on the holy cross of salvation, that you may have life eternal? No greater love has he that would give his only begotten son that all his children may have life eternal. Can you not comprehend the magnitude of love given to you from the Father, Son and Holy Spirit?"

Romans 1, cont'd:

⁵ **Through Him we have received the grace of apostleship, to bring about the obedience of faith, for the sake of his name, among all the Gentiles,**

⁶ **among whom are you also, who are called to belong to Jesus Christ.**

⁷ **To all the beloved of God in Rome called to be holy, grace to you and peace from God our Father and the Lord Jesus Christ.**

"I love you, my children. Shalom, my little one."

Approved by Rev. Sean Cronin,
Rev. John Neiman and Rev. Richard Hoynes

1996 July 26, Friday, 07:30
Feast of St. Joachim and St. Anne
EUCHARISTIC ADORATION

Jesus said: "Praise be to Jesus, for Jesus is Lord, Saviour, Redeemer and Messiah Deliverer. Thank you for coming to be with me today, my little one, and for coming to receive my teaching.

"Today is a very special day, my little one, as it is the feast of my holy grandparents; a sign of holiness and true example of the meaning of a holy family united with the Almighty Father, Son and Holy Spirit.

"My daughter, trust in me. I am your strength. It is through me, my little one, that all is accomplished. I only ask that you trust in me. Allow my mercy to flow, for it is in surrendering completely to me which allows you to be used to receive my teaching.

"Open to Sirach 1."

THE BOOK OF SIRACH
SIRACH 1: Praise of Wisdom

¹ **All wisdom comes from the Lord and with him it remains forever.**

Jesus said: "My children open your heart to receive my wisdom; but this wisdom can only be given to you if you remain in unity with my Holy Will.

"How, you ask, is this done?

"Through prayer, my children, and through keeping my commandments; in surrendering your will completely to the Father, Son, and Holy Spirit. I understand it is not easy to surrender your free will. You must first come to me in prayer with a daily commitment in the dialogue of love; then you receive my grace to help you to desire and accomplish a surrender of your free will.

"My beloved grandparents, Joachim and Anne, surrendered to the Will of the Father, as they gave their only child to be used mightily to the Will of the Father. And this holy innocence in surrendering her free will through the power of the Holy Spirit, the Son of the Father, was brought forth to set all humanity free. I surrendered to the Will of the Father when I died on the holy cross of salvation for all my children.

"Do you see the beauty of surrendering to the Will of the Father, Son and Holy Spirit? Do you see the magnitude of love evolved in the surrender of one's free will?

"I love you, my children. Shalom, my little one."

Approved by Rev. Sean Cronin

1996 July 30, Tuesday
EUCHARISTIC ADORATION

Jesus said: "Praise be to Jesus, for Jesus is Lord, Saviour, Redeemer, Holy One of Israel, who will deliver from all evil. Come to me, my children. Open your hearts to my teachings. Through my word you shall know me. For I am word and I shall set you free.

"I have come to give these teachings that you may see the love I have always had and will always have for each one of you. For no greater love can there be than the love that is mine for you.

"I shed my holy blood on the cross for each one of you, and I love not one more nor less than another.

"My love is unmeasurable and everlasting, and it is so little I ask in return. It is through my word, through the dialogue of love, prayer and the greatest prayer ever given, a reenactment of my death upon the holy cross, my holy sacrifice of the Mass. It is through the Sacraments, the greatest of all Holy Sacraments, my body, my blood, my soul, my divinity. I, who come to you alive in the holy Sacrament of the Eucharist to give you life everlasting. I give all of this to each of you with the many graces, I so willingly offer to each of you, that you may know me and have life everlasting. Won't you open your hearts to receive my gifts?

"Surrender yourselves completely and totally to me, for it is through me that you will know the Father Almighty, the Son Divine, and the Holy Spirit Eternal, three in one, Holy and Blessed Trinity."

THE BOOK OF PSALMS
PSALM 24: The Lord's Solemn Entry into Zion

1 **A Psalm of David. The earth is the Lord's and all it holds; the world and those who live there;**
2 **for God founded it on the seas, established it over the rivers.**
3 **Who may go up the mountain of the Lord? Who can stand in this holy place?**
4 **The clean of hand and pure of heart, who are not devoted to idols, who have not sworn falsely.**
5 **They will receive blessings from the Lord, and justice from their saving God.**
6 **Such are the people that love the Lord, that seek the face of the God of Jacob.**

Jesus said: "For I am the God of Jacob, my little one, and those who seek me shall find me; and I will live in them, and they shall live in me; and my heart their heart; my shield, their shield, and they shall know the Father as the Son and the Holy Spirit; and my love shall surround them in the glory of the Lord.

"Shalom, my little one; my peace unto you, my children."

Approved by Rev. Sean Cronin

1996 August 06, Tuesday
Feast of the Transfiguration
EUCHARISTIC ADORATION

Jesus said: "Precious one, praise be to Jesus, for Jesus is Lord, Saviour, Redeemer. Come to the font of my mercy. I shall give you rest. Do not fear the battles that surround you but reach out in my name, for I am your shield. Seek only me and I will defend you; for I do not betray, and my word is only truth. Come to me, my children, and I will give you rest. Open your hearts to me, and I shall fill them with my love, and your desire, my desire. Only seek me in all, for I will not leave you. I will never abandon you."

THE BOOK OF ZECHARIAH
ZECHARIAH 1: Necessity of Conversion

¹ **In the second year of Darius, in the eighth month, the word of the Lord came to the prophet Zechariah, son of Berechiah, son of Iddo.**
² **The Lord was indeed angry with your fathers;**
³ **and say to them: Thus says the Lord of hosts: Return to me, says the Lord of hosts, I will return to you, says the Lord of hosts.**
⁴ **Be not like your fathers whom the former prophets warned: Thus says the Lord of hosts: Turn from your evil ways and your wicked deeds. But they would not listen nor pay attention to me, says the Lord.**
⁵ **Your fathers, where are they? And the prophets, can they live forever?**
⁶ **But my words and my decrees, which I entrusted to my servants the prophets, did not these overtake your fathers? Then they repented and admitted: "The Lord of hosts has treated us according to our ways and deeds, just as he had determined he would."**

Jesus said: "My daughter, it is not easy to carry my cross. But as my children are willing to surrender to the will of the Father, Son and Holy Spirit, I carry their cross with them, and they shall see the love and the holiness of my cross.

"As I have said, I do not abandon my children, especially during these times of trials and sufferings, for it is not easy to walk the path of holiness; it is especially during these times that I surround them with my presence, my graces.

"Place my helmet, my armour of salvation on you, my children, and you shall bear all that is flung upon you. For the deceitful one shall not penetrate his woes through the armour of salvation.

"I am with you, my children. Pray and surrender completely unto my Holy Will.

"Thank you, my little one for responding to my call.

"Shalom, my little one. I love you, my children."

Approved by Rev. Sean Cronin

1996 August 12, Monday, 14:20
EUCHARISTIC ADORATION

Jesus said: "Welcome, my little one, thank you for coming to be with me and to receive my teaching. Praise be to Jesus, for Jesus is Lord, Saviour, Redeemer and King.

"Open, my daughter, to Exodus, chapter 4."

THE BOOK OF EXODUS
EXODUS 4: Aaron's Office as Assistant

¹¹ The Lord said to him, "Who gives one man speech and makes another deaf and dumb? Or who gives sight to one and makes another blind? Is it not I, the Lord?
¹² Go, then! It is I who will assist you in speaking and will teach you what you are to say.

Jesus said: "You see, my daughter, it took trust and faith for Moses to do as my Father requested, and as my Father spoke and taught Moses, so I speak and teach my children through my vessels and through my word.

"It is up to my children as it was in Moses time, to pray and obey the word of the Lord.

"So my children, I say unto you, pray. Visit me in my churches. Come to be with me in eucharistic adoration. Receive the sacraments often, that you may receive my grace to carry you through these trials, and especially during these days of upheaval and confusion. Without my grace you will not abide in my presence, your trials will become hardships and your cries unheard.

"Come to me, my children. I am here. I await your desire to seek me in all. I have never left you.

"I love you, my children. Shalom, my little one."

Approved by Rev. Sean Cronin

1996 August 13, Tuesday, 14:20
EUCHARISTIC ADORATION

Jesus said: "Praise be to Jesus, for Jesus is Lord, Saviour, and Deliverer. Welcome, my daughter. Thank you for opening your heart to my teachings.

"Be at peace, my beloved, for it is my peace that will give you rest. It is my peace that the world must realize without it they shall only know restlessness and overwhelming confusion. It is in seeking me and my love that they will find and know my peace.

"Open to Philippians 1. Yes, my little one, Philippians shows in seeking my love, my peace, Paul was able to withstand the imprisonment and injustice with such love, surrendering to the will of the Father, Son and Holy Spirit. It was through the anointing of the Holy Spirit that left Paul with such an enthusiastic and selfless perseverance of my truths, that he only wanted to relinquish to the will of the Father, leading all who would listen to him, to the love of the Almighty Father, Son and Holy Spirit."

THE EPISTLE OF PAUL TO THE PHILIPPIANS
PHILIPPIANS 1: Greeting

¹ Paul and Timothy, servants of Christ Jesus, to all the holy ones at Philippi, with their bishops and deacons in Christ Jesus.
² Grace and peace be yours from God our Father and from the Lord Jesus Christ.

Jesus said: "You see, my child, the overwhelming amount of love from my beloved Paul?"

Philippians 1 continued:

THE EXAMPLE OF PAUL
Gratitude and Hope

³ **I give thanks to my God at every remembrance of you —**
⁴ **which is constantly, in every prayer I utter — rejoicing, as I plead on your behalf,**
⁵ **at the way you have all continually helped promote the gospel from the very first day.**
⁶ **I am confident of this, that the one who began a good work in you will continue to complete it until the day of Christ Jesus.**

Philippians 1 continued:

¹⁰ **so that with a clear conscience and blameless conduct you may learn to value the things that really matter, up to the very day of Christ.**

Jesus said: "Oh my children, do you think that I would turn from you in time of sorrow, trial or persecution? No, my children; think back to all of the holy ones; those you read about in my word; those you have met through the word of others. Each carried their cross. I carried them and their crosses.

"How I love you, my children. Come to me and I will show you my love. I will carry you and your cross. I am the way, the light and the almighty; the Messiah; the Deliverer.

"I love you, my children. Shalom, my little one."

Approved by Rev. Sean Cronin

1996 August 30, Friday, 08:30
EUCHARISTIC ADORATION

Jesus said: "Praise be to Jesus, for Jesus is Lord, Saviour and Redeemer. I come to you my children that you may be refreshed in the springs of my eternal grace through the Holy Sacrament of the Eucharist. My living presence a gift for all mankind. I give you my word that through my teachings, through reading my word, you may grow in the richness and splendour of my truths. For I am the Father, the Son, and the Holy Spirit; and in me you shall find rest and eternal joy. For I love you, my children."

THE BOOK OF SIRACH
SIRACH 49: Josiah and the Prophets

¹ **The name of Josiah is like blended incense, made lasting by a skilled performer. Precious is his memory. Like honey to the taste, like music at a banquet.**

² **For he grieved over our betrayal, and destroyed the abominable idols.**

³ **He turned to God with his whole heart, and though times were evil, he practiced virtue.**

Jesus said: "This is what I ask of you, my children. Do not look around you, but within yourself; this is where it must begin. Though evil lurks around only trying to overcome and tempt, stray not away from me, but reach out to me. Seek me. I am the light within each of you. Though darkness may try to hinder your sight, through me you shall have eternal light. I love each of you, my children. Come to me. I await to give you life everlasting."

Sirach 49 continued:

⁹ **He also referred to Job, who always persevered in the right path.**

¹⁰ **Then too, the twelve prophets; may their bones return to life from their resting place! Gave new strength to Jacob and saved him by their faith and hope.**

"Shalom, my people. I love you, my little one."

Approved by Rev. Sean Cronin

1997 January 19, Sunday
EUCHARISTIC ADORATION

Jesus said: "Praise be to Jesus, for Jesus is Saviour, King, Reconciler. Welcome, my beloved. Thank you for responding to my call.

"Yes, my little one, I Who Am come to separate the evil from the righteous, for he that remains in me, remains in the springs of everlasting joy and peace. Only through my way can a person remain righteous.

"You have come to a crossroads of my teachings, my little one. You have requested my teaching, my direction, my path. Are you willing, my beloved, for my path is painful; but truth and victory shall overcome. I am your strength. Do not fear, my beloved, for as my Mother has promised, she will carry you as I lead you to my light eternal.

"Open to Jeremiah 10."

THE BOOK OF JEREMIAH
JEREMIAH 10: The Folly of Idolatry

1. **Hear the word which the Lord speaks to you, O house of Israel.**
2. **Thus says the Lord: learn not the customs of the nations, and have not fear of the signs of the heavens, though the nations fear them.**
3. **For the cult idols of nations are nothing, wood cut from the forest, wrought by craftsmen with the adze,**
4. **adorned with silver and gold. With nails and hammers they are fastened, that they may not totter.**
5. **Like a scarecrow in a cucumber field are they, they cannot speak; they must be carried about, for they cannot walk, fear them not, they can do no harm neither is it in their power to do good.**

Jesus said: "My beloved, as in worshipping idols that are not, so it is in unforgiveness that can not but rise to unrest of the spirit. Unforgiveness is as shallow as the idol that is stealth. There is nothing there but the stone of the idol maker, the spirit of the soul is stone, unable to be filled with my peace, my love. But, my beloved, through the prayers and offering of my children, this bondage can be removed. This is the beginning of reconciliation: prayer.

"As idolatry is the worship of false gods, so it is with the act of unforgiveness. They have filled themselves with the false god of lies and allowed the spirit of false ego to create their own god of unforgiveness within. So they must release this false god of idolatry they have created within themselves through prayer.

"I ask you, my children, to remove the blinders of truth and seek me; for I Am; and I will lead you home. Come to me my children. Do not delay. For you do not know the hour that you will be called to answer for your actions.

"I love you, my beloved little one. This is enough for today. I will await you, my children."

Approved by Rev. Sean Cronin

1997 January 22, Wednesday
Feast of St. Vincent
EUCHARISTIC ADORATION

Jesus said: "Praise be to Jesus, for Jesus is Lord, Saviour, Redeemer. Welcome, my little one. Open, my daughter, to Samuel 1."

THE FIRST BOOK OF SAMUEL
1 SAMUEL 26: Saul's Life Again Spared

⁸ **Abishai whispered to David, "God has delivered your enemy into your group this day. Let me nail him to the ground with one thrust of the spear; I will not need a second thrust."**

⁹ **But David said to Abishai, "Do not harm him, for who can lay hands on the Lord's anointed and remain unpunished?**

¹⁰ **As the Lord lives," David continued, "it must be the Lord himself who will strike him, whether the time comes for him to die, or he goes out and perishes in battle.**

¹¹ **But the Lord forbid that I touch his anointed!"**

Jesus said: "My daughter, reconciliation begins in one surrendering completely in prayer to the Lord. Trusting in me as Saul lay in a deep sleep, David could have taken it upon himself to allow the death of Saul; but David surrendered his will to my will. This, my child is what I seek of my children: total surrender to my will. This can only be accomplished as one begins to seek me in prayer.

Prayer; seeking my holy will through prayer; surrendering to my holy will. This will begin the process of reconciliation."

(Then Jesus asked that we read and meditate on Samuel 1 and 2)
"This is enough for today. I love you, my children."

Approved by Rev. Sean Cronin

1997 January 23, Thursday
EUCHARISTIC ADORATION

Jesus said: "Praise be to Jesus for Jesus is Lord, Saviour, Redeemer, Reconciler. Oh my precious child, thank you for coming to spend this time with me, for opening your heart to my teaching. Open, my daughter, to Samuel 1, Chapter 1 and 2.

"My little one, as my daughter Hannah bore her pain to me, I heard her pleas for a child. She trusted in me and I found favour in the purification of her pleas. Open your heart to me, my child; I will teach you! Do not dishearten, but continue seeking me. I am with you."

THE FIRST BOOK OF SAMUEL
1 SAMUEL 1: Hannah's Prayer

⁹ **Hannah rose after one such meal at Shiloh, and presented herself before the Lord; at the time, Eli the priest was sitting on a chair near the doorpost of the Lord's temple.**

¹⁰ **In her bitterness she prayed to the Lord, weeping copiously,**

¹¹ **and she made a vow, promising: "O Lord of hosts, if you look with pity on the misery of your handmaid, if you remember me and do not forget me, if you give your handmaid a male child, I will give him to the Lord for as long as he lives; neither wine nor liquor shall he drink, and no razor shall ever touch his head."**

¹² As she remained long at prayer before the Lord, Eli watched her mouth,

¹³ for Hannah was praying silently; though her lips were moving her voice could not be heard.

Approved by Rev. Sean Cronin

1997 February 3, Monday, 04:30
EUCHARISTIC ADORATION

Jesus said: "Welcome, my daughter, thank you for coming to be with me. Praise be to Jesus, for Jesus is Lord, Saviour, Reconciler. Open your heart to receive my teaching. For all who read my word will know me, for I am word, and he who desires and seeks my word, desires and seeks me. But it is only in prayer and sacrifice that will open the path to knowledge that is given from the word.

"Open to Isaiah 10, my beloved."

THE BOOK OF ISAIAH
ISAIAH 10: Social Injustice

¹⁰ Just as my hand reached out to idolatrous kingdoms that had more images than Jerusalem and Samaria,

¹¹ just as I treated Samaria and her idols, shall I not do to Jerusalem and her graven images?

¹² But when the lord has brought to an end all his work on Mount Zion and in Jerusalem, I will punish the utterance of the king of Assyria's proud heart,

¹³ and the boastfulness of his haughty eyes. For he says; "By my own power I have done it, and by my wisdom, for I am shrewd. I have moved the boundaries of peoples, their treasures I have pillaged, and like a giant, I have put down the enthroned."

Jesus said: "My daughter, open your heart for my teaching; do not worry about others around you. You are here to be with me. As I have spoken of the injustice that besieges the unforgiveness of the idolater of the god of ego, shall he who cannot forgive, expect my forgiveness. No, my child, for as I have said, he that cannot forgive has created his own downfall, and as the stonemaker who has created but an image of stone, does the idolater create his own house of stone that will crumble in the end to but grains of sand; and his house shall not be of mine but of the house of darkness, which spews forth idols of his own creation. No, his temple of unforgiveness is built of lies and deception.

"The temple which I enter must remain pure interiorly, and my truths the foundation which will stand firm.

"I bless you, my child, and I thank you for responding to my call."

Approved by Rev. Sean Cronin

1997 February 6, Thursday, 17:00
EUCHARISTIC ADORATION

Jesus said: "Praise be to Jesus, for Jesus is Lord, Saviour, Reconciler. Thank you, my daughter, for responding to my call. I Who Am, invite you, all my children, to come to the springs of everlasting grace. To renew yourselves in me, with me and through me. For only I can give you life eternal, and it is by asking me, seeking me in all you do, inviting me into your lives.

"As you partake in my Holy Mass, you partake in the greatest miracle ever given. The miracle of life and death, which I gave you as I died on the holy cross, crucified, to give you life eternal. And this reenactment takes place at each and every Holy Sacrifice of the Mass. I invite you to know me. I invite you to love me. I invite you to partake of my body, blood, soul and divinity. As I come alive to you. For I am the Sacrament of the Holy Eucharist. I *am* the Holy Eucharist, and it is in me, with me, and through me, that you are able to partake in the greatest miracle that is. Come back to me, my children.

"Open to Matthew 6."

THE GOSPEL ACCORDING TO MATTHEW
MATTHEW 6: True Riches

¹⁹ Do not store up for yourselves treasures on earth, where moth and decay destroy, and the thieves break in and steal.

²⁰ **But store up treasures in heaven, where neither moth nor decay, nor thieves break in and steal.**

²¹ **For where your treasure is there also will your heart be.**

Jesus said: "Receive me, my children. I am your treasure. I am the greatest of miracles. Your richness is I am. As you receive me, the richness is stored within the very depths of my being, and it is this richness that shall set you free. But know in order to receive the richness you must prepare yourselves. Have you prepared yourselves?

"I love you, my children."

"This is enough for today, my beloved little one. I love you."

Approved by Rev. Sean Cronin

1997 February 7, Friday, 04:20
EUCHARISTIC ADORATION

Jesus said: "Praise be to Jesus for Jesus is Lord, Saviour, Redeemer, Reconciler. Welcome, my little one, thank you for coming to spend this time with me.

"I am, my daughter, the Lord; the God of Jacob. I am the deliverer, who has given to all men, created in my image; the gift of life eternal.

"Open to Jeremiah 22."

THE BOOK OF JEREMIAH
Jeremiah 22: Oracles in the Last Years of Jerusalem

¹ **The Lord told me this: "Go down to the palace of the king of Judah, and there deliver this message:**

² **You shall say: Listen to the word of the Lord, king of Judah, who sits on the throne of David, you, your ministers, and your people that enter by these gates!**

³ **Thus says the Lord: Do what is right and just. Rescue the victim from the hand of his oppressor. Do not wrong or oppress the resident alien, the orphan, or the widow, and do not shed innocent blood in this place.**

⁴ **If you carry out these commands, kings who succeed to the throne of David will continue to enter the gates of this**

palace, riding in chariots or mounted on horses, with their ministers, and their people.

⁵ But if you do not obey these commands, I swear by myself, says the Lord, this palace shall become rubble.

Jesus said: "My beloved ones, soul must be always pure, that, as my temple, I may enter. It is the sacredness of the temple that must be guarded, and when one has fallen to the many temptations, he must then seek to cleanse the stain of sin through the Sacrament of Reconciliation, thus surrendering to comply with the teachings of the church. That sin must be removed and forgiveness sought through the Sacrament of Reconciliation. This surrender to my Holy Will is a beginning to the path of total surrender.

"Thank you, my child for responding to my call."

Approved by Rev. Sean Cronin

1997 February 11, Tuesday
Feast of Our Lady of Lourdes
EUCHARISTIC ADORATION

Message from Our Loving Mother: "Welcome, my beloved little one. How wonderful that my children gathered in the Holy Name of my Son, for prayer and sacrifice of the Holy Mass.

"My children, please my Holy Son and myself, for it can only be through prayer and sacrifice that the perdition this world is in can be changed.

"The evil can only run rampant in a society which remains in the coldness and deterioration of its own means through its evil and pernicious ways. The torture and killing of so many of my innocents has brought this decrease in moral value to such a horrific epidemic of paganism, that my Son has held back his hand of chastisement only because of the prayers and sacrifice of his children.

"But the hour glass has almost reached its fill, and justice for my tortured aborted innocents, who have been viciously murdered, must come forth for those who have refused to listen to our pleas.

"Those of my children who have continued to seek the reign of the Almighty Father, Son and Holy Spirit, as king of their hearts and their family, shall not fear, for they will be protected under the mantle of my love.

"The petals which are given are but a token of my love; but there are petals of graces which are showered forth, upon those of my children as they continue to seek the reign of the Almighty Father, Son, and Holy Spirit, through the sacrifice and prayer that I ask of my children.

"The greatest form of prayer is the Holy Sacrifice of the Mass. One should prepare to receive the Most Holy Eucharist through the Sacrament of Reconciliation.

"I ask for the daily recitation of the holy rosary, which brings reflections on the life of my holy crucified Son. I ask my children to wear the holy scapular in remembrance of the Holy Crucifixion, and as a reminder their total consecration to my Son's most wounded Sacred Heart. This sacramental is a testimony of our love to him, and a reminder to all that you have chosen the holy way of the cross.

"As I came to visit my beloved Simon, as the Mother of the redeemer on Mount Carmel, I come to remind you, my children, that my beloved son gave his life, so that all may have life eternal. And as you offer yourselves daily in sacrifice and prayer through my intercession, I promise to carry you forth to the 'doorsteps of heaven' where your groom awaits.

"I bless each in the Holy Name of the Father, Son, and Holy Spirit.

"Open to my beloved John 8."

THE GOSPEL ACCORDING TO JOHN
JOHN 8: Warning to Unbelievers

[28] **Jesus said to them, "When you lift up the Son of Man, you will realize that I Am, and that I do nothing on my own, but I say only what the Father taught me.**
[29] **The One who sent me is with me, he has not deserted me since I always do what pleases him.**

Approved by Rev. Sean Cronin

1997 February 12, Ash Wednesday
EUCHARISTIC ADORATION

Jesus said: "Praise to Jesus for Jesus is Savior, Lord, Redeemer, Reconciler. Welcome, my little one; thank you for responding to my call.

"I have called many, but many do not respond. It is your willingness to seek my love, your desire of me that pleases me. Many times my children are unwilling to take this time with me; but I still wait for them to open their hearts to my call.

"Total surrender to my Holy Will, my child, is not easy; but then to refrain from trying stifles the growth of the spiritual life of the soul. I only ask and desire that my children try, open their hearts to me, I will do the rest. The yearning, the desire to belong completely to me will grow as they come to me in prayer, but they must take the first step.

"This holy season of Lent can be a beginning for each of my children to respond to my call. It only takes the desire to begin this journey with me. The road of sanctity is a journey with me, and it begins at calvary for all who desire to belong completely to me.

"My holy Mother spoke yesterday of prayer, the steps she gave to draw each of you closer to me. It is not difficult to please me. I only ask that you try; this is a beginning to a lasting union with me.

"Now open, my daughter, to Luke 7."

THE GOSPEL ACCORDING TO LUKE
Luke 7: The Pardon of the Sinful Woman

36 A Pharisee invited him to dine with him; and he entered the Pharisee's house and reclined at table.

37 Now there was a sinful woman in the city who learned that he was at table in the house of the Pharisee. Bringing an alabaster flask of ointment,

38 she stood behind him at his feet with her tears, then she wiped them with her hair, kissed them and anointed them with the ointment.

39 When the Pharisee who had invited him saw this he said to himself, "If this man were a prophet, he would know who

and what sort of woman this is who is touching him, that she is a sinner."

[40] In answer to his thoughts Jesus said to him, "Simon, I have something to say to you." "Teacher," he said, "speak."

[41] "Two men owed money to a certain money lender; one owed a total of five hundred coins, the other fifty.

[42] Since neither was able to repay, he wrote off both debts. Which of them was more grateful to him?"

[43] Simon answered, "The one, I suppose, whose larger debt was forgiven." Jesus said to him, "You are right."

[44] Then he turned to the woman and said to Simon, "Do you see this woman? When I entered your house, you did not give me water for my feet, but she has bathed them with her tears and wiped them with her hair.

[45] You did not give me a kiss, but she has not ceased kissing my feet since the time I entered.

[46] You did not anoint my head with oil, but she has anointed my feet with perfume.

[47] So I tell you, that is why her many sins are forgiven — because of her great love. Little is forgiven the one whose love is small."

[48] He said to her then, "Your sins are forgiven."

[49] The others at the table said to themselves, "Who is this who even forgives sins?"

[50] Meanwhile he said to the woman, "Your faith has saved you. Now go in peace."

Jesus said: "Take the time to know me, my children, that I may know you when it is time for you to ask my forgiveness of your sins.

"I love you, my children; I await you; come to me, my children.

"Shalom, my little one."

1997 February 15, Saturday, 21:00
EUCHARISTIC ADORATION

Jesus said: "Welcome, my children. The holy peace of the Blessed Trinity I give to you. Praise be to Jesus, for Jesus is Lord, Saviour, Messiah.

"Your love appeases my wounded heart, my daughter. The wounds my children inflict upon me, through their misguided actions, leading them deeper into the hands of the evil one. Pray, my children. How many times I plead with all my children for more prayer, more sacrifice?"

THE GOSPEL ACCORDING TO LUKE
Luke 10: Mission of the Seventy-two

[13] **Woe to you, Chorazin! Woe to you, Bethsaida! For if the miracles done in your midst had been done in Tyre and Sidon, they would long ago have repented, sitting in sackcloth and ashes.**

[14] **But it will be more tolerable for Tyre and Sidon at the judgement than for you.**

[15] **And as for you Capernaum 'will you be exalted to heaven?' You shall be hurled down to the realm of death!**

[16] **Whoever listens to you, listens to me. Whoever rejects you, rejects me. And whoever rejects me, rejects the one who sent me.**

Jesus said: "Listen with your heart, my daughter. You wonder why my urgency in my pleas for my children to return to prayer? If a child loses a material item, these can be replaced; but if my child loses his or her soul, it is for all eternity. Repent and your sins will be forgiven. Pray and your voices will be heard. Surrender and your soul shall have life eternal. Read the word and you will know the word! Know the word, and you will know me.

"Shalom, my little one."

Approved by Rev. Sean Cronin

February 15, 1997, Saturday 1:15 a.m.
Eucharistic Adoration

Our Lady of the holy oils send me your love
In the purity and richness of the holy dove

The holy oils please send me from above
To spread His Healing grace, that all may see His Love
That all may see His glory as the holy dove
and change their ways to His, Your Redemptive Son
Hear my pleas, my Mama Mary please
and send me your gifts of holy oils never to cease
and with each drop that is given
may your wounded children enter into heaven
I close this prayer my Lady through the intercession of St.
Joseph and ask
your blessings upon us
Forever may we be holy children of thee and the Blessed
Trinity

I love you, St. Joseph
I love you, Mama Mary
Please intercede to Jesus, Holy Paraclete, Almighty God the
Father, the Blessed Trinity.

1997 February 17, Monday, 17:45, after Mass
EUCHARISTIC ADORATION

Jesus said: "Praise to Jesus, for Jesus is Lord, Saviour, Redeemer, Reconciler. Welcome, my little one, thank you for opening your heart for my message.

"In these beginning days of Lent, it pleases me to see so many of my children attending the Holy Sacrifice of the Mass. It is through this preparation of a soul's willingness to seek me through the most perfect prayer.

"As my children come to me in this perfect prayer, I open the gates of my Heart and shower each with graces to further their walk along the path to holiness. This testimony of their love to me unites their heart with mine; a perfect union as they receive me in the presence of my body and my blood. It is at this time that this perfect union of my children's heart with mine brings a special grace to the entire Mystical Body of Christ.

"Now open to Mark 4."

THE GOSPEL ACCORDING TO MARK
Mark 4: Seed Grows of Itself

²⁶ He said, "This is how it is with the kingdom of God. A man scatters seed on the ground.

²⁷ He goes to bed and gets up day after day. Through it all the seed sprouts and grows without his knowing how it happens.

²⁸ The soil produces of itself first the blade, then the ear, finally the ripe wheat in the ear.

²⁹ When the crop is ready he 'wields the sickle, for the time is ripe for the harvest.'"

Jesus said: "Do you not see, my children, how much I love each of you; that by whatever means I can share the wealth of the kingdom for your benefit, that all may belong to me, that each share in the light of life eternal! My love for you is incomparable to any other love, and it belongs to each of you.

"This is enough for today, my little one. Shalom, my beloved."

Approved by Rev. Sean Cronin

1997 February 18, Tuesday
EUCHARISTIC ADORATION

Jesus said: "Praise be to Jesus, for Jesus is Lord, Redeemer, Reconciler. Thank you, my beloved little one, for responding to my call.

"I Who Am, have given of my gifts abundantly, so that man, woman and child, all of my children have life eternal. Through my love, that shines forth in each of my children, who willingly surrender to my Holy Will, can lead others to the word, and in the word they shall find me, for I am word.

"Be examples of my love, my children, so that others may follow; and as you who have tried to be examples, know that I will open the doors of my most wounded Sacred Heart, that all of my mercy shall penetrate forth graces to sustain you through the tribulation ahead. It is this mercy that shall be your armour against all that comes against you and with this armour of my mercy nothing shall penetrate or destroy this armour.

"Open, my daughter, to Jeremiah 1:"

132

THE BOOK OF JEREMIAH
JEREMIAH 1: The Call of Jeremiah

⁴ The word of the Lord came to me thus:

⁵ Before I formed you in the womb, I knew you, before you were born I dedicated you, a prophet to the nations I appointed you.

⁶ "Ah Lord God!" I said, "I know not how to speak; I am too young."

⁷ But the Lord answered me, Say not, "I am too young." To whomever I send you, you shall go; whatever I command you, you shall speak.

⁸ Have no fear before them, because I am with you, to deliver you, says the Lord.

Jesus said: "I am love, my children; I am light, my children; I am peace, my children. He that lives in me shall have no fear. Know that it is only through your prayers and sacrifices that my wounded heart is soothed, and that it can only be through your prayers and sacrifices that many of those unwilling to succumb to the graces of my mercy can be saved. Pray my children, pray.

"I Love you, my children. Shalom my little one."

Approved by Rev. Sean Cronin

1997 February 28, Friday
EUCHARISTIC ADORATION

Jesus said: "Praise to you Lord Jesus Christ, for Jesus is Lord, Saviour, Messiah and King. He who worships and sings praise to the Lord, worships and sings praise to me. For I am the Holy One, the Almighty One, and he who comes to me shall have life eternal."

THE FIRST BOOK OF SAMUEL
SAMUEL 1: Hannah's Prayer

⁹ Hannah rose after one such meal at shiloh, and presented herself before the Lord; at the time, Eli the priest was sitting on a chair near the doorpost of the Lord's temple.

[10] In her bitterness she prayed to the Lord, weeping copiously,

[11] and she made a vow, promising: "O Lord of hosts, if you look with pity on the misery of your handmaid, if you remember me and do not forget me, if you give your handmaid a male child, I will give him to the Lord for as long as he lives; neither wine nor liquor shall he drink, and no razor shall ever touch his head."

[12] As she remained long at prayer before the Lord, Eli watched her mouth,

[13] for Hannah was praying silently; though her lips were moving, her voice could not be heard. Eli, thinking her drunk,

[14] said to her, "How long will you make a drunken show of yourself? Sober up from your wine!"

[15] "It isn't that, my lord," Hannah answered. "I am an unhappy woman. I have had neither wine nor liquor; I was only pouring out my troubles to the Lord.

[16] Do not think your handmaid a ne'er-do-well; my prayer has been prompted by my deep sorrow and misery."

[17] Eli said, "Go in peace, and may the God of Israel grant you what you have asked of him."

[18] She replied, "Think kindly of your maidservant." and left. She went to her quarters, ate and drank with her husband, and no longer appeared downcast.

[19] Early the next morning they worshipped before the Lord, and then returned to their home in Ramah.

Hannah Bears a Son

When Elkanah had relations with his wife Hannah, the Lord remembered her.

[20] She conceived, and at the end of her term bore a son whom she called Samuel, since she had asked the lord for him.

Jesus said: "As I have asked you to read Samuel 1, my daughter, do you see the love in which I, Who Am, gives to Hannah? Is it not possible that I, Who Am would not give in return much more love than what is offered to me? Then why do my children ignore my pleas for the salvation of their souls? Because they are caught up in a materialistic world which is self gratifying and unnecessary of my peace, my love, which they have convinced themselves of. For they do not see the unboundless love that I offer them. Through my love comes the peace and strength that is needed to live in this materialistic world of confusion and disarray. I am this unquenchable thirst of love they have within themselves, but they will never know this perfect love, which I have to offer them; this perfect love which can quench this unknown thirst, because they do not come to me.

"Come to me, my children. Remove the blinders you have allowed yourselves to remain in, which do not allow you to see the magnitude of my love. For you will never know the beauty of my love if you do not take the time to be with me, to teach you my love, to show you of my love; for I am Love.

"I love you, my children! Shalom, my little one."

Approved by Rev. Sean Cronin

1997 March 01, Saturday
EUCHARISTIC ADORATION

Jesus said: "Praise to Jesus, for Jesus is Lord, Saviour, Redeemer, Reconciler. Thank you, my little one, for coming to spend this time with me. Open your heart to receive my teaching. Open your heart to me, my children. Let me fill it with my love, my peace.

"In these days of tribulation, you shall only experience true peace and true love, through me. My love is everlasting. The peace that I give you is not of this world, and can only be found in me. Through me and with me.

"Changing one's life style is not easy, for happiness which is found in this materialistic society is but for a fleeing moment, and when this fleeing moment passes by, you search for other ways to appease this thirst for happiness. You find that there is nothing that lasts to quench this thirst and you continue to seek, but you will not find true happiness, peace or love in this world. That search continues into pleasures that deaden the soul, and soon you have found yourself in the evil errors of this world which blind you to truth, light and eternal life with me. Oh my children, turn from this unending search of happiness and wealth in this materialistic world of the abyss. Come to me and you shall know true wealth in the richness of my love, my peace, my joy everlasting.

"Open, my daughter, to Matthew 7."

THE GOSPEL ACCORDING TO MATTHEW
MATTHEW 7: Conclusion of the Sermon

[24] Everyone who listens to these words of mine and acts on them will be like a wise man who built his house on rock.

[25] The rain fell, the floods came, and the winds blew and buffeted the house. But it did not collapse; it had been built solidly on rock.

[26] And everyone who listens to these words of mine but does not act on them will be like a fool who built his house on sand.

[27] The rains fell, the floods came and the winds blew and buffeted the house. and it collapsed and was completely ruined.

Jesus said: "Listen to my words, my children. I do not come for my sake, but for yours; for these teachings have been repeated to you over and over. My word is everlasting. I am word. If you do not know the word, you do not know me. Do not let yourselves be misguided by the misconceptions of this world, for if you continue to remain in the materialistic values of this world, you stand to lose life eternal and the riches of the next.

"I love you, my children. Shalom, my little one."

Approved by Rev. Sean Cronin

1997 March 21, Friday, 08:30
EUCHARISTIC ADORATION

Jesus said: "Praise to you, Lord Jesus Christ, for Jesus is Lord, Saviour, Messiah, Reconciler. I give you my peace, my child. Open to Exodus 2, little one."

THE BOOK OF EXODUS
EXODUS 2: The Birth and Adoption of Moses

¹ Now a man belonging to the clan of Levi married a woman of his own tribe.

² She gave birth to a boy and seeing that he was a beautiful child, she kept him hidden for three months.

³ As she could not conceal him any longer, she made a basket out of papyrus leaves and coated it with tar and pitch. She then laid the child in the basket and placed it among the reeds near the bank of the Nile.

⁴ But the sister of the child kept at a distance to see what would happen to him.

⁵ Now the daughter of the pharaoh came down to bathe in the Nile and her maids walked along the river bank. Noticing the basket among the reeds she sent her handmaid to fetch it.

⁶ On opening it she looked, and lo, there was a baby boy, crying. She was moved with pity over him and said, "It is one of the Hebrews' children."

⁷ Then his sister asked Pharaoh's daughter, "Shall I go and call one of the Hebrew women to nurse the child for you?"

⁸ "Yes, do so," she answered. So the maiden went and called the child's own mother.

⁹ Pharaoh's daughter said to her, "Take this child and nurse it for me, and I will repay you." The woman therefore took the child and nursed it.

¹⁰ When the child grew, she brought him to Pharaoh's daughter, who adopted him as her son and called him Moses; for she said, "I drew him out of the water."

Jesus said: "My child, thank you for opening your heart to my teaching. As this child was placed in the water to escape death, so shall those of my children who are baptized with the springs of eternal life, be saved from eternal damnation. For only through the waters of Baptism, can the soul be free from original sin. It is my desire that all my children be freed from original sin, yet only a few are willing to respond to my gift of the grace which renews and cleanses the soul, freeing my children to receive my truths and gifts of love through the Holy Sacrament of Baptism. For these of my innocents who have been deprived of their life in abortion, they are brought to the springs of everlasting grace, through the many prayers and tears of my Holy Mother.

"Realize, my children, what this world of yours has come to. It is not a nation under God, but a materialistic upheaval of dissention and untruths; murderous, vengeful lies and deception; and through your own willingness to live in these deceptions, you have brought the wrath of my Father upon you!

"Return to the Sacraments, to prayer, so that you and your children may have life eternal.

"Come to me, my children! Shalom, my little one."

1997 June 20, Friday
EUCHARISTIC ADORATION

Jesus said: "Praise be to Jesus, for Jesus is Lord, Reconciler, Redeemer. Listen with your heart, my little one. It is precisely because of these messages, that you have come under such diabolical attack. But, my child, you must go forth, as you have given completely of yourself in such a way, that I, as the potter, you as the clay, will testify in my name.

"These are now the times of chastisement and diabolical warfare, which since 1981, my Holy Mother has come to warn and prepare my children for. For those who have opened their hearts to her warnings and have turned to prayer and supplication, these times will pass quickly; and they are under her mantle of protection. But those who closed their hearts and listened with a deaf ear, shall suffer what the rest of humanity will suffer.

"Open, my daughter, to Deuteronomy 7."

THE BOOK OF DEUTERONOMY
DEUTERONOMY 7: The Destruction of Pagans

¹ **When the Lord your God, brings you into the land which you are to enter and occupy, and dislodges great nations before you — the Hittites, Girgashites, Amorites, Canaanites,**

Perizzites, Hivites, and Jebusites: seven nations more numerous and powerful than you —

² and when the Lord, your God, delivers them up to you and you defeat them, you shall doom them. Make no covenant with them and show them no mercy.

³ You shall not intermarry with them, neither giving your daughters to their sons nor taking their daughters for your sons.

⁴ For they would turn your sons from following me to serving other gods, and then the wrath of the Lord would flare up against you and quickly destroy you.

⁵ But this is how you must deal with them: Tear down their altars, smash their sacred pillars, chop down their sacred poles, and destroy their idols by fire.

⁶ For you are a people sacred to the Lord, your God; he has chosen you from all the nations on the face of the earth to be a people peculiarly his own.

⁷ It was not because you are the largest of all nations that the Lord set his heart on you and chose you, for you are really the smallest of all nations.

⁸ It was because the Lord loved you and because of his fidelity to the oath he had sworn to your fathers, that he brought you out with his strong hand from the place of slavery, and ransomed you from the hand of Pharaoh, king of Egypt.

⁹ Understand, then, that the Lord, your God is God indeed, the faithful God who keeps his merciful covenant down to the thousandth generation toward those who love him and keep his commandments,

¹⁰ but who repays with destruction the person who hates him; he does not dally with such a one, but makes him personally pay for it.

¹¹ You shall therefore carefully observe the commandments, the statutes and the decrees which I enjoin on you today.

Jesus said: "My daughter, personally shall each person who willfully turned from me and denied my truths, see my wrath. For that which they have brought upon themselves, they shall desire that they had never been given life! Sodom and Gomorrah's cries from the nether world will not be as loud as the anguish from this generations' pleas for my mercy.

"Pray, my children, pray. For I have spoken.

"I love you, my little one."

Approved by Rev. Sean Cronin

1997 October 07, Tuesday
EUCHARISTIC ADORATION

Our Loving Mother said: "My dear little one, praise and all glory be to my holy crucified Son, for Jesus is Lord, Saviour and Redeemer.

"I am the Queen of Peace, my daughter, Lady of Divine Innocence, Mother of Sorrow. I have come, my daughter, to bring this message of urgency to all my children.

"Many times I have pleaded with my children to open their hearts to my cries of pleas, that none of my children be lost to the snares of the evil one. But to my dismay, my pleas of urgency seem to have been heard and forgotten through the attractions and ploys of the evil one.

"Now you have begun to see the many disasters and perils which are being allowed because of the murderous attacks and disseminations of my lost innocents which continues on.

"The hand of the Almighty Father has released the pangs of justice, and to my sorrow, many of my children will lose their souls to the ploys of the evil one.

"I do not come to warn now; the time of warning is over; the hour glass has passed its fill. I come, my children, to pray with you and for those of my children who have been continuous in their prayer life, surrendering the to the Holy Will of the Father, Son and Holy Spirit, do not fear; for you and your families are under my mantle of protection.

"For those who have turned away, I beg you turn back to the Father, Son and Holy Spirit in prayer, for the mercy of my Holy Son, the mercy of the Blessed Trinity is unboundless.

"Though at times many of you feel despair because of the trials, do not waver from your prayer life. Call out to the Blessed Trinity, the holy angels, the saints. Call out to me! We are all with you.

Though you feel your strength is gone, seek the strength of the Almighty Father, Son and Holy Spirit; their strength will never leave you.

"I bless each of you, my children, and each of your families, in the Almighty Name of the Father, Son and Holy Spirit.

"I love you, my children.

"Thank you, my daughter, for responding to my call."

Approved by Rev. Sean Cronin

1997 December 10, Wednesday
EUCHARISTIC ADORATION

Jesus said: "Praise be to Jesus, for Jesus is Lord, Saviour, Redeemer and Reconciler. Thank you, my little one, for opening your heart to my teaching.

"I thank my children for opening their hearts to my holy will. Release the anxiousness in your hearts my children; draw upon my strength, my love; and as you are firm in me, so shall I shower forth the grace of filial perseverance. My peace, my children, comes from within, and is to be shared with all who come into my presence.

"Open to Genesis 6, my daughter."

THE BOOK OF GENESIS
GENESIS 6: Warning of the Flood

⁸ **But Noah found favour with the Lord.**

⁹ **These are the descendants of Noah. Noah, a good man and blameless in that age,**

¹⁰ **for he walked with God, begot three sons: Shem, Ham, and Japheth.**

¹¹ **In the eyes of God the earth was corrupt and full of lawlessness.**

¹² **When God saw how corrupt the earth had become, since all mortals had depraved lives on earth,**

¹³ **he said to Noah: "I have decided to put an end to all mortals on earth; the earth is full of lawlessnes because of them. So I will destroy them and all life on earth."**

Jesus said: "My beloved ones, when my children allow themselves the willingness of surrendering to my holy will, they are releasing their free will to me, and my will is perfection. Why would I not give to my children what is in their best interest?

"Do you see how your willingness in accepting my Holy Will pleases me? Complete surrender must come through prayer, my children.

"My daughter, first must come the 'purification.' Open to Deuteronomy 1."

THE BOOK OF DEUTERONOMY
DEUTERONOMY 1: Threats of Revolt

³⁰ The Lord, your God who goes before you, will himself fight for you, just as he took part before your very eyes in Egypt, ³¹ as well as in the desert, where you saw how the Lord, your God, carried you, as a man carries his child, all along your journey until you arrived at this place.

Jesus said: "Do not be like my children whom Moses led out of slavery, who did not believe that the Lord God would take care of them. Know that what I speak of, 'the Purification,' is forthcoming. So that when the 'warning' comes, my children will be prepared through the purification; that they may see the error of their ways. This will be the final warning.

"I am merciful, my children. Seek my mercy now before the purification descends upon you."

Approved by Rev. Sean Cronin

1997 December 17, Wednesday
EUCHARISTIC ADORATION

Jesus said: "Praise be to Jesus, for Jesus is Lord, Saviour, Redeemer and Reconciler. Open your heart to me, my little one, I come that you may be refreshed in my splendour. Through my splendour, with my splendour, grace, my child; for my splendour is a grace given to all my children. Are you willing to surrender totally and completely to me?

"Striving to be a saint, my daughter, this should be the desire of all my children. How, my daughter? Through me, my child, through me. Coming to receive me in full splendour as the Sacrament of the Holy Eucharist. For as my children partake of me in this most holy, most perfect Sacrament.

"My child, for all who desire me, I come to them.

"Open, my daughter, to Jeremiah 7."

THE BOOK OF JEREMIAH
JEREMIAH 7: The Temple Sermon

³ **Thus says the Lord of hosts, the God of Israel: Reform your ways and your deeds, so that I may remain with you in this place.**
⁴ **Put not your trust in the deceitful words: "This is the temple of the Lord! The temple of the Lord!"**

Jesus said: "My children, the temple of the Lord is each of your souls who are in the state of grace; and as you receive me, I abide in this my Temple; but it is completely up to each of you the length of my stay! The splendour, my splendour, my grace given to you to be saints. But do you prepare yourselves to receive this grace, or do you refuse this grace, by the act of sin?"

Jeremiah 7 cont'd:

⁵ **Only if you thoroughly reform your ways and your deeds; if each of you deals justly with his neighbour;**
⁶ **if you no longer oppress the residential alien, the orphan, and the widow; if you no longer shed innocent blood in this place, or follow strange gods to your own harm,**
⁷ **will I remain with you in this place, in the land which I gave your fathers long ago and forever.**

Jesus said: "My daughter, it is this grace, this splendour which will be your strength and the strength of all those who desire me. The strength which will be needed for the days ahead. Come to me now, my children. Receive me now. In this holy, perfect Sacrament; for it is I alive you receive! It is I the Lord God of Hosts who will be your strength, your armour.

"Open to Ezekiel 7, my beloved one."

THE BOOK OF EZEKIEL
EZEKIEL 7: The End Has Come

1 **Thus the word of the Lord came to me:**
2 **Son of man, now say: Thus says the Lord God to the land of Israel: An end! The end has come upon the four corners of the land!**
3 **Now the end is upon you; I will unleash my anger against you and judge you according to your conduct and lay upon you the consequences of all your abominations.**
4 **I will not look upon you with pity nor have mercy; I will bring your conduct down upon you, and the consequences of your abominations shall be in your midst; then shall you know that I am the Lord.**
5 **Thus says the Lord God: Disaster upon disaster! See it coming!**
6 **An end is coming, the end is coming upon you! See it coming!**
7 **The climax has come for you who dwell in the land! The time has come, near is the day: a time of consternation, not of rejoicing.**
8 **Soon now I will pour out my fury upon you and spend my anger upon you: I will judge you according to your conduct and lay upon you the consequences of all your abominations.**

Jesus said: "My children, heed my words! Are you prepared?"
Approved by Rev. Sean Cronin

1997 December 19, Friday
MESSAGE FROM OUR LOVING MOTHER

Our Loving Mother said: "My precious children, praise be to my Beloved Son, Jesus Christ, in the Almighty Name of the Father, Son and Holy Spirit; for Jesus Is Lord, Saviour and Redeemer.

"I come to bless you with the holiness and peace at this dawn of the creation of birth; for the birth of my Holy Son was the beginning of everlasting life to all of creation.

"You, my children, have been asked by my beloved holy crucified Son to die unto yourselves, that you may receive this precious gift of salvation and life eternal.

"My Son has given you a final plea to surrender completely to the Holy Will of the Almighty Father, Son and Holy Spirit, through preparation with the holy and blessed Sacraments of Reconciliation and the true presence of my Son in the Holy Eucharist.

"Listen to my Holy Son, and do not take our words lightly, for you have come to the crossroads of final resignation to accept the Holy Will of the Father, or eternal damnation.

"I bless each of you in the Holy Name of the Father, Son and Holy Spirit.

"I love you my children, thank you, my little one, for responding to our call."

Approved by Rev. Sean Cronin and Rev. Richard Hoynes 1/6/98

1997 December 27, Saturday, 06:00
EUCHARISTIC ADORATION
MESSAGE FROM OUR LOVING MOTHER

Our Loving Mother said: "Welcome, my little one, thank you for coming to spend this time with my Son. Praise be to His Holiness, the Almighty Father, Son and Holy Spirit, for Jesus is Lord, Saviour and Redeemer.

"Once again, my children, I have come to bring the blessings of the Holy Father, Son and Holy Spirit to each of you, this holy season of my Son's birth and redemption.

"Each of you have been given a new life with the birth of my holy redemptive Son. A new beginning; but have you accepted this new life eternal, through dying unto yourselves and surrendering in complete submission to the Holy Will of the Father, Son, and Holy Spirit.

"Oh my precious children, know that as I am your Mother, I also plead with you for a change and a willingness to come in complete surrender and atonement to the Holy and Blessed Trinity. For it is only the strength and armour of protection from the Holy Blessed Trinity that will guide and withstand during the days ahead.

"As always I plead for you, my children, and with you my children, for the mercy of the Almighty Father, Son and Holy Spirit, to surround you for the coming days of tribulations ahead.

"Prepare, my children, through prayer, atonement, supplication; for if you do not heed the words of my holy crucified Son, you will not be able to withstand what is to come without the armour and protection of the Blessed Trinity.

"Know that my mantle of protection surrounds each of you and your families, as you are preparing to enter into a new season. May the mercy of the Holy and Blessed Trinity guide each of you to a total surrender of yourselves in love and will to the Holy Will of the Father, Son and Holy Spirit. For it is this release of love and surrender that will lead you to life eternal.

"I bless you each in the Almighty Name of the Father, the kingship of the Son, and the eternal spouse, the Holy Spirit.

"Thank you, my little one, for responding to our call. I love you, my children."

"*Jesus said:* "Now, my child, open to Isaiah 5.""

THE BOOK OF ISAIAH
ISAIAH 5: The Vineyard Song

¹ **Listen while I sing you this song, a song of my friend and his vineyard; my friend had a vineyard on a very fertile hill.**

² **He dug the soil and cleared it of stones; he planted the finest vines. He built a tower to guard them. Dug a pit for treading the grapes. He waited for the grapes to ripen, but every grape was sour;**

³ **so now my friend says, "You people who live in Jerusalem and Judah, judges between my vineyard and me.**

⁴ **Is there anything I failed to do for it? Then why did it produce sour grapes and not the good grapes I expected?**

⁵ **Here is what I am going to do to my vineyard; I will take away the hedge around it, break down the wall that protects it, and let wild animals eat it and trample it down.**

⁶ **I will let it be overgrown with weeds, I will not trim the vines**

or hoe the ground; instead I will let briers and thorns cover it; I will even forbid the clouds to let rain fall on it."

7 Israel is the vineyard of the Lord Almighty; the people of Judah are the vines he planted. He expected them to do what was good, but instead they committed murder. He expected them to do what was right, but their victims cried out for justice.

20 You are doomed! You call evil good and call good evil! You turn darkness into light and light into darkness. You make what is bitter, sweet; and what is sweet you make bitter.

30When that day comes, they will roar over Israel as loudly as the sea. Look at this country! Darkness and distress! The light is swallowed by darkness!"

Jesus said: "Come back to the Father, Son and Holy Spirit, my children. Pray, pray, pray.

"Shalom, my children. Peace unto you, my little one."

Approved by Rev. Sean Cronin
and Rev. Richard Hoynes, 1998 January 06

1998 January 06, Tuesday
EUCHARISTIC ADORATION
MESSAGE FROM OUR LOVING MOTHER

Our Loving Mother said: "Praise be to my holy redemptive Son, for Jesus is Lord, Saviour and Redeemer. I come, my beloved little one, through the merciful love of the Father, Son and Holy Spirit.

"Many times throughout history I was asked to come to plead with my children and for my children, that they would open their hearts to the merciful love of the Almighty to change their ways, in order that peace, the peace of the Holy and Blessed Trinity, would be brought into this world of deception. But to my dismay, very few children have responded to our pleas. Man is not willing to change the error of his ways, to turn away from the evil influences of power and the deceptions of money and pleasures; all of which is *not* of the holy and Blessed Trinity. Soon, my children, very soon, a great catastrophe shall not only awaken, but remind mankind, that money, pleasures, and materialistic values will not help or save them.

"The land will move, the grounds will open, and much of the coastline will be covered with water; mankind will plead for mercy and will recall the many warnings which we have given. Hearts will tremble with fear. Many lives will be lost, but more importantly, many souls will be lost to the snares of the evil one. And how, then, will all the materialistic wealth and pleasures of the world help them?

"How my heart breaks for what my children must suffer. Do not wait for this day to come upon you to seek the mercy of the Almighty. Come to the Sacrament of Reconciliation now; to the Holy Sacrament of the Eucharist now, before it is to late!

"'He comes as a thief in the night.' Are your souls prepared? You should always be prepared. Remain in the state of grace. Pray, my children, pray. Do not wait until it is too late, but seek and surrender to the Holy Will of the Blessed Trinity now.

"I bless each of you in the Almighty Name of the Father, Son and Holy Spirit. Thank you, my little one, for responding to our call."

Jesus said: "Open, my daughter, to Revelation 6."

THE BOOK OF REVELATION
REVELATION 6: The First Six Seals

⁹ **When the Lamb broke open the fifth seal, I saw underneath the altar the souls of those who had been slaughtered because of the witness they bore to the word of God.**

¹⁰ **They cried out in a loud voice, "How long will it be, holy and true master, before you sit in judgment and avenge our blood on the inhabitants of the earth?"**

¹¹ **Each of the martyrs was given a long white robe, and they were told to be patient a little while longer until the quota was filled of their fellow servants and brothers who were going to be killed as they had been.**

¹² **Then I watched while the Lamb broke open the sixth seal, and there was a great earthquake; the sun turned as black as goats-hair tentcloth and the moon grew red as blood.**

[13] The stars in the sky fell to the earth like unripe figs shaken loose from the tree in a strong wind.

[14] Then the sky disappeared as if were a scroll being rolled up; every mountain and island was uprooted from its base.

[15] The kings of the earth, the nobles, the military officers, the rich, the powerful and every slave and free person hid themselves in caves and among mountain crags.

[16] They cried out to the mountains and the rocks, "Fall on us and hide us from the face of the One who sits on the throne and from the wrath of the Lamb.

[17] The great day of their vengeance has come. Who can withstand it?"

"Are you listening my children?
"Pray, my children, pray.
"Shalom, my little one."

Approved by Rev. Sean Cronin and Rev. Richard Hoynes, 1998 January 06

1998 January 17, Saturday, 05:30
St. Dominic Savio Catholic Church
EUCHARISTIC ADORATION

Jesus said: "Praise be to Jesus, for Jesus is Lord, Saviour, Redeemer. Thank you, my little one, for coming to be with me. How I yearn for my children to visit me, pray with me, come to me.

"As you go where you have been invited to take mine and my holy Mother's teachings, I ask you to begin with the prayer of Mary's Way of the Cross. As my children are led through the passion with my Mother, each child who opens their heart to me will be given a special grace and feel the presence of my holy Mother.

"If each child releases to me their free will, conversions will happen, and peace will come to their families. Yes, my child, even in these times, for my mercy is never ending. It is my love, my mercy, my strength which will get you through these times.

"Open, my child, to Isaiah 6."

THE BOOK OF ISAIAH
ISAIAH 6: The Call of Isaiah

1. In the year king Uzziah died, I saw the Lord seated on a high and lofty throne with the train of his garment filling the temple.

2. Seraphim were stationed above; each of them had six wings; with two they veiled their faces, and with two they veiled their feet, and with two they hovered aloft.

3. "Holy, holy, holy is the Lord of hosts!" they cried one to the other. "All the earth is filled with his glory!"

4. At the sound of that cry, the frame of the door shook and the house was filled with smoke.

5. Then I said, "Woe is me, I am doomed! For I am a man of unclean lips, living among a people of unclean lips; yet my eyes have seen the King, the Lord of hosts!"

6. Then one of the seraphim flew to me, holding an ember which he had taken with tongs from the altar.

7. He touched my mouth with it. "See," he said, "now that this has touched your lips your wickedness is removed, your sin is purged."

8. Then I heard the voice of the Lord saying, "Whom shall I send? Who will go for us?" "Here I am," I said; "send me!"

9. And he replied, "Go and say to this people: Listen carefully, but you shall not understand! Look intently, but you shall know nothing!

10. You are to make the heart of this people sluggish, to dull their ears and close their eyes; else their eyes will see, their ears hear, their heart understand, and they will turn and be healed."

11. "How long O Lord?" I asked. And he replied: until the cities are desolate, without inhabitants, houses without a man, and the earth is a desolate waste.

12. Until the Lord removes men far away, and the land is abandoned more and more.

13. If there be still a tenth part in it, then this in turn shall be laid waste; as with at terebinth or an oak whose trunk remains when its leaves have fallen. (Holy offspring is the trunk.)

Jesus said: "My beloved one, go in my name as my vessel. Give my children my teachings. As you have pleaded they will see only me; they will hear only me; for I Am, and as I Am, I Am word; and the word shall be for all.

"Bend your knees my children, surround yourselves in my mercy. I love each one of you. I Am, my children. Have no fear, but come to me.

"I love you, my little one. Shalom, my people."

*Approved by Rev. Sean Cronin and
Rev. Paul Caporali, 1998 January 17*

1998 January 20, Tuesday
AFTER MASS AT HOLY TRINITY

Jesus said: "My beloved little one, praise be to Jesus, for Jesus is Lord, Saviour, Redeemer, Messiah.

"Daughter do not worry about this project and the place of recording. You will seek the advice of my children at Follow Me Communications.

"Tell my children this, Follow me my children; I will lead you; I will guide you. This my holy work; my teachings will reach many. I desire 3300 recordings of my teachings. Are you willing to surrender to my Holy Will? Then follow me my children, I will lead.

"My son Michael knows in his heart my desire. He shall be my voice; his composition of music for this recording, I have placed within.

"Thank you, my children, for your willingness to follow me. I love you, my little one. I bless you, my children.

"Open, my children, to Jeremiah 1 and 2."

JEREMIAH 1

⁴ **The Lord said to me,**
⁵ **"I knew you before you were formed within your mother's womb; before you were born I sanctified you and appointed you as My spokesman to the world.**
⁶ **"O Lord God," I said, "I can't do that! I'm far too young! I'm only a youth!"**

⁷ "Don't say that," He replied, "for you will go wherever I
send you and speak whatever I tell you to.

⁸ And don't be afraid of the people, for I, the Lord, will be
with you and see you through.

⁹ Then He touched my mouth and said, "See, I have put My
words in your mouth!

¹⁰ Today your work begins, to warn the nations and the
kingdoms of the world."

*Approved by Rev. Sean Cronin
& Rev. Paul Caporali 1/28/98*

1998 January 21, Wednesday, 07:00
EUCHARISTIC ADORATION

Jesus said: "Praise be to Jesus, for Jesus is Lord Almighty
Saviour, King and Messiah. Open your heart, my children, for my
teachings. I bring many graces to my children especially in these
times, for my children to persevere through prayer to guard their
faith; for it will be through my strength and the many graces I
shower upon my children during these very difficult times.

"My children, surrender to me in prayer; but not only in prayer,
but in all that you do. Invite me to be with you. Offer all to me, for
me and through me.

"You want dates, times, a quick remedy; this you call preparation?

"No, my children, preparation for all times is prayer, supplication, sacrifice. Even the littlest sacrifice if offered with love can be
the biggest sacrifice in my eyes.

"You are not on this earth to please others or yourselves. Your
life was a gift from the Heavenly Father. A gift of yourselves for
Him. Through Him and with Him.

"Understand, my child, it takes no great theologian to understand the meaning of life. Life is a gift from the Heavenly Father.
The purpose of life is to honour the Father with mind, body and soul;
and when you die unto yourselves, you will have life eternal. This
is the whole purpose of life.

"Now, open my little one, to Romans 1."

THE EPISTLE OF PAUL TO THE ROMANS
ROMANS 1: Punishment of Idolatry

[17] For in the gospel is revealed the justice of God which begins and ends with faith; as Scripture says, "The just man shall live by faith."

[18] The wrath of God is being revealed from heaven against the irreligious and perverse spirit of men who, in this perversity of theirs, hinder the truth.

[19] In fact, whatever can be known about God is clear to them; he himself made it so.

[20] Since the creation of the world, invisible realities, God's eternal power and divinity, have become visible, recognized through the things he has made. Therefore these men are inexcusable.

[21] They certainly had knowledge of God, yet they did not glorify him as God nor give him thanks; they negated themselves through speculating to no purpose, and their senseless hearts were darkened.

[22] They claimed to be wise, but turned into fools instead;

[23] they exchanged the glory of the immortal God for images representing mortal man, birds, beasts, and snakes.

[24] In consequence, God delivered them up in their lusts to unclean practices; they engaged in the mutual degradation of their bodies,

[25] these men who exchanged the truth of God for a lie and worshipped and served the creature rather than the Creator — blessed be he forever, amen!

[26] God therefore delivered them up to disgraceful passions. Their women exchanged natural intercourse for unnatural,

[27] and the men gave up natural intercourse with women and burned with lust for one another. Men did shameful things with men, and thus received in their own persons the penalty for their perversity.

[28] They did not see fit to acknowledge God, so God delivered them up to their own depraved sense to do what is unseemly.

[29] They are filled with every kind of wickedness: maliciousness, greed, ill will, envy, murder, bickering, deceit, craftiness. They are gossips

[30] and slanderers, they hate God, are insolent, haughty, boastful, ingenious in their wrongdoing and rebellious towards their parents.

[31] One sees in them men without conscience, without loyalty, without affection, without pity.

[32] They know God's just decree that all who do such things deserve death; yet they not only do them, but approve them in others."

ROMANS 2: God's Last Judgement

[7] He will give eternal life to those who strive for glory, honour, and immortality by patiently doing right;

[8] wrath and fury to those who selfishly disobey the truth and obey wickedness.

[9] Yes, affliction and anguish will come upon every man who has done evil, the Jew first, then the Greek.

[10] But there will be glory, honour, and peace for everyone who has done good, likewise the Jew first, then the Greek.

[11] With God there is no favouritism.

[16]On the day when in accordance with the Gospel I preach, God will pass judgment on the secrets of men through Christ Jesus.

Jesus said: "I bless each of you my children, in the Almighty Name of the Father, Son and Holy Spirit.

"I love you, my little one. Shalom, my people."

Approved by Rev. Sean Cronin and
Rev. Paul Caporali, 1998 January 21

1998 January 22, Thursday
EUCHARISTIC ADORATION

Jesus said: "Peace unto you, my beloved children. Once again I come that you may be given my word. Open, my children, to Isaiah 9 and 10.

"As you place yourselves in my presence to read my word, you will be fed from the tree of knowledge.

"The spirit is willing but the flesh is weak; this, my children, is why my teachings are given; to stir the weak and fill the mind with my word.

THE BOOK OF ISAIAH
ISAIAH 9: The Prince of Peace

¹ **The people who walk in darkness have seen a great light; upon those who dwelt in the land of gloom a light has shone.**

Jesus said: "Oh, my children, do you not see how without my word, you remain in darkness; your mind is closed to the light; your heart cannot be filled? These times, my children, you have brought them down upon yourselves; but I Am, and I will lead you out of the darkness. I am truth, and I am the light.

"My presence in the Holy Sacrament of the Eucharist will be the strength of your spirit, and give you life eternal. Yes, the flesh is weak, but I will be your strength. Do not continue in this barren desert, but refresh yourselves in my splendour, the springs of everlasting grace.

"Open my Beloved to Psalm 28."

THE BOOK OF PSALMS
PSALM 28: Petition and Thanksgiving

⁶ **Blessed be the Lord, for he has heard the sound of my pleading;**
⁷ **the Lord is my strength and my shield. In him my heart trusts, and I find help; then my heart exults, and with my song I give him thanks.**
⁸ **The Lord is the strength of his people, the saving refuge of his annointed.**
⁹ **Save your people, and bless your inheritance; feed them, and carry them forever!"**

Jesus said: "I love you, my little one. Shalom, my people."
Approved by Rev. Sean Cronin and
Rev. Paul Caporali, 1998 January 22

1998 January 25, Sunday
MESSAGE FROM OUR LOVING MOTHER

Our loving Mother said: "Thank you, my little one, for opening your heart to our call. Praise be to Jesus, for Jesus is Lord, Saviour Redeemer.

"I have been asked by my Holy Crucified Son to come to teach you, my beloved one.

"These are very crucial and decisive times; but, my little one, not only have I come during these times to give warning, but throughout time I have been asked by the Almighty to come to plead with my children to change their ways; to return to the Father, Son and Holy Spirit. Always to prepare themselves through the Holy Sacraments that their souls will always be ready; for no one knows the hour nor time they will be called.

"As I have told you in my other teaching, 'he comes as a thief in the night.' You and others have been drawn together, as many other visionaries and locutionists in these times have been drawn together, because these times are so crucial to all of humanity. As I have told others, times, dates are *never* given, and my children should not worry about these things. What my children should do to prepare is what they should always have been doing, and that is prayer, sacrifice, surrendering to the Holy Will of the Father, Son and Holy Spirit; and receive the Holy Sacraments.

"Yes, my children, signs are being given, have been given, and will be given, so that all may see the mercy of the Father, Son and Holy Spirit. But unless your souls are prepared through prayer, sacrifice and reception of the Holy Sacraments, how will you be able to surrender to the Holy Will of the Father, Son and Holy Spirit? How will you be able to know the signs?

"When my holy Son walked this earth, many did not believe nor want to believe that he was and *is* the Messiah. Instead they crucified him! They were not prepared through their own willingness of unpreparation. They closed their hearts, will and mind, to the teachings and directions of the Father.

"Where did this get them my children? They crucified the Lamb and hailed the thief and murderer.

"As my heart broke then for my Son and for my people, it breaks now for all my children. As it was then, it *is* now. Do not close your heart to my holy Son's word or to his teachings. Do not be like the children who shouted, 'crucify him, crucify him!'

"Save your souls, my children. Save the souls of your children. Pray, pray, pray."

Jesus said: "Open, my daughter, to Revelation 3."

THE BOOK OF REVELATION
REVELATION 3: To Sardis

¹ **To the angel of the church in Sardis; write this: "The One who holds the seven spirits of God, the seven stars, says this; I know your conduct; I know the reputation you have of being alive, when in fact you are dead!**

² **Wake up and strengthen what remains before it dies. I find that the sum of your deeds is less than complete in the sight of my God.**

³ **Call to mind how you accepted what you heard; keep to it, and repent. If you do not rouse yourselves I will come upon you like a thief at a time you cannot know.**

⁴ **I realize you have in Sardis a few persons who have not soiled their garments; these shall walk with me in white because they are worthy.**

⁵ **The victor shall go clothed in white. I will never erase his name from the book of the living, but will acknowledge him in the presence of my Father and his angels.**

⁶ **Let him who has ears heed the Spirit's word to the churches!"**

Jesus said: "Pray, my children, pray! I love you."

Approved by Rev. Sean Cronin and
Rev. Paul Caporali, 1998 January 25

1998 January 27, Tuesday
EUCHARISTIC ADORATION

Jesus said: "Praise be to Jesus for Jesus is Lord, Saviour and Redeemer. My daughter, thank you for opening your heart for my teaching

"My beloved earthly father, St. Joseph, was the perfect example of surrender. As he was told by the Angel Gabriel that my Holy

Mother was to be his wife, even though she was with child, he accepted the Father's Holy Will. Once again when he was led by the Angel Gabriel to take Mother and myself away from Herod's land, he surrendered completely to the Holy Will of the Father. Then when it was time for him to come home with the Father, though he was saddened at leaving us, again he surrendered to the Holy Will of the Father.

"My children, surrendering of yourselves in complete obedience to the Holy Will of the Father, is not an easy task because you are being asked to go against the ways of the world. As many of my children are trying to live according to the Holy Will of the Father in complete surrender, they are outcast from a society which soon will not only shun my children, but many of you will be martyrs if you go against the one-world government, which is led by the antichrist himself.

"You, my children are being called to total surrender as my beloved Joseph was called to total surrender as he led us out of danger from Herod's killing spree. Now you, my children, will soon be asked in order to save your souls from eternal damnation to surrender completely to the holy will of the Father, Son and Holy Spirit in order that you may have life eternal.

"This is why I beg you now. Pray, surrender, sacrifice. That you will be able to withstand that which is ahead of you.

"Open, my beloved one, to Revelation 13."

THE BOOK OF REVELATION
REVELATION 13: The First Beast

¹ **Then I saw a wild beast come out of the sea with ten horns and seven heads; on its horns were ten diadems, and on its heads blasphemous names.**

² **The beast I saw was like a leopard, but it had feet like a bear, and the mouth of a lion. The dragon gave it its power and throne, together with great authority.**

³ **I saw that one of its heads seemed to have been mortally wounded, but this mortal wound was healed. Fascinated, the whole world followed after the beast.**

⁴ They worshipped the dragon because it gave its authority to the beast; they also worshipped the beast and said, "Who can compare with the beast or who can fight against it?"

⁵ The beast was given a mouth uttering proud boasts and blasphemies, and it was given authority to act for forty-two months.

⁶ It opened its mouth to utter blasphemies against God, blaspheming his name and his dwelling, and those who dwell in heaven.

⁷ It was also allowed to wage war against the God's people and conquer them, and it was granted authority over every tribe, people, tongue and nation.

⁸ The beast will be worshipped by all those inhabitants of earth who did not have their names written at the world's beginning in the book of the living, which belongs to the Lamb who was slain.

⁹ Let him who has ears heed these words!

¹⁰ If one is destined for captivity, into captivity he goes! If one is destined to be slain by the sword, by the sword he will be slain! Such is the faithful endurance that distinguishes God's holy people.

Jesus said: "My beloved little one, I am with you. My people, I am with you. I bless you in the Almighty Name of the Father, Son and Holy Spirit."

Approved by Rev. Sean Cronin and
Rev. Paul Caporali, 1998 January 27

1998 January 28, Wednesday
EUCHARISTIC ADORATION

Jesus said: "Praise be to Jesus for Jesus is Lord, Saviour and Redeemer and Holy is the Almighty Father, Son and Holy Spirit. Thank you, my beloved little one, for opening your heart to my teaching.

"As I have spoken, so shall it be!

"You, my children, continue in this waste land of barren desert. My Holy Mother pleads for mercy for all of our children; but do you listen? Have you opened your hearts to my whisperings upon each of your hearts? These teachings, as those of my Holy Mother's, have been given to you for many years. I have promised all my children shall hear my words, for no one shall have the excuse that I did not try to reach all my children. But do you turn a deaf ear? How long will it take for your hearts to realize this is your last opportunity to receive my mercy before the pangs of justice fall upon each one of you.

"I have said many times, I do not come to bring these teachings for my sake, but for each one of your soul's. Do not let another minute go by before you realize you did not heed my words, for that minute may be to late.

"I come that you may know my mercy, my love.

"The evil one has torn apart and broken the foundation of your families. I come to unite the family, each of your families, with my love, my peace. It only takes one member of each family to unite in prayer, sacrifice, the Holy Sacraments and surrender of your will to the will of the Holy Blessed Trinity, and I will unite your families as a chain, intermingling with each other, and holding you together. Is that not my mercy?

"Oh, my children, how I love each one of you. I have never left you. Why do you leave me? Come back to me, my children. I love each one of you. I am the God of mercy.

"Open, my daughter, to Daniel 3."

THE BOOK OF DANIEL
DANIEL 3: The Fiery Furnace

¹⁹ King Nebuchadnezzar's face became livid with utter rage against Shadrach, Meshach, and Abednego. He ordered the furnace to be heated seven times more than usual

²⁰ and had some of the strongest men in his army bind Shadrach, Meshach, and Abednego and cast them into the white-hot furnace.

²¹ They were bound and cast into the white-hot furnace with their coats, hats, shoes and other garments,

²² For the king's order was urgent. So huge a fire was kindled in the furnace that the flames devoured the men who threw Shadrach, Meshach, and Abednego into it.

²³ But these three fell bound into the midst of the white-hot furnace.

²⁴ They walked about in the flames, singing to God and blessing the Lord.

²⁵ In the fire Azariah stood up and prayed aloud:

²⁶ "Blessed are you, and praiseworthy, O Lord, the God of our fathers, and glorious forever is your name.

²⁷ For you are just in all you have done; all your deeds are faultless, all your ways right, and all your judgments proper."

Jesus said: "My children, have I not shown you my mercy? Do not delay. Do not continue in the abyss where the evil one's ploys have swayed you; he has only brought destruction to you, to your families. I will raise you up from this nether world. I love you, my children.

"I bless you, my child. Thank you, my little one, for remaining obedient to our call.

"In this little shrine of the Holy Family I will shower many graces of spiritual and corporal healings. As the little petals are given out with the prayer of the consecration, I ask my children to consecrate themselves through the intercession of the Holy Family to my most Sacred Heart, and the Immaculate Heart of my Holy Mother.

"Shalom my people."

Approved by Rev. Sean Cronin and Rev. Paul Caporali

1998 January 29, Thursday
EUCHARISTIC ADORATION

Jesus said: "Praise be to Jesus, for Jesus is Lord, Saviour, Redeemer, Messiah. Thank you, my beloved little one, for opening your heart for my teaching.

"Open, my daughter, to Isaiah 15. In Isaiah, my children cry out with bitterness in their hearts because they have justly been punished by the Father because they remained in disobedience to the Father."

THE BOOK OF ISAIAH
ISAIAH 15: Moab

¹ **Oracle on Moab; laid waste in a night, Ar of Moab is destroyed; laid waste in a night, Kir of Moab is destroyed.**
² **Up goes daughter Dibon to the high places to weep; over Nebo and over Medeba Moab wails. Every head is shaved, every beard sheared off.**
³ **In the streets they wear sackcloth, lamenting and weeping; on the rooftops, and in the squares everyone wails.**

Jesus said: "Wailing in bitterness, my child, after they had been warned, as my children have been warned. It has never been the Almighty Father's desire to punish; but when the errors of the children lead them to lose their souls through their own free will, then it is necessary for the Almighty Father's justice.

"Listen my people! Listen with the truth of your hearts, for this I pray now, that you may know I lived that you may live and have life eternal. I died so you may live and have life eternal. I come to you, my children, now, in these teachings and with these teachings, for I am Word; I Am; I will always be, for I am word. I come to you body, blood, soul and divinity, alive in the Holy Sacrament of the Eucharist that you may have life eternal. Partake of me and you partake of the greatest miracle that will give you strength, my strength; love, my love; peace, my peace; and life eternal. You partake in a reenactment of my death upon the cross which gave you life eternal. Surrender to me, my children. Surrender completely to the Holy Will of the Father, Son and Holy Spirit, so that you may not suffer as those of my children in Moab suffered.

THE GOSPEL ACCORDING TO JOHN
JOHN 17: The Completion of Jesus' Work

¹ **After he had spoken these words, Jesus looked up to heaven and said, "Father, the hour has come! Give glory to your son that your son may give glory to you,**
² **inasmuch as you have given him authority over all mankind, that he may bestow eternal life on those you gave him.**

³ Now this is eternal life, that they should know you, the only true God, and the one whom you sent, Jesus Christ.

⁴ I glorified you on earth by accomplishing the work that you gave me to do.

⁵ Now glorify me, Father, with you, with the glory that I had with you before the world began.

⁶ I revealed your name to those whom you gave me out of the world. They belonged to you, and you gave them to me, and they have kept your word.

⁷ Now they know that everything you gave me is from you.

⁸ Because the words you gave to me I have given to them, and they accepted them and truly understood that I came from you, and they have believed that you sent me.

⁹ I pray for them. I do not pray for the world but for the ones you have given me, because they are yours.

¹⁰ And everything of mine is yours and everything of yours is mine, and I have been glorified in them.

¹¹ And now I will no longer be in the world, but they are in the world, while I am coming to you. Holy Father, keep them in your name that you have given me, so that they may be one just as we are.

¹² When I was with them I protected them in your name that you gave me, and I guarded them, and none of them was lost except, the son of destruction, in order that the scripture might be fulfilled.

¹³ But now I am coming to you. I speak this in the world so that they may share my joy completely.

¹⁴ I gave them your word, and the world hated them, because they do not belong to the world anymore than I belong to the world.

¹⁵ I do not ask that you take them out of the world but that you keep them from the evil one.

¹⁶ They do not belong to the world anymore than I belong to the world.

¹⁷ Consecrate them in the truth. Your word is truth.

¹⁸ As you sent me into the world, so I sent them into the world.

¹⁹ And I consecrate myself for them, so that they also may be consecrated in truth.

²⁰ I pray not only for them, but also for those who will believe in me through their word,

²¹ that they may all be one, as you, Father, are in me and I in you, that they also may be in us, that the world may believe that you sent me.

²² And I have given them the glory you gave me, so that they may be one, as we are one —

²³ I in them and you in me, that they may be brought to perfection as one, that the world may know that you sent me, and that you loved them even as you love me.

²⁴ Father, they are your gift to me. I wish that where I am they also may be with me, that they may see my glory that you gave me, because you loved me before the foundation of the world.

²⁵ Righteous Father, the world also does not know you, but I know you, and they know you sent me.

²⁶ I made known to them your name and I will make it known, that the love with which you loved me may be in them and I in them.

Jesus said: "This I pray for each one of you, my children. I bless you in the Almighty Name of the Father, Son and Holy Spirit. I love you, my children. I love you, my little one. Shalom, my people."

Approved by Rev. Paul Caporali

1998 January 30, Friday
EUCHARISTIC ADORATION
St. Bridgit's Eucharistic Chapel, Las Vegas

Jesus said: "Praise be to Jesus, for Jesus is Lord, Saviour, Redeemer, Reconciler. Thank you, my beloved one for remaining obedient to our call.

"Do you see, my little one, what the youth of this world are being taught through television and video games, this electronic technology, the evil one's tool to thwart and confuse the minds of my children? Technology that man has created to advance the world, but destroys the minds and takes possession of my children's souls. How do my little ones stand a chance when the parents themselves have brought this evil into their homes?

"My children must return to me, to the Holy Blessed Trinity, in order to save their souls and the souls of their children. I continue to plead with you, my children, for prayer, sacrifice and a return to the Sacraments, or you will lose your children to the ploys of the evil one. How can you, my children, expect me to allow you to continue in this abyss, this destruction of the souls of my children?

"Open, my beloved, to Jeremiah."

THE BOOK OF JEREMIAH
JEREMIAH 7: Abuses in Worship

¹⁸ The children gather wood, their fathers light the fire, and the women knead dough to make cakes for the queen of heaven, while libations are poured out to strange gods in order to hurt me.

¹⁹ Is it I whom they hurt, says the Lord; is it not rather themselves, to their own confusion?

²⁰ See now, says the Lord God, my anger and my wrath will pour out upon this place, upon man and beast, upon the trees of the field and the fruits of the earth; it will burn without being quenched.

JEREMIAH 50: The First Prophecy Against Babylon

⁶ Lost sheep were my people, their shepherds mislead them, straggling on the mountains; from mountain to hill they wandered, losing the way to their fold.

⁷ Whoever came upon them devoured them, and their enemies said, "We incur no guilt, because they sinned against the Lord, the hope of their fathers, their abode of Justice."

Jesus said: "My beloved little one, the parents were to be the teachers and protectors of my innocents. Instead they lead their children astray and allow their own gods to create havoc in the family. What a curse, oh my people, you have brought upon yourselves! Television and games, your children's sitters, are now the idols of your children and yourselves. The materialistic values you set before you are your idols and your gods. Will these idols save your souls or those of your children?

"You, the caretakers of my children, have bequeathed their souls to the evil one as a dowry for your pleasures!

"Lament for your children's souls; and for your own souls.

"I love you, my beloved little one. Pray, pray, pray, for these my people, my little one."

Approved by Rev. Paul Caporali

1998 February 01, Sunday
EUCHARISTIC ADORATION
St. Bridgit's Eucharistic Chapel, Las Vegas

Jesus said: "Praise be to Jesus, for Jesus is Lord, Saviour and Redeemer.

"Thank you, my beloved little one, for coming to be with me. My precious children, do you remember the story of King Solomon, and the choice the two women were given when they each claimed to be the mother of the child? His answer was to kill the child and each would receive what they desired.

"How many of you are allowing the evil one to kill the souls of your children through misguided attempts in giving choices of freedom to the children? Babies killing babies, mothers killing children; fathers killing spouse and children; children killing parents. Which of the women are you in King Solomon's court?

"Open, my little one, to 1 Kings 3."

THE FIRST BOOK OF KINGS
1 KINGS 3: Solomon's Judgment

16 Later, two harlots came to the king and stood before him.

17 One woman said: "By your leave, my lord, this woman and I live in the same house, and I gave birth in the house while she was present.

18 On the third day after I gave birth, this woman also gave birth. We were alone in the house; there was no one there but us two.

19 This woman's son died during the night; she smothered him by lying on him.

[20] Later that night she got up and took my son from my side, as I, your handmaid, was sleeping. Then she laid him in her bosom, after she had laid her dead child in my bosom.

[21] I rose in the morning to nurse my child, and I found him dead. But when I examined him in the morning light, I saw it was not the son whom I had borne.

[22] The other woman answered, "It is not so! The living one is my son, the dead one is yours." But the first kept saying, "No, the dead one is your child, the living one is mine!" Thus they argued before the king.

[23] Then the king said: "One woman claims, 'This, the living one, is my child, and the dead one is yours.' The other answers, "No! The dead one is your child; the living one is mine.'"

[24] The king continued, "Get me a sword." When they brought the sword before him,

[25] he said, "Cut the living child in two, and give half to one woman and half to the other."

[26] The woman whose son it was, in the anguish she felt for it, said to the king, "Please, my lord, give her the living child — please do not kill it!" The other, however, said, "It shall be neither mine nor yours. Divide it!"

[27] The king then answered, "Give the first one the living child! By no means kill it, for she is the mother."

[28] When all Israel heard the judgment the king had given, they were in awe of him, because they saw that the king had in him the wisdom of God for giving judgment."

Jesus said: "I bless you, my people. Shalom, my little one."
Approved by Rev. Paul Caporali

1998 March 03, Tuesday
EUCHARISTIC ADORATION

Jesus said: "Praise be to Jesus, for Jesus is Lord, Saviour, and Redeemer.

"My children, come to the font of my mercy. I am your Jesus of mercy. I give you the graces necessary to redeem yourselves; to surrender completely and totally to me. I give you the Sacrament of Reconciliation to cleanse your souls from all error of sin, that you may ready yourself to receive me alive in the Holy Sacrament of the Eucharist, in order that you may have my salvation and eternal life. *Now* is the time for you to open your hearts to my mercy. For you do not know the hour that I come 'as a thief in the night'; that you come before my Father for judgment. Are you ready? Are you prepared?

"Oh, my children, time is short. Time, not as you know it, but as God the Father Almighty wills it. It is not of chastisement we speak; nor is it of the end times we speak. But you were created to remain for a period of time on this earth. Have you used your time wisely, or have you squandered it away with the wiles of worldly ways?

"You were created in the image and likeness of the Father, Son and Holy Spirit. Did you remain obedient to the Will of the Father, so that at the time of judgment when you come before the Father, you may remain in the presence of the Almighty? Or will you be sent to the eternal fires of Gehenna, where, because you refused the gifts of the Almighty to assure your place in the heavenly kingdom, you squandered these gifts; turned away these gifts for the worldly errs and pleasures of lucifer?

"You were created children of God the Father Almighty. I died for each one of you. Was my death in vain for your soul?

"As I carried the cross on the path of the Via Dolorosa, it was as if I carried each one of you, holding you close to my Heart.

"As I was kicked and beaten, I held each one of you in my arms, never wanting to let you go.

"As they spat in my face, I held on to the thought of the kiss I would give each of you, with the love I have for each of you, from the deepest crevices of my being; and as they crowned me with the thorns which pierced my head, with the trickles of blood streaming down my face, I thought of each one of you, and the true and pure love only I was willing to surrender for you by dying on the cross for you.

"And as I drew the last of my dying breath in pleading with the Father Almighty, "Father, forgive them for they know not what they do!" I plead for each of you now: "Father, forgive all these my children, for they know not what they do!"

"Come to me, my children. I love you. I died for you!

"Open, my beloved little one, to John 19."

THE GOSPEL ACCORDING TO JOHN
JOHN 19: The Trial Before Pilate

¹ Pilate's next move was to take Jesus and have him scourged.
² The soldiers then wove a crown of thorns and fixed it on his head, throwing around his shoulders a cloak of royal purple.
³ Repeatedly they came up to him and said, "All hail, king of the Jews!," slapping his face as they did so.

John 19 cont'd: *The Crucifixion and Death of Jesus*

¹⁷ Jesus was led away and, carrying the cross by himself, went out to what is called the Place of the Skull (in Hebrew, *Golgotha*).
¹⁸ There they crucified him, and two others with him: one on either side, Jesus in the middle.
¹⁹ Pilate had an inscription placed on the cross which read, "Jesus the Nazorean, The King of the Jews."

THE GOSPEL ACCORDING TO LUKE
LUKE 23: The Crucifixion

³⁴ Then Jesus said "Father, forgive them; they do not know what they are doing."

THE GOSPEL ACCORDING TO MARK
MARK 15: The Death of Jesus

³³ When noon came, darkness fell on the whole countryside and lasted until mid-afternoon.
³⁴ At that time Jesus cried out in a loud voice, "Eloi, Eloi, lama sabachthani?" which means, "My God, my God, why have you forsaken me?"

Jesus said: "My beloved children, why have you forsaken me? Open your hearts and I will fill them. Come to me. I will give you the graces necessary to surrender completely and totally to the Holy Will of the Father, as I surrendered on the Hill of Golgotha, so that you would have life eternal.

"I am your Jesus of Mercy."

Approved by Rev. Paul Caporali

1998 March 16, Monday
EUCHARISTIC ADORATION

Jesus said: "Praise be to Jesus for Jesus is Lord, Saviour, Redeemer, Reconciler.

"I am your Jesus of Mercy. My beloved little one, as you see personally, the persecutions of my children continues on, but I am your Jesus of mercy and I am your strength.

"To succumb to the attacks of the evil one through an unwillingness to surrender completely to the will of the Almighty Father, Son and Holy Spirit, is the ploy of Lucifer to destroy mankind. Lucifer knows that when a surrendering of one's will to the Holy Blessed Trinity is accomplished, he can no longer influence or destroy what is willingly mine. He will still try to influence or deter this soul from my haven, but he knows that my strength and my protection now surrounds the soul who has surrendered to me.

"Open, my beloved little one, to Matthew 3, v16."

THE GOSPEL ACCORDING TO MATTHEW
MATTHEW 3: The Baptism of Jesus

[16] After Jesus was baptized, he came directly out of the water. Suddenly the sky opened and he saw the Spirit of God descend like a dove and hover over him.
[17] With that, a voice from heavens said, "This is my beloved Son. My favour rests on him."

MATTHEW 4: The Temptation

[1] Then Jesus was led onto the desert by the Spirit, to be tempted there by the devil.

² **He fasted forty days and forty nights, and afterward was hungry.**

³ **The tempter approached and said to him, "If you are the Son of God, command these stones to turn into bread."**

⁴ **Jesus replied, "Scripture has it: not on bread alone is man to live but on every utterance that comes from the mouth of God."**

Jesus said: "My children, Satan tried to get me to go against the holy will of the Father, as he does you. He wanted my surrender to him, not to the Father Almighty, just as he wants and ploys for your surrender to him. Do not surrender to Satan, but know that in releasing yourselves to the Holy Will of the Father, your soul is being saved from the eternal fires of Gehenna. You will have life eternal with the Almighty Father, Son and Holy Spirit.

"Open to Luke Ch 3, v7."

THE GOSPEL ACCORDING TO LUKE
LUKE 3: John the Baptizer

⁷ **Here is a sample of John's preaching to the crowds that came for baptism: "You brood of snakes! You are trying to escape hell without truly turning to God. That is why you want to be baptized!**

⁸ **First go and prove by the way you live that you really have repented. And don't think you're safe because you are descendants of Abraham. That isn't enough. God can produce children of Abraham from these desert stones!**

⁹ **The axe of his judgment is poised over you, ready to sever your roots and cut you down. Yes, every tree that does not produce good fruit will be chopped down and thrown into the fire."**

Jesus said: "Oh my daughter, I bring these teachings to my children though many are not willing to listen; to open their hearts to my teachings; but I continue to show you, my children, this love I have for each one of you is merciful and boundless. I come to plead with you, my precious children, for you do not realize eternal is timeless and I want you to spend this eternity with me. Will you not listen?

"Open, my beloved, to Zechariah Ch 1, v2."

THE BOOK OF ZECHARIAH
ZECHARIAH 1: The Necessity of Conversion

² **The Lord was indeed angry with your fathers...**
³ **and say to them: thus says the Lord of hosts: return to me, says the Lord of Hosts, and I will return to you, says the Lord of Hosts.**
⁴ **Be not like your fathers whom the former prophets warned: thus says the Lord of hosts: turn from your evil ways and your wicked deeds. But they would not listen nor pay attention to me.**

Jesus said: "My beloved children, won't you please listen? I *am* your Jesus of mercy.

"I love you, my beloved little one. I am with you. Thank you for remaining obedient to my call."

Approved by Rev. Sean Cronin

1998 March 28, Saturday
EUCHARISTIC ADORATION

Jesus said: "Praise be to Jesus, for Jesus is Lord, Saviour, and Redeemer. I am with you, my daughter. Open your heart for my teaching, for I am teacher and messiah. I am your Jesus of mercy.

"It is difficult for my children to understand why I would bring these teachings, this preparation; for they do not know me or understand the love which I, your Jesus crucified, surrendered to the Will of the Father Almighty; the merciful love of the Father in giving His only begotten Son to die on a cross, so that all his children could have life eternal. My love given completely to each of you through my death on a cross.

"If this much I would do for each of you, why can you not see my mercy, my justice, in coming to give you my teachings, my preparation, in order that you will not lose your soul to the evil one, the conspirator of death for all eternity?

"If you truly knew me, you would not need this preparation nor my teachings. For your love for me would bring you to know truth, and this truth would set you free; because you would know the word as you know me.

"Understand, my children, that each of you have your own free will, and the choices you make through this free will either give life eternal to the soul, or eternal death in the flames of Gehenna!

"As I said before, eternity is timeless, so the choices you make now are choices that can mean life forever or death forever.

"Open, my beloved one, to Jonah."

THE BOOK OF JONAH
JONAH 2: Psalm of Thanksgiving

1 **The Lord sent a large fish that swallowed Jonah; and he remained in the belly of the fish three days and three nights.**

2 **From the belly of the fish Jonah said this prayer to the Lord, his God:**

3 **Out of my distress I called to the Lord, and he answered me; from the midst of the nether world I cried for help, and you heard my voice.**

4 **For you cast me into the deep, into the heart of the sea, and the flood enveloped me; all your breakers and your billows passed over me.**

5 **Then I said, "I am banished from your sight! Yet would I again look upon your holy temple?"**

6 **The waters swirled about me, threatening my life; the abyss enveloped me; seaweed clung about my head.**

7 **Down I went to the roots of the mountains; the bars of the nether world were closing behind me forever, but you brought up my life from the pit, O Lord, my God.**

8 **When my soul fainted within me, I remembered the Lord; my prayer reached you in your holy temple.**

9 **Those who worship vain idols forsake their source of mercy.**

10 **But I, with resounding praise, will sacrifice to you; what I have vowed, I will pay: deliverance is from the Lord.**

¹¹ Then the Lord commanded the fish to spew Jonah upon the shore."

Jesus said: My children, as Jonah was taken by the fish to wallow in his misery, that he would see the errors of his time spent upon this earth, the warning will show you *all* your errors as I have seen them; that you will be given this chance to renew your life in me, with me, and for me; a surrender of your will, in order that you may have life eternal; as Jonah was given my mercy to see and renew his life in me, with me and for me, so that *he* would have Life eternal, and not remain in the abyss for which he himself knew he was headed.

"Why would you not think, as I gave Jonah this preparation, that I would do less for each of you? Is not my mercy your gift of my love for each of you?

"Question not why I bring this preparation to you; but question why you doubt my love!

"Is it that you do not really know me because you have not taken the time to read my word; taken the time to visit me in Eucharistic Adoration, where I await each one of you; taken the time to know me in the Holy Sacrament of the Eucharist, where I come to you alive, body, blood, soul and divinity?

"Why do you not know me, my children? Why do your children not know me?

"Open, my daughter, to Matthew 23."

THE GOSPEL ACCORDING TO MATTHEW
MATTHEW 23: Hypocrisy of the Scribes and Pharisees

³⁷ O Jerusalem, Jerusalem, murderess of the prophets and stoner of those who were sent to you! How often have I yearned to gather your children, as a mother bird gathers her young under her wings, but you refused me.
³⁸ Recall the saying, "You will find your temple deserted."
³⁹ I tell you, you will not see me from this time on until you declare, "Blessed is he who comes in the name of the Lord!"

Jesus said: I love you, my little one. Shalom, my people."
Approved by Rev. Paul Caporali

1998 April 30, Thursday
EUCHARISTIC ADORATION

Jesus said: "My precious children, praise be to Jesus, for Jesus is Lord. I am the Messiah; I am your Jesus of mercy; and they that come to me shall have life everlasting.

"I have given you my teachings that you may see my mercy; that you may open your hearts to my mercy; that you may repent and change from the error of your ways; for you who remain in the world will only go deeper into the error of your ways; for you are not willing to accept that you are *in* this world, not *of* this world.

"My children, you do not realize that for many of you, you are at a crossroad of faith and error. You are beginning to realize this world is in extreme chaos; yet you want to believe what you hear through the media that things are changing; times are better. But if you look around you, you will see the utter despair that many are in. You will see the children bringing out their despair in violence.

"No, my children, mankind itself is on the brink of destruction through its own pernicious ways. This you already know; but you want to believe the media and close your hearts and minds to the truths.

"My children, I do not bring you my words that you turn a deaf ear; for I know many of you are willing to open your hearts to my words, to my teachings; but it is easier to believe the media and hope in the best, than to see truth for what is really is.

"But I do not turn away from you and let you waste away in this evil destruction you are bringing yourselves into. For I am your merciful Jesus and your loving Jesus. So I continue to plead with you. I continue to shower you with my mercy. For if just one of you opens your heart to my mercy, to my teachings, and returns to me, I tell you, all of heaven rejoices.

"My children, these are the times spoken of in my holy word. The times where signs will be given; when you will see and hear prophets. Oh, my children, do you not see how much I love you? How much I plead for your return to me? Open your hearts to me. Surrender to me, your Jesus of mercy.

"Open, my beloved one, to Revelation 7."

THE BOOK OF REVELATION
REVELATION 7: Triumph of the Elect

9 After this I saw before me a huge crowd which no one could count from every nation and race, people and tongue. They stood before the throne and the Lamb, dressed in long white robes and holding palm branches in their hands.

10 They cried out in a loud voice, "Salvation is from Our God, who is seated on the throne, and from the Lamb!"

11 All the angels who were standing around the throne and the elders and the four living creatures fell down before the throne to worship God. They said:

12 "Amen! Praise and glory, wisdom and thanksgiving and honour, power and might, to our God forever and ever. Amen!"

13 Then one of the elders asked me, "Who are these people all dressed in white? And where have they come from?"

14 I said to him, "Sir, you should know better than I." He then told me, "These are the ones who have survived the great period of trial; they have washed their robes and made them white in the blood of the Lamb.

15 It was this that brought them before God's throne: day and night they minister to him in his temple; he who sits on the throne will give them shelter.

16 Never again shall they know hunger or thirst, nor shall the sun nor its heat beat down on them,

17 for the Lamb on the throne will shepherd them. He will lead them to springs of life-giving water, and God will wipe every tear from their eyes.

Jesus said: "My children, will you wear the white robes of eternal life? Will you let me wipe away every tear from your eyes? Open your heart to me. Surrender to me.

"I love you, my children. Shalom, my people.

"Thank you, my beloved one, for remaining obedient to my call."

Approved by Rev. James L. Swenson, 1998 April 30

1998 May 02, 1st Saturday
The Greensides' Farm, Marmora, Ontario, Canada

Message given by Jesus to Patricia Soto
at the Greenside's Farm

Praise be to Jesus, for Jesus is Lord, Saviour, Redeemer.
Jesus said: "My precious children, thank you for coming to my holy ground. I have opened the way for many places like this holy land of Marmora that My children may see the mercy of my love, the love of my Holy Mother who pleads for mercy for her children, and is the true example of surrender. She comes to her children in obedience to the Father Almighty, surrendering to the Holy Will of the Father Almighty, the Holy Will of the Blessed Trinity. Are you willing, my children, to surrender totally to the Holy Will of the Father, Son, and Holy Spirit?

"This holy land of Marmora will have in my time the chapel of prayer, love, sacrifice, and my mercy. You must remember, my children, when obstacles are put in place there is a reason, for nothing is done without authority of the Father Almighty, and done according to the Holy Will of the Father.

"Remember, my children, as you come to visit my holy places of mercy and love, open your hearts to seek my Holy Will, and in seeking my Holy Will, you learn surrender. But not only come to me in these holy places of apparitions, but come to me in the greatest miracle of time, my presence in the Holy Sacrament of the Eucharist where I await you, body, blood, soul and divinity.

"You seek answers, miracles, in these holy places of apparitions; but first, seek your answers through me in the most Holy Sacrament of the Eucharist, Eucharistic Adoration, where I await you, my children.

"Yes, as I have stated, special graces are given as you come to visit these holy places, such as Marmora, where I shower my love upon you, my children. But it is up to each of you to use these graces given to come to me in the Holy Sacrifice of the Mass, The Holy Sacrament of the Eucharist, Eucharistic Adoration.

"I love you, my children; I await you, my children; come to me, my children.

"Yes, my beloved little one, this will be one of many safe havens where my children will be protected. But my children need not worry of the future. They need not worry of the past. They are to be with me now, surrender now to the Father Almighty.

"I love you, my children. Shalom, my people.

"Thank you, my beloved little one, for remaining obedient to my call."

(The following verses are taken from The Catholic Living Bible. Bible has imprimatur from Leo A. Pursley; Bishop of Fort Wayne - South Bend 1/9/76)

[22] Then turning to his disciples he said, "Don't worry about whether you have enough food to eat or clothes to wear

[23] for life consists of far more than food and clothes

[24] Look at the ravens — they don't plant or harvest or have barns to store away their food, and yet they get along all right, for God feeds them. And you are far more valuable to him than any birds!

[25] And besides, what's the use of worrying? What good does it do? Will it add a single day to your life? Of course not!

[26] And if worry can't even do such little things as that, what's the use of worrying over bigger things?

[27] Look at the lilies! They don't toil and spin, and yet Solomon in all his glory was not robed as well as they are.

[28] And if God provides clothing for the flowers that are here today and gone tomorrow, don't you suppose that he will provide clothing for you, you doubters?

[29] and don't worry about food - what to eat and drink; don't worry at all that God will provide it for you.

[30] All mankind scratches for its daily bread, but your heavenly Father knows your needs.

[31] He will always give you all you need from day to day if you will make the Kingdom of God your primary concern.

[32] So don't be afraid, little flock. For it gives your Father great happiness to give you the Kingdom.

³³ Sell what you have and give to those in need. This will fatten your purses in heaven! And the purses of heaven have no rips or holes in them. Your treasures there will never disappear; no thief can steal them; no moth can destroy them.

³⁴ Wherever your treasure is, there your heart and thoughts will also be.

Luke Chapter 13 - verse 1:

¹ About this time, he was informed that Pilate had butchered some Jews from Galilee as they were sacrificing at the Temple in Jerusalem.

² Do you think they were worse sinners than other men from Galilee?"

³ Not at all! And don't you realize that you also will perish unless you leave your evil ways and turn to God?

⁴ "And what about the eighteen men who died when the Tower of Siloam fell on them? Were they the worst sinners in Jerusalem?

⁵ Not at all! And you, too, will perish unless you repent!

⁶ Then he used this illustration. "A man planted a fig tree in his garden and came again and again to see if he could find any fruit on it, but he was always disappointed.

⁷ Finally he told his gardener to cut it down, I've waited three years and there hasn't been a single fig!" he said. "Why bother with it any longer! It's taking up space we can use for something else."

⁸ "Give it one more chance," the gardener answered. "Leave it another year, and I'll give it special attention and plenty of fertilizer.

⁹ If we get figs next year, fine; if not, I'll cut it down."

Approved by Rev. Paul Caporali (5/4/98)

1998 May 02, 1st Saturday
At the 10th Station
The Greensides' Farm, Marmora, Ontario, Canada

Jesus said: "Praise be to Jesus, for Jesus is Lord, Saviour, Redeemer.

"My precious children, thank you for coming to my holy ground. I have opened the way for many places like this holy land of Marmora that my children may see the mercy of my love, the love of my Holy Mother, who pleads for mercy for her children, and is the true example of surrender. She comes to her children in obedience to the Father Almighty, surrendering to the Holy Will of the Father Almighty, and the Holy Will of the Blessed Trinity. Are you willing, my children, to surrender totally to the Holy Will of the Father, Son, and Holy Spirit?

"This holy land of Marmora will have in my time, the chapel of prayer, love, sacrifice, and my mercy. You must remember, my children, when obstacles are put in place there is a reason; for nothing is done without authority of the Father Almighty, and done according to the Holy Will of the Father.

"Remember, my children, as you come to visit my holy places of mercy and love, open your hearts to seek my Holy Will, and in seeking my Holy Will, you learn surrender. But not only come to me in these holy places of apparitions, but come to me in the greatest miracle of time, my presence in the Holy Sacrament of the Eucharist where I await you body, blood, soul and divinity.

"You seek answers, miracles, in these holy places of apparitions; but first, seek your answers through me in the most Holy Sacrament of the Eucharist, Eucharistic Adoration, where I await you, my children.

"Yes, as I have stated, special graces are given as you come to visit these holy places, such as Marmora, where I shower my love upon you, my children. But it is up to each of you to use these graces given to come to me in the Holy Sacrifice of the Mass, the holy Sacrament of the Eucharist, Eucharistic Adoration.

"I love you, my children; I await you, my children; come to me, my children.

"Yes, my beloved little one, this will be one of many safe havens where my children will be protected. But my children need not worry of the future. They need not worry of the past. They are to be with me now. Surrender now to the Father Almighty.

"I love you, my children. Shalom, my people.

"Thank you, my beloved little one, for remaining obedient to my call."

THE GOSPEL ACCORDING TO LUKE
LUKE 12: Dependence on Providence

22 He said to his disciples: "That is why I warn you, do not be concerned for your life, what you are to eat, or for your body, what you are to wear.

23 Life is more important than food and the body more than clothing.

24 Consider the ravens: they do not sow, they do not reap, they have neither cellar nor barn — yet God feeds them. How much more important you are than the birds!

25 Which of you by worrying can add a moment to his life-span?

26 If the smallest things are beyond your power, why be anxious about the rest?

27 Or take the lilies: they do not spin, they do not weave; but I tell you, Solomon in all his splendour was not arrayed like any one of them.

28 If God clothes in such splendour the grass of the field, which grows today and is thrown in the fire tomorrow, how much more will be provided for you, O weak in faith!

29 It is not for you to be in search of what you are to eat or drink. Stop worrying.

30 The unbelievers of this world are always running after these things. Your Father knows that you need such things.

31 Seek out instead his kingship over you, and the rest will follow in turn.

32 Do not live in fear, little flock. It has pleased your Father to give you the kingdom.

³³ Sell what you have and give alms. Get purses for yourselves that do not wear out, a never-failing treasure with the Lord which no thief comes near nor any moth destroys.

³⁴ Wherever your treasure lies, there your heart will be.

LUKE 13: Providential Calls to Penance

¹ At that time, some were present who told him about the Galileans whose blood Pilate had mixed with their sacrifices.

² He said in reply, "Do you think that these Galileans were the greatest sinners in Galilee just because they suffered this?

³ By no means! But I tell you, you will all come to the same end unless you reform.

⁴ Or take those eighteen who were killed by a falling tower in Siloam. Do you think they were more guilty than anyone else who lived in Jerusalem?

⁵ Certainly not! But I tell you, you will all come to the same end unless you reform.

⁶ Jesus spoke this parable: "A man had a fig tree growing in his vineyard, and he came out looking for fruit on it but did not find any.

⁷ He said to the vinedresser, 'Look here! For three years now I have come in search of fruit on this fig tree and found none. Cut it down. Why should it clutter up the ground?'

⁸ In answer, the man said, 'Sir, leave it another year, while I hoe around it and manure it;

⁹ then perhaps it will bear fruit. If not, it shall be cut down.'"

Approved by Rev. Paul Caporali, 1998 May 04

1998 May 06, Wednesday
EUCHARISTIC ADORATION

Jesus said: "Praise be to Jesus, for Jesus is Lord, Redeemer, and Reconciler.

"Open your heart, my precious daughter, for my teaching. In this time, man has left all morals and reasoning, where brother is against brother, sister against sister, children against parents, where all human dignity and respect have betrayed the Holy Will of the Father, to make themselves gods in their own eyes. Where the pleading of my Holy Mother to all her children turns a deaf ear. What is left but for the Father Almighty to destroy this bondage of evil?

"The Father Almighty has allowed the pleadings of my Holy Mother to her children, through His all-goodness and mercy, as the teachings have also been allowed to my children. Yes, my beloved one, children are now beginning to listen, but are they willing a complete surrender of their will to the Holy Will of their Triune God?

"I have given my teachings that they may see and understand my love and my mercy. But they do not want to hear the decisiveness of change they must make to the errs of their existence. So, instead, they close a deaf ear and continue on in the worldly existence that Satan has decreed though worldly pleasures, which deaden the soul and the mind to the existence of the Father Almighty. They remain in the abyss of evil in this world. But for my children who open their hearts to the Blessed Trinity, who are willing to close their hearts and minds to their worldly ways and to try, my child, it just takes a child to *desire* to change and surrender to the Holy Will of the Blessed Trinity — I open the gates of my mercy upon them.

"I open the gates to my holy lands chosen as a refuge for my children; and they will see signs, signs of my mercy, and signs of my justice.

"As I now gather my children, I prepare my children, for I am a merciful God; I am a loving God. I am he who comes in the Almighty Name of the Father, Son and Holy Spirit.

"Return to me, my children. Soon the time for mercy will be the time of my justice!

"Will it be too late for you, my beloved ones? Too late because you were not willing to open your hearts to my mercy and instead will reap my justice?

"You have a free will. Choose, my beloved children. Where will your souls spend eternity?

"Open, my beloved one, to Revelation, Chapter 9."

THE BOOK OF REVELATION
REVELATION 9: The Fifth Trumpet

⁴ **The locusts were commanded to do no harm to the grass in the land or to any plant or tree but only to those men who had not the seal of God on their foreheads.**
⁵ **The locusts were not allowed to kill them but only to torture them for five months; the pain they inflicted was like that of a scorpion's sting.**
⁶ **During that time these men will seek death but will not find it; they will yearn to die but death will escape them.**

Jesus said: "Oh, my children, *you* make this choice. Open your hearts to me. Surrender to me. I love you, my people.

REVELATION 19:

²⁰ **The beast was captured along with the false prophet who performed in its presence the prodigies that led men astray, making them accept the mark of the beast and worship its image. Both were hurled down alive into the fiery pool of burning sulphur.**
²¹ **The rest were slain by the sword which came out of the mouth of the One who rode the horse, and all the birds gorged themselves on the flesh of the slain.**

So, I tell you, my children, for those of you who open your hearts to me, who relinquish the ways of the world and surrender completely to me, you shall have the fill of my mercy and the holy lands I have prepared for you.

"Do not turn from me, my children, but come to me, where I await you alive, body, blood, soul and divinity, in the Holy Sacrament of the Eucharist, for I am your Jesus of mercy.

"Shalom, my people. Thank you, my beloved little one, for remaining obedient to my call."

Approved by Rev. Richard Hoynes, 1998 May 06

1998 May 11, Monday
EUCHARISTIC ADORATION

Jesus said: "Praise be to Jesus, for Jesus is Lord, Saviour, Messiah.

"Thank you, my beloved one, for opening your heart for my teaching. It is up to each of my children to open their hearts to me, for their spiritual growth. Their walk with me is accomplished through me, with me, and for me. That is a part of surrendering. It is learning *how* to surrender.

"My children cannot, or are not willing to comprehend the boundless graces I am willing to give them to accomplish a total surrender.

"My child *[a woman in the presentation audience]* said it best, as she contemplated my mercy, when she felt my presence within her and she felt the gentle and loving touch of my hand upon her shoulder at my presentation last evening. She said it was not as she had thought in looking to follow my way, and it was not in spectacular things, nor difficult tasks. But she learned what I was asking for was very simple: just loving me, visiting me in Eucharistic Adoration; opening your heart to me in the Holy Sacrifice of the Mass and the Holy Sacrament of the Eucharist.

"It is nothing difficult I ask of my children, but they seem to think as my daughter did, that there was so much more that I was asking for.

"Oh, my children, why can you not see? Open your eyes to me. Open your hearts to me. I am a loving God, and a merciful God. I want nothing but the best for you; but it is up to each one of you to decide how much are you willing to give me of your time, of your love.

"Open, my beloved little one, to Matthew 9."

THE GOSPEL ACCORDING TO MATTHEW
MATTHEW 9: The Mission of the Twelve

[35] **Jesus continued his tour of all the towns and villages. He taught in their synagogues, he proclaimed the good news of God's reign, and he cured every sickness and disease.**

³⁶ At the sight of the crowds, his heart was moved with pity. They were lying prostrate from exhaustion, like sheep without a shepherd.

³⁷ He said to his disciples: "The harvest is good but labourers are scarce.

³⁸ Beg the harvest master to send out labourers to gather his harvest."

Jesus said: "Oh, my precious children, do you not see for yourselves the chaos this world is in? Yes, the evil one continues to deceive you through the materialistic enticements of this world; but I come to remove your blinders, to lead you back to my flock as the shepherd who cares for his sheep. I bring you these, my teachings, to all who will listen. I send you, my beloved little one, to bring these teachings. I come to you as you open your hearts to me, to listen to my word to receive my abundance of mercy and love, as your Jesus of mercy.

"Yes, my children, as I showed my presence to my child who opened her heart to me, who invited me to her home to listen to my word, I opened her eyes to the mercy of my love.

"I invite you, my children, to open your hearts to me. I listen to each of you as you call out to me. I never refuse your invitation to come into your hearts. Why do you refuse my invitation to come into my Heart?

"I love you, my children. Shalom, my people. Thank you, my beloved little one, for remaining obedient to my call."

Approved by Rev. Richard Hoynes

1998 May 15, Friday
EUCHARISTIC ADORATION

Jesus said: "Praise be to Jesus, for Jesus is Lord, Messiah, and King.

"My precious daughter, peace be unto you, my little one. Thank you for opening your heart for my teaching. I am your Jesus of mercy, and as I have told you before many times, I come to prepare my children through my love and through my mercy. As a shepherd who gathers his flock before the storm, I come to gather my children that they will not perish into the flames of Gehenna.

"What do I ask of my children? A change of their hearts, my daughter, that they focus on me, not on the materialistic values this world sets before them to draw them away from me, from truth which will show them the dissention and chaos that is destroying mankind. The deceiver unleashes his henchmen through worldly desires, while I bring truth and love, and the grace to change from the pernicious enticements of the world. I bring you peace my children; the peace this world cannot give you, and I only ask in return your love, a surrender of your will to the Holy Will of the Father, Son and Holy Spirit.

"Yes, my children, soon the time asked of my Holy Mother, to come to teach my children, to renew the breath of the Holy Spirit, through prayer, reconciliation, sacrifice; all that she has come to plead for with her children; her time to teach my children, will be over; for the Father, in His almighty love, gave his only begotten Son, to die on the cross for all children, that all may be set free to have eternal life, as he sent my Holy Mother to teach and prepare all children, that they may turn from their evil and perditious ways, in order that mankind would return to the Triune God.

"Did you listen, my children? Are you listening, my children?

"Now, in his almighty love God the Father sends his Son to you once again, to show you his merciful love, as he sends the Holy Spirit to renew the souls of all who are willing to receive this outpouring of gifts. For this is the onset of a new pentecost; it is now at the brink of dawn as I ready my children for the return of my second coming. Yes, the world must be cleansed and purified before this great manifestation of the love of the Father Almighty.

"So, I ask you once again my children, are you prepared through a total surrender to the Holy Will of the Father; and if not, then open your hearts to me, that you may receive the graces to fulfil the Holy Will of the Triune God. Prepare yourselves through a willingness to conversion through prayer, sacrifice, and the Holy Sacraments, so that you may receive this outpouring of the gifts of the Holy Spirit. For the new pentecost is upon you and the time for salvation is at hand.

"You, my children, will always have the love and prayers of my Holy Mother. You were granted the graces to know and see the greatest saint ever. In her love and her peace she manifested a total surrender to the Holy Will of the Father. Use her example that you may come to know the realization of her desire for each one of you her children. As the Almighty Father wills it, so it will be done, as she is given the title, "Mediatrix of All Graces," for she has fulfilled the Holy Will of the Father, Son and Holy Spirit. Deceive yourselves no longer that what has been spoken of in my holy word is coming to pass.

"Open, my beloved one, to Revelation 12."

THE BOOK OF REVELATION
REVELATION 12: The Woman and the Dragon

1 **A great sign appeared in the sky, a woman clothed with the sun, with the moon under her feet, and on her head a crown of twelve stars.**

2 **Because she was with child, she wailed aloud in pain as she laboured to give birth.**

3 **Then another sign appeared in the sky: it was a huge dragon, flaming red, with seven heads and ten horns; on his heads were seven diadems.**

4 **His tail swept a third of the stars from the sky and hurled them down to earth. Then the dragon stood before the woman about to give birth, ready to devour her child when it should be born.**

5 **She gave birth to a son, a boy, destined to shepherd all the nations with an iron rod. Her child was caught up to God and to his throne.**

6 **The woman herself fled into the desert where a special place had been prepared for her by God; there she was taken care of for twelve hundred and sixty days.**

Jesus said: "I tell you, my children, as scripture has been written, so it shall be, and you, my children, must open your hearts to me. Open your hearts to the Holy Spirit, that you will be prepared, for I am your Jesus of mercy. I am the Way, the Light and the Truth. With me you shall not fear.

"Shalom, my people. I love you, my beloved little one. Thank you for remaining obedient to my call."

Approved by Rev. James L. Swensen, 1998 May 15

1998 May 19, Tuesday
EUCHARISTIC ADORATION

Jesus said: "Praise be to Jesus, for Jesus is Lord, Saviour, and Redeemer.

"I am your Jesus of mercy, my children, and I come that you may have life eternal. I come to you alive; body, blood, soul and divinity, my children. How you do not realize the very depth of my love for each one of you. But then if you remain blinded to my truths through the errors of your ways, you will never see nor know truth. You will never know love as only I can give love, nor will you know true peace as only I can give; the peace this world cannot give.

"Oh, my wayward children, as lambs lost in a storm, bewildered and overcome by the enticements of this world, you follow each other not knowing where you are going; one lost lamb leading another, and you don't see the cliff ahead of you; but I as your shepherd go ahead of you, to lead you back to my fold. But how many of you are willing to go over that cliff?

"Oh, my children, do not continue in this barren desert of worldly enticements, materialistic values set before you to lead you astray, continuously looking for self gratification, and falling deeper into the clutches of the evil one, the conspirator of death for all eternity.

"Are you willing to descend into the pit of Gehenna for what is timeless, just for moments of pleasures of this world? For you must remember, time on earth are but moments in eternity. Do not justify your moments of pleasures for an eternity of death to your souls.

"I have come to prepare you, my children, through the love and mercy of your Triune God. But you have a free will, and that will never be taken away from you. It will be your own final decision as to the life or death of your soul.

"Open, my daughter, to Job 4."

THE BOOK OF JOB
JOB 4: Eliphaz's First Speech

[15] **Then a spirit passed before me, and the hair of my flesh stood up.**

^{16}It paused, but its likeness I could not discern; a figure was before my eyes, and I heard a still voice:

^{17} "Can a man be righteous as against God? Can a mortal be blameless against his maker?

^{18} Lo he puts not trust in his servants, and with his angels he can find fault.

^{19} How much more with those that dwell in houses of clay, whose foundation is in the dust, who are crushed more easily than the moth!

^{20} Morning or evening they may be shattered; with no heed paid to it, they perish forever.

^{21} The pegs of their tent are plucked up; they die without knowing Wisdom."

Job 5:

^{6} For mischief comes not out of the earth, nor does trouble spring out of the ground;

^{7} But man himself begets mischief, as sparks fly upward.

Jesus said: "Oh, my children, do not deceive yourselves into thinking your soul's immortality is only a fabrication, that a soul neither lives nor dies. That which you feel as conscience is the life of the soul showing right or wrong. You will know you are either in eternal glory with me or in the eternal fires of Gehenna; and once your earthly life is over, you will have made the choice for eternal life or eternal death.

"My children, your worst nightmare is not one tenth of what the eternal fires of Gehenna will be!"

(Patsy: at this point I had the most horrific fear which weakened me physically, I had to stop taking the teaching. Jesus later told me I was allowed to feel not even for a moment what is suffered in hell. I was unable to go on with the teaching.)

Approved by Rev. Richard Hoynes, 1998 May 19

1998 May 27, Wednesday
EUCHARISTIC ADORATION

Jesus said: "Praise be to Jesus, for Jesus is Lord, Saviour, and Messiah.

"My beloved daughter, thank you for opening your heart for my teaching. It is my mercy, my gentle one, that I bring to my people. My mercy and salvation, for I, your Jesus of mercy, am love, the pure undefiled love, which only 'I' can give you, and which will fill your empty hearts. But to my saddened heart, many will never feel this love nor desire this love, for they only see their love of self, which is a non-existent, fruitless love. This type of love, self gratification, will dwindle away to an emptiness which will never be filled, which will ultimately destroy the life of the soul.

"Open, my beloved one, to 2 Corinthians, Chapter 6, verse 11."

THE SECOND EPISTLE OF PAUL TO THE CORINTHIANS
2 CORINTHIANS 6: The Temple of the Living God

[11] Men of Corinth, we have spoken to you frankly, opening our hearts wide to you.
[12] There is no lack of room for you in us; the narrowness is in you.
[13] In fair exchange, then (I speak as a father to his children), open wide your hearts!
[14] Do not yoke yourselves in a mismatch with unbelievers. After all, what do righteousness and lawlessness have in common or what fellowship can light have with darkness?
[15] What accord is there between Christ and Belial, what common lot between believer and unbeliever?
[16] Tell me what agreement there is between the temple of God and idols.

Jesus said: "Oh, my precious children, these idols you have created within yourselves when you choose love of self over the love of God, the materialistic enticements of this world, instead of the Holy Gifts of the Holy Spirit!

"The idols of man, money and power, are the enticements which prevent my children from realizing the importance of one's soul. They distract one from seeking God and truth.

"Again, my children, 'and what union can there be between God's temple and idols'? For you are God's temple, the home of the living God, and God has said of you, 'I will live in them and walk among them, and I will be their God, and they shall be my people.'

"My precious children, my teachings are given to you so that you may return to me through the sacraments, reconciliation, opening to my word and reading my word. And as this is my word, as you invite my teachings, my presentation, I have told you, my children, my presence you have invited, and graces shall be given, for you are allowing yourselves to be used as my vessels to reach others.

"Open your hearts to me, my children, and you shall receive the graces necessary to remove the blinders from your eyes. As in my word, 'I will live in them, and walk among them.'

"My daughter, as you have seen the graces given to the children who attended my presentation, I will continue to pour forth my graces at all the presentations where I am invited. I will pour forth my mercy and my graces to all my children who open their hearts to me, to my Holy Will.

"Now is the time of my mercy! Receive now, my children, for I am your Jesus of mercy. Receive before it is *your* time for my justice.

"Open, my beloved one, to Corinthians 2 Chapter 6, verse 17."

2 CORINTHIANS 6 *cont'd:*

¹⁷ Therefore, **"Come out from among them and separate yourselves from them," says the Lord; "and touch nothing unclean. I will welcome you**
¹⁸ **and be a father to you and you will be my sons and daughters," says the Lord Almighty.**

2 CORINTHIANS 7:

¹ **Since we have these promises, beloved, let us purify ourselves from every defilement of flesh and spirit, and in the fear of God strive to fulfil our consecration perfectly."**

Shalom, my people. Thank you, my little one, for remaining obedient to my call."

Approved by Rev. Paul Caporali, 1998 May 27

1998 June 02, Tuesday
EUCHARISTIC ADORATION

Jesus said: "Praise be to Jesus for Jesus is Lord, Saviour, and Redeemer.

"Thank you, my little one, for opening your heart for my teaching. Come to the font of my mercy now, my children, for you do not want to see the utter chaos this world is in. Countries deceiving each other, thinking that by showing strength through nuclear technology they are rebuking the other's theory of ultimate power. Oh, my children, this chaos and confusion if not stopped through prayer and sacrifice, will ultimately destroy much of your world.

"I have told you, my children, through prayer and sacrifice, even wars can be mitigated. Oh, my children, will you not listen. Open your hearts to me. I, your Jesus of mercy, surround you with my love, my strength. You, my children, have not accepted my gifts. Your churches remain empty and only a few churches offer the availability of twenty-four hour Eucharistic Adoration. Seek my children, to fill the empty-time spaces, so that the churches will continue with twenty-four hour Eucharistic Adoration.

"Many of you are not even aware of where your churches are that offer my presence in Eucharistic Adoration. Why do you not know this, my children? When is the last time you gathered your family together and prayed as a family? And you wonder why there is so much conflict and despair in this world.

"You criticize my shepherds instead of praying for my shepherds. You are unhappy with change in the church, but most of you only enter the church as an obligation, or when it suits your needs. When is the last time you entered my house out of love and desire?

"My children, obedience to my Holy Magisterium of the Church has become discarded and confusing because you want to decree yourselves as to how the church must be. My beloved John Paul II is still the Pope, and as head of my church he needs your prayers and your obedience.

"I have told you, my people, pray! Pray for discernment. Pray for unity. Instead, you criticize and find fault with my shepherds. Oh, my children, you, yourselves have brought upon you this chaos and confusion."

"Open, my daughter, to 1 John 5."

THE FIRST EPISTLE OF JOHN
1 JOHN 5:

1 **Everyone who believes that Jesus is the Christ has been begotten of God. Now, everyone who loves the father loves the child he has begotten.**

2 **We can be sure that we love God's children when we love God and do what he has commanded.**

3 **The love of God consists in this: that we keep his commandments — and his commandments are not burdensome.**

4 **Everyone begotten of God conquers the world, and the power that has conquered the world is this faith of ours.**

Jesus said: "And as you remain obedient to my beloved John Paul II, you remain obedient to me. But my church needs much prayer as this world needs much prayer, and only you, my children, can do this. Do you pray? Have you prayed? Why do you not listen, my children? It is for your souls out of love I come to you. Alive; body, blood, soul and divinity; the Sacrament of the Holy Eucharist; and many times I have repeated this is the greatest miracle, but do you partake of me in this Holy Sacrament? This is where your strength is: in me; with me; for me; and through me. But unless you come to me and partake of me in this Holy Sacrament, you will not have the strength, my strength, to withstand the chaos, tribulation and confusion that is in this world.

"Open now, my daughter, to Luke 12."

THE GOSPEL ACCORDING TO LUKE
LUKE 12: Signs of the Times

54 **He said to the crowds: "When you see a cloud rising in the west, you say immediately that rain is coming — and so it does.**

⁵⁵ When the wind blows from the south, you say it is going to be hot — and so it is.

⁵⁶ You hypocrites! If you can interpret the portents of earth and sky, why can you not interpret the present time?

⁵⁷ Tell me, why do you not judge for yourselves what is just?

"I love you, my people. Shalom, my children. Thank you for remaining obedient to my call, my little one."

Approved by Rev. Richard Hoynes, 1998 June 02

1998 June 05, Friday
EUCHARISTIC ADORATION

Jesus said: "My beloved one, thank you for opening your heart to me. Praise be to Jesus, for Jesus is Lord, King, merciful. Yes, my beloved one, I am all merciful, all loving, and when the trials come, the attacks come, I am with you. I am your strength, my children, for you cannot see what is beyond you; nor do you see what is around you. You must put the armour of protection on you daily my children.

"Open, my beloved one, to Ephesians 6."

THE EPISTLE OF PAUL TO THE EPHESIANS
EPHESIANS 6: Christian Warfare

¹⁰ **Finally, draw your strength from the Lord and his mighty power.**

¹¹ **Put on the armour of God so that you may be able to stand firm against the tactics of the devil.**

¹² **Our battle is not against human forces but against the principalities and powers, the rulers of this world of darkness, the evil spirits in regions above.**

¹³ **You must put on the armour of God if you are to resist on the evil day; do all that your duty requires, and hold your ground.**

¹⁴ **Stand fast, with the truth as the belt around your waist, justice as your breastplate,**

¹⁵ **and zeal to propagate the gospel of peace as your footgear.**

16 In all circumstances hold faith up before you as your shield; it will help you extinguish the fiery darts of the evil one.
17 Take the helmet of salvation and the sword of the spirit, the word of God.

Jesus said: "My precious children, the word of God is your strength; and as I am word, I am your strength; and as I am the word, so shall it be what has been prophesied.

"Are you ready? Are you prepared? For you must call on me, my children. You must return to me, my children, or you will not be able to withstand what is ahead of you.

"Just over the horizon the beast prepares for his entrance and you do not see the horrendous attacks he prepares for my children. But I am your strength, and you only need to come to me. Open your hearts to me.

"Read Ephesians 6, verses 10 through 17, daily, my children, for I am preparing you. But it is up to you whether you are willing to surrender to me completely.

"Remember the preparation in Noah's time, Lot's time, and when Lots' wife was disobedient, she was not willing to surrender. Do not be like Lots' wife or your suffering shall be greater. This is not what I want for you, my children, but you have a free will and you must make the choice. I come as the light in this darkness that surrounds your world.

"In these present times you see disaster upon disaster, yet you refrain from opening your hearts to my truths and to what has been prophesied, because it is easier to close your eyes to what is around you with the materialistic enticements swaying you to ignore the signs. But will these materialistic enticements save you when disaster strikes you? No, my children, the evil one's henchmen are ready to strike and your souls will not be prepared, and the deceiver will take with him as many souls unwilling to see and change the error of their ways.

"Pray, my children, pray. I am your Jesus of mercy. Shalom, my people."

(NOTE: Jesus' voice was very stern, and I was given to feel overwhelming sadness over this teaching; and then Mama Mary spoke and the sadness once more was overwhelming — she came as Our Lady of Sorrows.)

Our Blessed Mother said, "My daughter, open your heart to me. I come to you as your Sorrowful Mother, my child, for these are sorrowful times, and as my beloved Son has spoken. I beg you my children, to listen.

"Will you not listen, my children? Pray, my children pray! Pray for the many souls of my children being lost to the prey of the evil one; my children who have become entangled in the web spun by the evil one's worldly enticements, drawing young and old alike away from my Son who is truth and love. I as your Sorrowful Mother see the many lost souls that are unwilling to release themselves from the bondage of evil they have become entangled in, and my Son, all loving and all merciful, coming to plead for all to return to him; for you have the free will given to you to make this choice.

"Open your hearts to my Son, my children. He died for each one of you that you may have life eternal. Please, I beg of you and for you, my children. Return to prayer; return to the sacraments; return to your Triune God, that He may have mercy on you, my children. I love each of you, my children. I surround you with the mantle of my protection."

Jesus said: "Open, my beloved little one, to Isaiah 4:"

THE BOOK OF ISAIAH
ISAIAH 4: The Messianic Branch

¹ **Seven women will take hold of one man on that day, saying: "We will eat our own food and wear our own clothing; only let your name be given us, put an end to our disgrace!"**

² **On that day, the branch of the Lord will be lustre and glory, and the fruit of the earth will be honour and splendour for the survivors of Israel.**

³ **He who remains in Zion and he that is left in Jerusalem will be called holy; every one marked down for life in Jerusalem.**

⁴ **When the Lord washes away the filth of the daughters of Zion, and purges Jerusalem's blood from her midst with the blast of searing judgment,**

⁵ **Then will the Lord create, over the whole site of Mount Zion and over her place of assembly, a smoking cloud by day and a light of flaming fire by night.**

⁶ **For over all, his glory will be shelter and protection: shade from the parching heat of day, refuge and cover from storm and rain."**

Approved by Rev. Paul Caporali, 1998 June 05

1998 June 09, Tuesday
EUCHARISTIC ADORATION

Jesus said: "My precious child, praise be to Jesus, for Jesus is Lord, Saviour, Reconciler. I, your Jesus of mercy, come to heal your broken hearts, your broken spirit; for you, my children, do not understand the need for prayer, reconciliation, and sacrifice; and because you do not take the time to pray, you have stifled the spiritual life of your soul. Prayer is your substance for the soul. Without prayer the senses of the soul become deadened and the spiritual life is slowly dwindled away. It is imperative, my children, that you renew your prayer life in me, with me and through me. For you have been told by many of my vessels that only through prayer can you mitigate the justice of your Triune God. But more importantly, it is prayer that will help you to surrender to the Holy Will of the Father, Son and Holy Spirit.

"Soon the words of my Holy Mother will no longer be heard, for her time to visit my children and to prepare my children will be over. Everything she has been asked to do for our children on this earth by the Father has been accomplished. She has called our children to preparation for her Eternal Spouse, the Holy Spirit. She has asked for prayer, sacrifice, a return to the Holy Sacraments; and has asked you, my children, to surrender to me. Have you done what she has asked? Are you ready, my children?

"Open, my beloved, to John 3."

THE GOSPEL ACCORDING TO JOHN
JOHN 3: Nicodemus

¹**A certain Pharisee named Nicodemus, a member of the Jewish Sanhedrin,**

² came to him at night. "Rabbi," he said, "we know you are a teacher from God, for no man can perform signs and wonders such as you perform unless God is with him."

³ Jesus gave him this answer: "I solemnly assure you, no one can see the reign of God unless he is begotten from above."

⁴ "How can a man be born again once he is old?" retorted Nicodemus. Can he return to his mother's womb and be born over again?"

⁵ Jesus replied, "I solemnly assure you, no one can enter into God's kingdom without being begotten of water and Spirit.

⁶ Flesh begets flesh, spirit begets spirit.

⁷ Do not be surprised that I tell you you must all be begotten from above.

⁸ The wind blows where it will. You hear the sound it makes but you do not know where it comes from, or where it goes. So it is with everyone begotten of the spirit."

⁹ "How can such a thing happen?" asked Nicodemus.

¹⁰ Jesus responded: "You hold the office of teacher of Israel and still you do not understand these matters?

¹¹ I solemnly assure you, we are talking about what we know, we are testifying to what we have seen, but you do not accept our testimony.

¹² If you do not believe when I tell you about earthly things, how are you to believe when I tell you about those of heaven?"

Jesus said: "My children, my Holy Mother who has come from heaven to you because she, as the Holy Queen and Mother of all, teaches and pleads with you that you change your ways through prayer and sacrifice, and that you may return to me and have life eternal.

"As a mother, she wanted only the best for each of you. Why did you not listen? Why will you not listen? Surrender is living to the Holy Will of the Father; living in the Holy Will of your Triune God; living as a child of the Triune God, and not as children of darkness.

"How can you remain in the light when you are willing to continue in the darkness of the worldly enticements of Lucifer?

How can you surrender to the Holy Will of your Triune God when you surrender to the ways of the world, and how can you become born again in the Spirit, if your soul remains deadened with the error of sin? The Holy Spirit cannot reign in your heart when you have sin as your master.

"My Holy Mother's time on earth was your gift in order to prepare yourselves for the reign of the Holy Spirit within your hearts and souls; to ready yourselves for this period of time spoken of by the prophets. But as I told my beloved Nicodemus, 'we speak of what we know and we testify to what we have seen, but you people do not accept our testimony.'

"Shalom, my people. I love you, my little one, thank you for responding to our call."

Approved by Rev. Paul Caporali, 1998 June 10

1998 June 11, Thursday
EUCHARISTIC ADORATION

Jesus said: "Jesus said: "Praise be to Jesus for Jesus is Lord, Saviour, Redeemer, Reconciler!

I, your Jesus of mercy, come that I may abide in your hearts, in the holy temple of the Holy Spirit, where I come to you alive through the Holy Sacrament of the Eucharist. Are your temples ready for me, unstained from the error of sin, so that I may abide in you and you in me? This is where your strength will be: in me, with me, for me, and through me. But only if you refrain from the error of sin am I able to reside within this temple.

"Oh, my children, I want to surround you with my love, and in my love, but are you willing to surrender? For surrender is what I ask, in order that you may remain with me, in the light, in eternal glory.

"My children, these days have the chaos and confusion spoken of in my word, where you see the horrendous crimes being committed against each other; and it will only get worse. The 'peace' spoken of through the media is a false peace, recognized only by those who walk in my grace, for I open your eyes to truth, that you may continue to seek my mercy.

"Continue to seek my wisdom through prayer, the Holy Sacraments, and sacrifice.

"Open, my beloved to Wisdom, Chapter 2, verse 1."

THE BOOK OF WISDOM
WISDOM 2: The Wicked Reject Immortality and Justice Alike

¹ **They who said among themselves, thinking not aright, "Brief and troublous is our lifetime: neither is there any remedy for man's dying nor is anyone known to have come back from the nether world."**

Wisdom 2 cont'd:

¹⁸ **"For if the just one be the son of God, he will defend him and deliver him from the hand of his foes.**
¹⁹ **With revilement and torture let us put him to the test that we may have proof of his gentleness and try his patience.**
²⁰ **Let us condemn him to a shameful death, for according to his own word, God will take care of him."**
²¹ **These were their thoughts, but they erred; for their wickedness blinded them,**
²² **and they knew not the hidden counsels of God; neither did they count on recompense of holiness nor discern the innocent souls' reward.**
²³ **For God formed man to be imperishable; the image of his own nature he made him.**
²⁴ **But by the envy of the devil, death entered the world, and they who are in his possession experience it.**

Jesus said: "You, my children, who have opened your hearts to me, who are doing as I have asked, must continue to seek me in all. Continue in your walk with me that you may be examples to others.
"Pray for all my children, for what is to befall your world is what man has created through his continuous error in sin."

WISDOM 6: Exhortation to Seek Wisdom

⁴ **Because, though you were ministers of his kingdom, you judged not rightly and did not keep the law, nor walked according to the will of God.**

⁵ Terribly and swiftly shall he come against you, because judgment is stern for the exalted

⁶ For the lowly may be pardoned out of mercy but the mighty shall be mightily put to the test.

⁷ For the Lord of all shows no partiality, nor does he fear greatness, because he himself made the great as well as the small, and he provides for all alike;

⁸ But for those in power a rigorous scrutiny impends.

⁹ To you, therefore, O princes, are my words addressed, that you may learn wisdom and that you may not sin.

¹⁰ For those who keep the holy precepts hallowed shall be found holy, and those learned in them will have ready a response.

¹¹ Desire therefore my words; long for them and you shall be instructed.

Jesus said: "My precious children, have I not kept my word? Am I not giving you my teachings that you may understand; that you may see the words spoken of in my word *are* truth, and that I *am* truth.

"I love you, my children. Shalom, my people.

"Thank you, my beloved little one, for remaining obedient to my call."

Approved by Rev. Paul Caporali, 1998 June 11

1998 June 16, Tuesday
EUCHARISTIC ADORATION

Jesus said: ""Praise be to Jesus, for Jesus is Lord, Redeemer, Saviour, Messiah!

"My precious daughter, I, your Jesus of mercy, come to you, my children, to invite you to the font of all mercy and grace, my most wounded Sacred Heart. I ask you, my children, to now open your hearts to my mercy, for as spoken to many of my vessels, this period of history is coming to a consequential climax. But you must first know and realize in your hearts that I am not a God of doom. I am your Jesus of mercy. I am pure love, and I am justice.

"Your time, you must remember, is not mine, you must understand. Do not allow pride and stubbornness to cloud your decisions, your actions. What I ask of you, my children, is to center your hearts, your minds, on the truths and love which I, your Triune God, have always given you.

"Yes, it is imperative that you prepare yourselves for future events of catastrophic consequences, but it must all be done with me, through me and for me, in order that you may receive the graces necessary to be your strength.

"Prayer, my children, will clear the path to receive my peace. Sacrifice will open the gates of my mercy, and the Holy Sacraments your armour and protection during all trials and afflictions.

"Man will never superimpose what your Triune God has decreed. And all is done according to the holy will of your Triune God, not according to the desires of man.

"Again, my children, I come to plead with you for a return to my Holy Sacraments, prayer and sacrifice. Come to me in holy adoration of the Blessed Sacrament, for all your answers to the questions you have are there. Today's answer today, tomorrow's answer tomorrow. I am your Jesus of mercy.

"My child, open to Daniel Chapter 9, verse 27, and all of Ch 10 through Ch 12. Read it, pray over it, and open your hearts to the Holy Spirit, and your discernment will be given."

THE BOOK OF DANIEL
DANIEL 9: Gabriel and the Seventy Weeks

²⁷ This king will make a seven-year treaty with the people, but after half that time, he will break his pledge and stop the Jews from all their sacrifices and their offerings; then, as a climax to all his terrible deeds, the enemy shall utterly defile the sanctuary of God, but in God's time and plan, his judgment will be poured out upon this evil one.

Daniel 10: Vision of the Hellenistic Wars

¹ In the third year of Cyrus, king of Persia, a revelation was given to Daniel, who had been named Belteshazzar. The revelation was certain: a great war; he understood it from the vision.

² In those days, I, Daniel, mourned three full weeks.

³ I ate no savory food, I took no meat or wine, and I did not anoint myself at all until the end of the three weeks.

⁴ On the twenty-fourth day of the first month I was on the bank of the great river, the Tigris.

⁵ As I looked up, I saw a man dressed in linen with a belt of fine gold around his waist.

⁶ His body was like chrysolite *[or topaz, a yellowish precious stone - JMc]*, his face shone like lightning, his eyes were like fiery torches, his arms and feet looked like burnished bronze, and his voice sounded like the roar of a multitude.

⁷ I alone, Daniel, saw the vision; but great fear seized the men who were with me; they fled and hid themselves, although they did not see the vision.

⁸ So I was left alone, seeing this great vision. No strength remained in me; I turned the colour of death and was powerless.

⁹ When I heard the sound of his voice, I fell face forward in a faint.

¹⁰ But then a hand touched me, raising me to my hands and knees.

¹¹ "Daniel beloved," he said to me, "understand the words which I am speaking to you; stand up, for my mission now is to you." When he said this to me, I stood up trembling.

¹² "Fear not, Daniel," he continued; "from the first day you made up your mind to acquire understanding and humble yourself before God, your prayer was heard. Because of it, I started out,

¹³ but the prince of the kingdom of Persia stood in my way for twenty-one days, until finally Michael, one of the chief princes, came to help me. I left him there with the prince of the kings of Persia,

¹⁴ and came to make you understand what shall happen to your people in the days to come; for there is yet a vision concerning those days."

¹⁵ While he was speaking thus to me, I fell forward and kept silent.

[16] Then something like a man's hand touched my lips; I opened my mouth and said to the one facing me, "My lord, I was seized with pangs at the vision and I was powerless.

[17] How can my lord's servant speak with you, my lord? For now no strength nor even breath is left in me."

[18] The one who looked like a man touched me again and strengthened me, saying,

[19] "Fear not, beloved, you are safe; take courage and be strong."

[20] When he spoke to me, I grew strong and said, "Speak, my lord, for you have strengthened me." "Do you know," he asked, "why I have come to you? Soon I must fight the prince of Persia again. When I leave, the prince of Greece will come;

[21] but I shall tell you what is written in the truthful book. No one supports me against all these except Michael, your prince,

Daniel 11:

[1] standing as a reinforcement and a bulwark for me.

[2] Now I shall tell you the truth. "Three kings of Persia are yet to come; and a fourth shall acquire the greatest riches of all. Strengthened by his riches, he shall rouse all the kingdom of Greece.

[3] But a powerful king shall appear and rule with great might, doing as he pleases.

[4] No sooner shall he appear and his kingdom shall be broken and divided in the four directions under heaven; but not among his descendants or in keeping with his mighty rule, for his kingdom shall be torn to pieces and belong to others than they.

[5] The king of the south shall grow strong, but one of his princes shall grow stronger still and govern a domain greater than his.

[6] After some years they shall become allies: the daughter of the king of the south shall come to the king of the north in the interest of peace. But her bid for power shall fail: and

her line shall not be recognized, and she shall be given up, together with those who brought her, her son and her husband. But later

7 a descendant of her line shall succeed to his rank, and shall come against the rampart and enter the stronghold of the king of the north, and conquer them.

8 Even their gods with their molten images and their precious vessels of silver and gold, he shall carry away as booty into Egypt. For years he shall have nothing to do with the king of the north.

9 Then the latter shall invade the land of the king of the south, and return to his own country.

10 But his sons shall prepare and assemble a great armed host, which shall advance like a flood, then withdraw. When it returns and surges around the stronghold,

11 the king of the south, provoked, shall go out to fight against the king of the north, whose great host shall make a stand but shall be given into his hand

12 and be carried off. In the pride of his heart, he shall lay low tens of thousands, but he shall not triumph.

13 For the king of the north shall raise another army, greater than before; after some years he shall attack with this large army and great resources.

14 In those times many shall resist the king of the south, and outlaws of your people shall rise up in fulfilment of vision, but they shall fail.

15 When the king of the north comes, he shall set up siegeworks and take the fortified city by storm. The power of the south shall not withstand him, and not even his picked troops shall have the strength to resist.

16 He shall attack him and do as he pleases, with no one to withstand him. He shall stop in the glorious land, dealing destruction.

17 He shall set himself to penetrate the entire strength of his kingdom. He shall conclude an agreement with him and give him a daughter in marriage in order to destroy the kingdom, but this shall not succeed in his favour.

¹⁸ He shall take to the coastland and take many, but a leader shall put an end to his shameful conduct, so that he cannot renew it against him.

¹⁹ He shall turn to the strongholds of his own land, but shall stumble and fall, to be found no more.

²⁰ In his stead one shall arise who sent a tax collector through the glorious kingdom, but he shall soon be destroyed, though not in conflict or in battle.

²¹ There shall rise in his place a despicable person, to whom the royal insignia shall not be given. By stealth and fraud he shall seize the kingdom.

²² Armed might shall be completely overwhelmed by him and crushed, and even the prince of the covenant.

²³ After allying with him, he shall treacherously arise to power with a small party.

²⁴ By stealth he shall enter prosperous provinces and do that which his father nor grandfathers never did; he shall distribute spoil, booty, and riches among them and devise plots against their strongholds; but only for a time.

²⁵ He shall call out his strength and cleverness to meet the king of the south with a great army; the king of the south shall prepare for battle with a very large and strong army, but he shall not succeed because of the plots devised against him.

²⁶ Even his table companions shall seek to destroy him, his army shall be overwhelmed, and many shall fall slain.

²⁷ The two kings, resolved on evil, shall sit at table together and exchange lies, but they shall have no success, because the appointed end is not yet.

²⁸ He shall turn back towards his land with great riches, his mind set against the holy covenant; he shall arrange matters and return to his land.

²⁹ At the time appointed he shall come again to the south, but this time it shall not be as before.

³⁰ When ships of the Kittim *[the Romans - JMc]* confront him, he shall loose heart and retreat. Then he shall direct his rage and energy against the holy covenant; those who forsake it he shall once more single out.

³¹ Armed forces shall move at his command and defile the sanctuary stronghold, abolishing the daily sacrifice and setting up the horrible abomination.

³² By his deceit he shall make some who were disloyal to the covenant apostatize; but those who remain loyal to their God shall take strong action.

³³ The nation's wise men shall instruct the many; though for a time they will become victims of the sword, of flames, exile, and plunder.

³⁴ When they fall, few people shall help them, but many shall join them out of treachery.

³⁵ Of the wise men, some shall fall, so that the rest may be tested, refined, and purified, until the end time which is still appointed to come.

³⁶ The king shall do as he pleases, exalting himself and making himself greater than any god; he shall utter dreadful blasphemies against the God of gods. He shall prosper only until divine wrath is ready, for what is determined must take place.

³⁷ He shall leave no regard for the gods of his ancestors or for the one in whom women delight; for no god shall he have regard, because he shall make himself greater than all.

³⁸ Instead, he shall give glory to the god of strongholds; a god unknown to his fathers he shall glorify with gold, silver, precious stones, and other treasures.

³⁹ To defend the strongholds he shall station a people of a foreign god. Whoever acknowledges him he shall provide with abundant honour; he shall make them rule over the many and distribute the land as a reward.

⁴⁰ At the appointed time the king of the south shall come to grips with him, but the king of the north shall overwhelm him with chariots and horsemen and a great fleet, passing through the countries like a flood.

⁴¹ He shall enter the glorious land and many shall fall, except Edom, Moab, and the chief part of Ammon, which shall escape from his power.

⁴² He shall extend his power over the countries, and not even the land of Egypt shall escape.

⁴³ He shall control the riches of gold and silver and all the treasures of Egypt; Libya and Ethiopia shall be in his train.

⁴⁴ When news from the east and the north terrifies him, he shall set out with great fury to slay and to doom many.

⁴⁵ He shall pitch the tents of his royal pavilion between the sea and the glorious holy mountain, but he shall come to his end with none to help him.

Daniel 12:

¹ At that time there shall arise Michael, the great prince, guardian of your people; it shall be a time unsurpassed in distress since nations began until that time. At that time your people shall escape, everyone who is found written in the book.

² Many of those who sleep in the dust of the earth shall awake; some shall live forever, others shall be an everlasting horror and disgrace.

³ But the wise shall shine brightly like the splendour of the firmament, and those who lead the many to justice shall be like the stars forever.

⁴ As for you, Daniel, keep secret the message and seal the book until the end of time; many shall fall away and evil shall increase."

⁵ I, Daniel, looked and saw two others, one standing on either bank of the river.

⁶ One of them said to the man clothed in linen, who was upstream, "How long shall it be to the end of these appalling things?"

⁷ The man clothed in linen, who was upstream, lifted his right and left hands to heaven; and I heard him swear by him who lives forever that it should be for a year, two years, a half year; and that, when the power of the destroyer of holy people was brought to an end, all these things should end.

⁸ I heard, but I did not understand; so I asked, "My Lord, what follows this?"

⁹ "Go Daniel," he said, "because the words are to be kept secret and sealed until the end of time.

 ¹⁰ Many shall be refined, purified, and tested, but the wicked shall prove wicked; none of them shall have understanding, but the wise shall have it.
 ¹¹ From the time that the daily sacrifice is abolished and the horrible abomination is set up, there shall be one thousand two hundred and ninety days.
 ¹² Blessed is the man who has patience and perseveres until the one thousand three hundred and thirty five days.
 ¹³ Go, take your rest, you shall rise for your reward at the end of days."

Approved by Rev. James L. Swensen, 1998 June 16

1998 June 17, Wednesday
EUCHARISTIC ADORATION

Jesus said: "My precious little one, praise be to Jesus, for Jesus is Lord, Saviour, Redeemer, Reconciler.

"Oh my precious children, open your hearts to me. Open your hearts to my mercy. It is very difficult for my children who do not desire to know me, to know their Triune God as a loving, merciful God, for they have closed their hearts and minds to truth and the realization that there is a God, and that someday there will be a judgement. They question if heaven or hell exists. They have come to believe this world is the beginning and end for their souls. How sadly mistaken they are. Oh my children, unless you pray for these lost souls, they will be lost forever in the pits of Gehenna. Your prayers, my children, given to me in love for these lost souls, will open the gates of my mercy upon them.

"Realize, my children, that many of these souls can be in your family; someone you know and are not aware of the utter desolation these souls are in. I have given you my teaching, explaining how easy it becomes to lose the spiritual strength of your soul; how the soul can be deadened spiritually without the grace given through prayer. Imagine the soul that never prays, or has even an inkling of what prayer is. But in my mercy, I take the prayers offered to me in love for all my children, and as your Jesus of mercy, I allow the graces needed for these children with the slightest desire to know truth, and release this grace to them. This is why my Holy Mother pleads. I plead for more prayer and more sacrifice, for your prayers may save a lost soul from the fires of Gehenna.

"Open, my beloved one, to Sirach 14."

THE BOOK OF SIRACH
SIRACH 14: The Use of Wealth

1 Happy is the man whose mouth brings him no grief, who is not stung by remorse for sin.
2 Happy is the man whose conscience does not reproach him, who has not lost hope.
3 Wealth ill becomes the mean man; and to the miser, of what use is gold?
4 What he denies himself, he collects for others, and in his possessions a stranger will revel.
5 To whom will he be generous who is stingy with himself and does not enjoy what is his own?
6 None is more stingy than he who is stingy with himself; he punishes his own miserliness.
7 If ever he is generous, it is by mistake; and in the end he displays his greed.
8 In the miser's opinion his share is too small;
9 he refuses his neighbour and brings ruin upon himself.
10 The miser's eye is rapacious for bread, but on his own table he sets it stale.
11 My son, use freely whatever you have and enjoy it as best you can;
12 remember that death does not tarry, nor have you been told the grave's appointed time.

"My children, I your Jesus of mercy beg you to release totally to me your iniquities; rather, surrender completely to me that you may have life eternal. Surround yourself in my light that you may shine forth in this world of darkness, and that through your light you may be that ember of light for a soul lost in the darkness.

"I love you, my beloved little one.

"Shalom, my people.

"Thank you for remaining obedient to my call."
Approved by Rev. James L. Swensen, 1998 June 17

1998 June 18, Thursday
EUCHARISTIC ADORATION

Jesus said: "Praise to the Triune God, the Almighty Father, Son and Holy Spirit, for Jesus is Lord, Redeemer, Reconciler of all nations.

"My beloved children, open your hearts to my teaching in order that you may prepare yourselves for the events unfolding which will lead now to the beginning of my prophesies foretold.

"You, my children, do not see ahead the corruption your government has decreed through this one world order: the decay of unity — not the beginning. You are unprepared, my children, through your own unwillingness to return to truth, to your Triune God, who is the only Supreme Being, Creator; not man.

"You my children still have the chance to secure the means of victory in complete surrender to the Holy Will of the Father, Son and Holy Spirit. Victory over death eternal of your souls, my children. Come to the font of my mercy, your salvation. For I *am* your Jesus of mercy. I died that you may have life eternal. As you see now the events unfold before your very eyes. You will know you have come to the crossroads of truth and deceit. Which road you take, my children, is entirely up to you. For it is your free will given to you from the Almighty. This is what the deceitful one, the father of all lies, is trying to take from you. Do not be deceived any longer. For eternal damnation of one's soul is timeless. Understand my words, my children. Pray, pray, pray!

"My precious one, open to Daniel, Ch. 11."

THE BOOK OF DANIEL
DANIEL 11:

[11] **The king of the south, provoked, shall go out to fight against the king of the north, whose great host shall make a stand but shall be given into his hand**

[12] **and be carried off. In the pride of his heart, he shall lay low tens of thousands, but he shall not triumph.**"

Jesus said: "My precious children, I your Jesus of mercy await you in the Holy Sacrament of the Eucharist. I am your strength. I am the font of mercy.

"I love you, my children. Shalom, my people. Thank you, my beloved little one, for remaining obedient to my call."

Approved by Rev. James L. Swenson, 1998 June 18

1998 June 19, Friday
EUCHARISTIC ADORATION

Jesus said: "Thank you for opening your heart to my call, my beloved little one. Praise be to Jesus, for Jesus is Lord, Messiah, King.

"Oh my children, on this day, I desire to be King of your hearts, through my most wounded Sacred Heart, scourged by the sin from the erroneous deceptions my children are plagued with. They are unwilling to remove the blinders from sin which keep my childrens' hearts and minds closed to my light, my love. My children, you cannot remain in this darkness from the error of sin and not expect to lose your soul to the deceiver of lies who is leading you to the pits of Gehenna."

"Today, my children, as you read my word, if you open your hearts to me, through the Holy Sacrament of Reconciliation, through Sacrifice, through the Holy Sacraments, you will be given the grace to seek me and to renew in me, with me and through me a total commitment in surrendering yourselves to your Triune God; and I only ask you to open your hearts to me. That you may see I am all loving, all merciful, for I am your Jesus of mercy, and my love knows no bounds.

"Make my most wounded Sacred Heart your shelter and protection from all the evil corruption which plagues this earth, and you will know true peace and true love as you have never known it."

"Open, my beloved little one, to 1 John, ch. 4."

THE FIRST EPISTLE OF JOHN
1 JOHN 4: Testing the Spirits

¹ Beloved, do not trust every spirit, but put the spirits to a test to see if they belong to God, because many false prophets have appeared in the world.

² This is how you can recognize God's spirit: every spirit that acknowledges Jesus Christ come in the flesh belongs to God,

³ while every spirit that fails to acknowledge him does not belong to God. Such is the spirit of the antichrist which, as you have heard, is to come; in fact, it is in the world already.

Jesus said: "Do you, my children, not see the rays coming from my most wounded Sacred Heart in the Jesus of mercy images? Once you open your heart to me, I fill you with these rays, quenching all who thirst for me. How, you ask? By receiving me alive; body, blood, soul and divinity.

"By the everlasting waters flowing from the font of my mercy shall you be filled.

"Open, my beloved one, to Luke, Ch. 6."

THE GOSPEL ACCORDING TO LUKE
LUKE 6:

⁴⁵ A good man produces goodness from the good in his heart; an evil man produces evil out of his store of evil. Each man speaks from his heart's abundance.

⁴⁶ Why do you call me "Lord, Lord," and do not put into practice what I teach you?

⁴⁷ Any man who desires to come to me will hear my words and put them into practice. I will show you with whom he is to be compared.

⁴⁸ He may be likened to the man who, in building a house, dug deeply and laid the foundation on a rock. When the floods came the torrent rushed in on that house, but failed to shake it because of its solid foundation.

⁴⁹ On the other hand, anyone who has heard my words but not put them into practice is like the man who built his house on

the ground without any foundation. When the torrent rushed upon it, it immediately fell in and was completely destroyed."

Jesus said: "Shalom, my people. Thank you, my beloved little one, for remaining obedient to my call."

Approved by Rev. James L. Swenson

1998 June 21, Sunday
MESSAGE FROM OUR LADY OF SORROWS

Our Loving Mother said: "My beloved daughter, praise be to Jesus, my holy crucified Son. For He is Lord, Saviour, Messiah, Redeemer.

"I come to you, my beloved little one, as requested by my Holy Son, to give this teaching, for soon my words shall no longer be heard on earth, for very soon my time of teaching will be over. But through my Son's most holy and most wounded Sacred Heart, I, your Mother of Sorrows, will intercede for all my children.

"You do not realize, my children, that this perdition of erroneous sacrileges, which is being committed against your Triune God, is at such a horrific and epidemic level throughout this, your world, that without divine intervention, men would have destroyed the world.

"I have pleaded with all of you, my children, for more prayer; more sacrifice; and for a return to your Triune God. For those of you who have listened, you are under my mantle of protection. For those who continue in this abyss, I plead for mercy for your souls.

"Oh, my precious children, listen to what my Holy Son has promised during this hour of his mercy, for he is all-loving and all-merciful.

"In remembrance of our holy feast days, that of my Son's most holy and most wounded sacred heart, and my Immaculate Heart, I ask you to unite yourselves in remembrance of the two hearts, consecrating yourselves with your families; and that through this consecration which I ask of you, to take most seriously dedicating yourselves daily to refrain from the error of sin; that by doing this daily you will return to a more prayerful and holy example of daily living, examples which will draw others to do the same in order to cleanse this corruption of error and sin, before it must be done through divine intervention.

"Oh, my precious children, open your hearts to my holy and crucified Son; that his mercy and love may fill your hearts; that you may be examples of this love and mercy for each other; examples which will lead others to return to your Triune God.

"Open, my daughter, to Jeremiah, Chapter 24, verse 2."

THE BOOK OF JEREMIAH
JEREMIAH 24: The Two Baskets of Figs

² **One basket contained excellent figs, the early-ripening kind. But the other basket contained very bad figs, so bad they could not be eaten.**

³ **Then the Lord said to me: "What do you see, Jeremiah?" "Figs," I replied; "the good ones are very good, but the bad ones very bad, so bad they cannot be eaten."**

⁴ **Thereupon this word of the Lord came to me:**

⁵ **Thus says the Lord, the God of Israel: "Like these good figs, even so will I regard with favour Judah's exiles whom I sent away from this place into the land of the Chaldeans.**

⁶ **I will look after them for their good, and bring them back to this land, to build them up, not to tear them down; to plant them, not to pluck them out.**

⁷ **I will give them a heart with which to understand that I am the Lord. They shall be my people and I will be their God, for they shall return to me with their whole heart.**

⁸ **And like the figs that are bad, so bad they cannot be eaten — yes, thus says the Lord — even so will I treat Zedekiah, king of Judah, and his princes, the remnant of Jerusalem remaining in this land and those who have settled in the land of Egypt.**

⁹ **I will make them an object of horror to all the kingdoms of the earth, a reproach and a byword, a taunt and a curse, in all the places to which I will drive them.**

¹⁰ **I will send upon them the sword, famine, and pestilence, until they have disappeared from the land which I gave them and their fathers."**

Our Loving Mother said: "How I pray for you, my children, with a motherly heart broken and wounded for each of you. Oh, that only you would listen and return to your Triune God, that he may have mercy upon each of you, my children.

"I bless each of you, my children, in the Almighty Name of the Father, in the Almighty Kingship of the Son, and in the glory and outpouring of grace from the Holy Spirit.

"I love you, my children.

"Thank you, my beloved little one, for remaining obedient to our call."

1998 July 02, Thursday
EUCHARISTIC ADORATION

Jesus said: "Praise be to Jesus, for Jesus is Lord, Redeemer Supreme; and I, as your Jesus of mercy, draw you to my resplendent joy, peace and love.

"My children, have I not taught you that all is done through me, with me and for me? Yes, my children, I have allowed the evil one his pursuant reign of evil for a period of time. As with Job, he was and is only allowed a certain time to reign over his evil deeds. But you seem to forget that you have a free will. Your free will has never, nor will it *ever* be, taken away from you. So the choice you make for the surrender of your soul to Lucifer, the deceiver and father of all lies, or to your Triune God, the Father of truth and the Supreme Being, will be yours entirely, my children.

"Open, my beloved little one, to Job Ch 1."

THE BOOK OF JOB
JOB 1: Job's Wealth and Piety

6 **One day, when the sons of God came to present themselves before the Lord, Satan also came among them.**

7 **And the Lord said to Satan, "Whence do you come?" Then Satan answered the Lord and said, "From roaming the earth and patrolling it."**

8 **And the Lord said to Satan, "Have you noticed my servant Job, and that there is none on earth like him, blameless and upright, fearing God and avoiding evil?"**

⁹ But Satan answered the Lord and said, "Is it for nothing that Job is God-fearing?

¹⁰ Have you not surrounded him and his family and all that he has with your protection? You have blessed the work of his hands, and his livestock are spread over the land.

¹¹ But now put forth your hand and touch anything that he has, and surely he will blaspheme you to your face."

¹² And the Lord said to Satan, "Behold, all that he has is in your power; only do not lay a hand upon his person." So Satan went forth from the presence of the Lord.

Jesus said: "My beloved children, look to the right of you; look to the left of you; what do you see? Chaos and corruption. In front and behind you, evil and destruction. If you fear it, it is because you do not trust in me and do not know me. For if you had done what I have spoken to you of, surrounding yourselves in my love and my protection, as Job, you would know all is done through me; and if done through me, it is done with me and for me. You would be sure of my strength and my protection.

"Yes, my children, the messages you hear have dire consequences; but you must always remember to surround yourself in my presence in order to receive my peace, my love. I do not ask much of you, for I love you unconditionally. I *am* your Jesus of mercy. I ask for prayer and resignation to my Holy Will; to the Holy Sacraments; to sacrifice. Know me and you will know love and peace within your hearts. Know me, and you shall not fear, as my beloved Job knew me.

"You seek the signs; and I have asked you: how will you know my sign if you do not know me? How can you know me if you do not seek me? You ask, my beloved children, what was the sign? Was the sign given? For all those present were touched by me with a special grace of my love and my mercy; and they can testify, as all who have been present and opened their hearts to me at my presentations can testify, to my presence of love within.

"Seek me, my children; I am never far from any one of you. Call out to me, my children; I will answer.

"Open, my beloved one, to Hebrews, Ch. 3."

THE EPISTLE TO THE HEBREWS
HEBREWS 3: Israel's Infidelity, a Warning

⁷ **Therefore, as the Holy Spirit says: "Oh, that today you would hear his voice,**

⁸ **harden not your hearts as at the revolt in the day of testing in the desert,**

⁹ **when your fathers tested and tried me, and saw my works**

¹⁰ **for forty years. Because of this I was angered with that generation and I said, "They have always been of erring heart, and have never known my ways.**

¹¹ **Thus I swore in my anger, "They shall never enter into my rest."**

¹² **Take care, brothers, that none of you may have an evil and unfaithful heart, so as to forsake the living God.**

¹³ **Encourage one another daily while it is still 'today,' so that no one grows hardened by the deceit of sin."**

Jesus said: "My beloved children, I come to you today asking you to open your hearts to my request. I have asked my daughter to open a house of prayer, to bring my little shrine of the Holy Family to this house of prayer. Direction has been given. My children chosen to oversee this my holy project of the house of prayer. I have chosen the site next to my holy ground of St. Bridget's. My house of prayer is to be built next to my holy chapel of twenty-four-hour Eucharistic Adoration at St. Bridget's in Las Vegas.

"To all of you, my children, I have given; now I ask you to open your hearts to this request of building my holy house of prayer. This will be a place of refuge for many after the time of my warning. Open your hearts to me, my children. I bless you each in the Almighty Name of the Father, Kingship of His Crucified Son, and the Redemption of the Holy Spirit.

"I love you, my people. Shalom, my children. Thank you, my children, for remaining obedient to my call.

"Open, my beloved little one, to Hebrews, Ch. 2."

THE EPISTLE TO THE HEBREWS
HEBREWS 2: Exhortation to Faithfulness

¹ **Therefore we must attend all the more to what we have heard, so that we may not be carried away.**
² **For if the Word announced through angels proved firm, and every transgression and disobedience received is just recompense,**
³ **how shall we escape if we ignore so great a salvation? Announced originally through the Lord, it was confirmed for us by those who had heard him.**
⁴ **God added his testimony by signs, wonders, various acts of power, and distribution of the gifts of the Holy Spirit according to his will.**

Approved by Rev. Richard Hoynes, 1998 July 02

1998 July 04, Saturday
MESSAGE FROM OUR LOVING MOTHER

Our Loving Mother said: "My beloved daughter, praise be to Jesus, for Jesus is Lord, Saviour, Holy Redeemer. Praise to the Holy Paraclete, and praise to the Father Almighty.

"Oh my precious children, how my heart breaks for my children. They unite today to celebrate freedom, but they celebrate a false peace, a total fabrication of security. When instead all should bend their knees and plead for the mercy of the Almighty Father, Son and Holy Spirit.

"My precious children, you see the fires burning out of control, the weather causing complete damage in many areas, wars in many parts of the world, and you, my children, continue to bury your heads in the sand celebrating a false freedom. How my heart breaks, my children, for you continue in this abyss refusing to turn from evil, all the while falling deeper and deeper into the clutches of the evil one.

"Oh my precious children, why do you continue to persecute and scourge my Holy Crucified Son with the error of your sinful ways? Has not my son shown you his love and mercy as he hung crucified for each one of you? Why do our pleas continue to fill empty hearts, as you continue in this destruction of humanity? When will you open your eyes and hearts to the realization that you have now gone beyond a self-decaying morality of inhumane and animalistic behaviour?

"Yes, my children, I shed tears of blood for you as a sign of the corruption and evil times you are in. I shed tears of blood for the great loss of souls to the evil one, which you have forgotten, and many are of your own. You celebrate this false security you are blinded with as you see flames covering much of your land. Do not celebrate, my precious children, but fall to your knees in supplication, for you have not seen nor realized the purgation ahead! There are no words left; only my tears of anguish for all those who will not return to your Triune God. May he have mercy on you, my children."

Jesus said: "Open, my beloved little one, to Revelation Ch 14."

THE BOOK OF REVELATION
REVELATION 14: The Harvest of the Earth

¹⁴ Then, as I watched, a white cloud appeared, and on the cloud sat one who looked like a Son of Man, wearing a gold crown on his head and holding a sharp sickle in his hand.

¹⁵ Another angel came out of the temple crying out in a loud voice to the one sitting on a cloud, "Use your sickle and reap the harvest, for the time to reap has come, because the earth's harvest is fully ripe."

¹⁶ So the one who was sitting on the cloud swung his sickle over the earth, and the earth harvested.

¹⁷ Then another angel came out of the temple in heaven who also had a sharp sickle.

¹⁸ Then another angel came from the altar who was in charge of the fire, and cried out in a loud voice to the ones who had the sharp sickle, "Use your sharp sickle and cut the grapes from the earth's vines, for the clusters are ripe."

¹⁹ So the angel swung his sickle over the earth and cut the earth's vintage. He threw it into the great wine press of God's fury.

[20] The wine press was trodden outside the city and blood poured out of the wine press to the height of the horses' bridle for two hundred miles.

Our Loving Mother said: "Thank you, my beloved little one, for remaining obedient to our call."

Approved by Rev. James J. Swenson, 1998 July 06

1998 July 05, Sunday
EUCHARISTIC ADORATION

Jesus said: "My precious child, praise be to Jesus for Jesus is Lord, Redeemer, Reconciler. I am your Jesus of mercy, my beloved children. I have come to prepare you through the mercy and love of your Almighty Triune God. But have you listened? How many times have you said this is the same message repeated over and over. You think that my messengers and my vessels repeat themselves, but it is because you have not listened! It is because you have not opened your heart to me that you question.

"As my Mother continues to plead with you, sheds her tears for you, because of the many loss of souls to the eternal fires of Gehenna, you continue to avoid truth. You continue to remain with a closed heart, and my messengers continue to bring the same messages. But if even one child opens his heart to me, returns to me, all of heaven rejoices. As my Holy Mother has spoken, there are no words left, only her tears of anguish, pleading for her children; our children; that a surrender of your will to your Triune God will open the doors of my mercy upon you. Upon your children. Upon your families.

"Do not look for dates or times. Instead, pray, my children!

"Do not waste your time looking for signs, for the greatest sign is among you and you don't even see me or know me in the Sacrament of the Holy Eucharist. I have told you, I have pleaded with you. Come to me in the Holy Sacrament of the Eucharist. Come to me in Eucharistic Adoration. Here is where your answers are. Here is where the greatest of all miracles is. And you do not ever open your hearts to the realization of this. You continue to look in other directions, you continue to wander in this barren desert of deceit and lies which plague this world with materialistic blindness.

"Open, my beloved one, to Sirach Chapter 15."

THE BOOK OF SIRACH
SIRACH 15: Man's Free Will

[11] **Say not: "It was God's doing that I fell away;" for what he hates most he does not do.**

[12] **Say not: "It was he who set me astray;" for he has no need of wicked man.**

[13] **Abominable wickedness the Lord hates, he does not let it befall those who fear him.**

[14] **When God, in the beginning, created man he made him subject to his own free choice.**

[15] **If you choose you can keep the commandments; it is loyalty to do his will.**

[16] **There are set before you fire and water; to whichever you choose, stretch forth your hand.**

[17] **Before man are life and death, whichever he chooses shall be given him.**

Jesus said: "My children, my messengers speak of the chastisements you have brought upon yourselves; they bring you the teachings of my warning, but you do not look to change your ways. Instead, you occupy your minds with dates. Soon or sooner? What does it matter if you have overlooked the purpose of my message, my teaching?

"Prayer, sacrifice, sacraments, the Holy Eucharist. Open your hearts to me. Surrender yourselves completely and totally to me. For I *am* the answer.

"If you overlook the road in the forest to find the opening above the trees, you lose your way out of the forest.

"I love you, my children. Shalom, my people.

"Thank you, my beloved little one, for remaining obedient to my call."

Approved by Rev. James J. Swenson, 1998 July 06

1998 July 09, Thursday
EUCHARISTIC ADORATION

Jesus said: "Praise be to Jesus, for Jesus is Lord, King, Saviour, and Messiah.

"My beloved little one, I come to you once again as your Jesus of mercy, for I have but one desire, my beloved one, for all my children to live eternally with me, their Triune God. It is precisely why my holy Mother and I come to so many of our children, that through the opening their hearts to our messages, to our teachings, many will receive and open their hearts to me, their Triune God, surrendering completely to me; changing their ways, that they may have life everlasting.

"My beloved one, surrendering of one's will is a gift to their Triune God. But it is also a gift to that child surrendering, relinquishing his way of life to have life eternal: the most important gift he shall ever receive. It is not hard my beloved one; it only seems hard, because they feel that once they surrender to me, they will have to change their life style. But what has this life style given them that I cannot replace with my eternal love, my eternal joy, and my eternal peace? Nothing in my paradise is momentary but is for all eternity.

"Open, my beloved one to Psalm 23."

THE BOOK OF PSALMS
PSALM 23: The Lord, Shepherd and Host

1. Because the Lord is my shepherd, I have everything I need.
2. He lets me rest in the meadow grass and leads me besides the quiet streams.
3. He restores my failing health. He helps me do what honours him the most.
4. Even when walking through the dark valley of death I will not be afraid, for you are close beside me, guarding, guiding all the way.
5. You provide delicious food for me in the presence of my enemies. You have welcomed me as your guest, blessings overflow.

⁶ **Your goodness and unfailing kindness shall be with me all of my life, and afterwards I will live with you forever in your home.**

Jesus said: "My children, rescind your ways, that you may reign in eternal bliss with me. Do you not see what you have on this earth does not satisfy you but for moments? You will never be satisfied and as you go deeper and deeper into the error of the abyss, you will not be able to see clearly truth, honour and justice. Nor will you have the ability to seek my truth, my love, or my peace, for you will descend deeper and deeper into the clutches of the evil one.

"Open to Psalm 49, my beloved one."

PSALM 49: The Vanity of Worldly Riches

¹ **Listen everyone! High and low, rich and poor, all around the world.**
² **Listen to my words,**
³ **for they are wise and filled with insight.**
⁴ **I will tell in song accompanied by harps the answer to one of life's most perplexing problems:**
⁵ **There is no need to fear when times of trouble come, even though surrounded by enemies.**
⁶ **They trust in their wealth and boast about how rich they are,**
⁷ **yet not one of them, though rich as kings, can ransom his own brother from the penalty of sin. For God's forgiveness does not come that way;**
⁸ **for a soul is far too precious to be ransomed by mere earthly wealth. There is not enough of it in all the earth to buy eternal life for just one soul, to keep it out of hell.**

Jesus said: "My beloved children, if you do not open your hearts to me, your Triune God, and remain with the worldly ways, the materialistic bondage, you decree your soul to the everlasting fires of Gehenna. Then you will call out to me to save you, but it will be too late!

"Won't you listen now to your Triune God? Won't you come to me now before it is too late? I am a merciful and loving God. I wait for you, my children. It is not I that create havoc and confusion, and bring corruption and destruction to your world in order to take souls to the abyss, the fires of Gehenna."

Psalm 49 cont'd:

¹⁴ **This is the way of those who trust in folly, the end of those contented with their lot:**

¹⁵ **like sheep they are herded into the nether world; death is their shepherd, and the upright rule over them. Quickly their form is consumed; the nether world is their palace.**

¹⁶ **But God will redeem me from the power of the nether world by receiving me. Fear not when a man grows rich, when the wealth of his house becomes great,**

¹⁷ **for when he dies, he shall take none of it; his wealth shall not follow him down.**

¹⁸ **Though in his lifetime he counted himself blessed, "They will praise you for doing well for yourself,"**

¹⁹ **he shall join the circle of his forebears who shall never more see light.**

²⁰ **Man, for all his splendour, if he have not prudence, resembles the beasts that perish.**

Jesus said: "Again, I ask you my children, change your ways! Come to me. Come to the Holy Sacraments. Come to me in the Holy Sacrament of the Eucharist, Eucharistic Adoration, where I await you. Come to me in prayer and sacrifice.

"I love you my, children."

Approved by Rev. James J. Swenson, 1998 July 09

1998 July 11, Saturday
EUCHARISTIC ADORATION

Jesus said: "Praise be to Jesus, for Jesus is Lord, Saviour, Redeemer, Reconciler.

"My beloved, come to the font of my most merciful Sacred Heart, that I may fill you with the graces of my love, my peace, my joy. In this world plagued by such evil contempt and mistrust for each other, there is no remedy other than my mercy and my love, which I shall pour forth over each one of my children who comes to seek me to reign as king of their hearts.

"Do not wallow in this self-decaying, chaotic and destructive misconception the devil dwells in. He is the conspirator of lies and deceit, only wanting to destroy all of humanity, taking with him as many lost souls as he can to the eternal fires of Gehenna.

"No, my children, linger no longer in this evil destructive plan of Lucifer to destroy your souls, condemning your soul for all of eternity to the pits of hell. This is solely your decision, for you have a free will, and that free will no one has the power or decision over. Only you, yourselves, can willingly give up this free will. As I have told you many times, pleaded with you many times, the choice is completely yours.

"Come to me. Know me in the Holy Sacrament of the Eucharist, Eucharistic Adoration, where it is I, alive, waiting to soothe your broken hearts. I will mend them with the balm of my eternal love. I will soothe them with the grace of everlasting joy and peace! But you must open your hearts to me. That is all I ask of you. Open your hearts to me, through prayer, sacrifice, supplication, and the holy sacraments, and I will give you life eternal.

"Open, my beloved little one, to John, Chapter 12 verse 30."

THE GOSPEL ACCORDING TO JOHN
JOHN 12: The Coming of Jesus' Hour

30 **Jesus answered, "That voice did not come for my sake, but for yours.**
31 **Now has judgment come upon this world, now will this world's prince be driven out,**
32 **and I — once I am lifted up from the earth — will draw all men to myself."**
33 **(This statement indicated the sort of death he had to die.)**
34 **The crowd objected to his words: "We have heard it said in the law that the Messiah is to remain forever. How can you claim that the Son of Man must be lifted up? Just who is this 'Son of Man'?"**

³⁵ Jesus answered: "The light is among you only a little longer. Walk while you still have it or darkness will come over you. The man who walks in the dark does not know where he is going.

³⁶ While you have the light, keep faith in the light; thus you will become sons of light." After this utterance, Jesus left them and went into hiding.

Evaluation of the Ministry

³⁷ Despite his many signs performed in their presence, they refused to believe him.

³⁸ This was to fulfill the word of the prophet Isaiah: "Lord, who has believed what has reached our ears? To whom has the might of the Lord been revealed?

³⁹ The reason they could not believe was that, as Isaiah says elsewhere:

⁴⁰ he has blinded their eyes, and numbed their hearts, lest they see or comprehend, or have a change of heart — and I should heal them.

⁴¹ Isaiah uttered these words because he had seen Jesus' glory, and it was of him he spoke.

⁴² There were many, even among the Sanhedrin, who believed in him; but they refused to admit it because of the Pharisees, for fear they might be ejected from the synagogue.

⁴³ They preferred the praise of the men to the glory of God.

"Jesus said: "Shalom, my people."
Approved by Fr. James J. Swenson, 1998 July 11

1998 July 12, Sunday
EUCHARISTIC ADORATION

Jesus said: "My beloved daughter, praise be to Jesus, for Jesus is Lord, Saviour, Reconciler of all nations.

"I, your Jesus of mercy, have open the gates of my most wounded Sacred Heart. Yet you, my children, remain in the coldness and deceitfulness of your hearts. Such an easy choice, many of you say: I give you life eternal, while the evil one, master of lies and corruption, seeks only to destroy your souls and take your souls to the eternal fires of Gehenna for all eternity! If it is such an easy choice, then why do you continue in this evil conspiracy with the destroyer of souls? Then, it is not as easy a choice as you think! For before you are put materialistic mayhem, the gods you set before you: wealth, fame, pleasures of the mind and body, fulfilling your every whim and desire, these your gods; leading you deeper and deeper into the nether world, and causing eternal death to your soul; and taking with you none of this wealth, none of this fame and pleasures of this world. For when you die, it all stays behind.

"Why do you not listen, my children?

"For you, it is much easier to turn a deaf ear and live in total blindness, than to what you hear as truth and see what is all around you.

"My children, it is you in the final end who will suffer. Do you not see I bring these teachings for each of you? For the good of your soul?

"But it is your choice.

"Many of my children speak of safe havens, places of refuge, protection. Have I not prepared these places for you? But most important and most safest with all guarantees, is my most wounded Sacred Heart.

"And how do you receive this protection? Through the most holy Sacrament of the Eucharist. Eucharistic Adoration; prayer; sacrifice. I have told you many times, this is where all your answers are. But do you listen? Have you listened? Have you opened your heart to me? Have you done what I have asked?

"Many of you have heard this plea to your hearts. Have you done what I have asked? If Noah had not listened when he was asked to build the Ark, do you realize what would have happened? I ask you again my children, open your hearts for my direction. Build my house of prayer.

"Open, my daughter, to Ezekiel 20."

THE BOOK OF EZEKIEL
EZEKIEL 20: Israel's History of Infidelity

[39] As for you, house of Israel, thus says the Lord God: come, each one of you, destroy your Idols! Then listen to me, and never again profane my holy name with your gifts and your Idols.

[40] For on my holy mountain, on the mountain height of Israel, says the Lord God, there the whole house of Israel without exception shall worship me; there I will claim your tributes and the first fruits of your offerings and all that you dedicate.

[41] As a pleasing odour I will accept you, when I have brought you from among the nations and gathered you out of the countries over which you were scattered; and by means of you I will manifest my holiness in the sight of the nations.

[42] Thus you shall know that I am the Lord, when I bring you back to the land of Israel, the land which I swore to give your fathers.

[43] There you shall recall your conduct and all the deeds by which you defiled yourselves; and you shall loathe yourselves because of all the evil things you did.

[44] And you shall know that I am the Lord when I deal with you thus, for my name's sake, and not according to your evil conduct and corrupt actions, O house of Israel, says the Lord God.

Jesus said: "My children, come to me. I am your Jesus of mercy. I love you. I will protect you. Will you not listen?

"Shalom my people.

"Thank you, my beloved little one, for remaining obedient to my call."

Approved by Rev. James J. Swenson, 1998 July 15

1998 July 21, Tuesday
EUCHARISTIC ADORATION

Jesus said: "My beloved little one, praise be to Jesus, for Jesus is Lord, Saviour, Reconciler of all nations. Come, my precious children, into my temple of mercy and love, where there are no bounds to my mercy. You ask where, my children? The sanction of all grace, my most wounded Sacred Heart."

"You have seen the graces flow, the mercy of my love, as I have promised, at all my presentations. I tell you now as I have told you in the past, it only takes opening your heart to me. To my mercy. You have witnessed testimony upon testimony, as my children testify to the presence of my love, my mercy.

"I ask you my children, continue to open your heart to me, continue to seek me, in the Holy Sacrament of the Eucharist, Eucharistic Adoration, prayer and sacrifice and you will find me. You will know me. Open to my word and you shall be filled from the tree of knowledge. It is I who will quench your thirst in this barren desert, where the evil one preys upon my children seeking to destroy souls. But I am here. I am your salvation and protection, and you only need to open your hearts to me.

"Open, my daughter, to John, Ch. 10."

THE GOSPEL ACCORDING TO JOHN
JOHN 10: Feast of the Dedication

²² It was winter and the time came for the feast of the Dedication in Jerusalem.

²³ Jesus was walking in the temple area, in Solomon's Portico,

²⁴ When the Jews gathered around him and said, "How long are you going to keep us in suspense? If you really are the Messiah, tell us so in plain words."

²⁵ Jesus answered: "I did tell you, but you do not believe. The works I do in my Father's name give witness in my favour,

²⁶ but you refuse to believe because you are not my sheep.

²⁷ My sheep hear my voice. I know them, and they follow me.

²⁸ I give them eternal life, and they shall never perish. No one shall snatch them out of my hand.

²⁹ My Father is greater than all, in what he has given me, and there is no snatching out of his hand.

³⁰ The Father and I are one."

Jesus said: "My beloved children, as you opened your hearts to me, I filled them with my love, my peace, my joy, and yes, my sorrow. For you did not understand the sorrow you felt was for those of my children who will never know me, because they would not open their hearts to me. Now you can testify in my name, to what you felt so that others may know of me.

"I love you, my children. Shalom, my people.

"Thank you, my beloved little one, for remaining obedient to my call."

Approved by His Excellency Bishop Roman Danylak,
Toronto, Canada, 1998 July 21

1998 September 15, Tuesday
Feast of Our Lady of Sorrows
EUCHARISTIC ADORATION

Jesus said: "Praise be to Jesus, for Jesus is Lord, Redeemer and Reconciler, the Reconciler of all nations, my beloved one. Thank you for coming to spend this time with me.

"Yes, my beloved one, Reconciler of all peoples; but they, all my children, have a free will; this free will is never taken away.

"These times, my beloved one, my children have brought upon themselves. Through their own misguided misconception of 'freedom.' The freedom of choice. The freedom of right to life. The freedom of dignity of one's death. The freedom of speech. The freedom of the press. Man's own free will. And where my children, has this gotten you?

"Let's begin with the freedom of choice: the 'right' of life in a woman's choice to bear the child or to kill the innocent. 'Freedom' you call this satanic ritual. Sacrificing the unborn. One of Satan's tricks to take your soul.

"Another of Satan's ploys for your souls: the 'dignity' of death; killing one's self in the name of dignity. This is suicide. Nothing less than suicide!

"'Freedom of speech;' 'freedom of the press;' 'freedom of voice;' the manipulative structure of putting filth onto the air waves, into television and magazines; broadcasting venomous, sadistic pornography to the minds of your children.

"This 'freedom' you call out for is under total control of evil influence. This so-called 'freedom;' your free will has allowed this manipulation from the evil one; the evil one's manipulation through 'freedom,' self centerdness, power, and materialistic enticements.

"Where has all this freedom gotten you, my children?

"But, my beloved ones, your free will is never taken away. You still have a chance to redeem yourselves. You still have my love and my mercy. Prayer, sacrifice, the Holy Sacraments, and surrendering to the Holy Will of your Triune God, can bring you the safe haven of my love and my mercy.

"Pray not for change, but pray for all to remain in the Holy Will of the Father, Son and Holy Spirit. For I, as your Triune God, am a merciful God. A loving God. I died for each one of you. Have you forgotten this?

"My holy Mother watched her only Son placed on a cross, pierced not only by nails on my hands and my feet for each one of you, but also pierced by a lance in order that you each would have life eternal. This for each one of you, my children; my free will, given in total surrender to the holy will of the Father, God Almighty, in order that each of you would have life eternal. This, my free will, un-denied to the Father, given in total conformity to the Holy Will of the Father in love, my love for each of you.

"Now, my beloved one, open to Exodus, Chapter 3, verse 13."

THE BOOK OF EXODUS
EXODUS 3: The Call of Moses

[13] "But," said Moses to God, "when I go to the Israelites and say to them, 'The God of your fathers has sent me to you,' if they ask me, 'What is your name?' what am I to tell them?"

[14] God replied, "I am who am." The he added, "This is what you shall tell the Israelites: I Am sent me to you."

THE BOOK OF JEREMIAH
JEREMIAH 21: Oracles Regarding the Kings

[11] To the royal house of Judah:

[12] hear the word of the Lord, O house of David! Thus says the Lord: each morning dispense justice, rescue the oppressed

from the hand of the oppressor, lest my fury break out like fire which burns without being quenched, because of the evil of your deeds."

JEREMIAH 22:

⁷ Against you I will send destroyers, each with his axe: They shall cut down your choice cedars, and cast them into the fire.

⁸ Many people will pass by this city and ask one another, "Why has the Lord done this to so great a city?"

⁹ And the answer will be given: "Because they have deserted their covenant with the Lord, their God, by worshipping and serving strange gods."

JEREMIAH 31: The New Covenant

³⁰ But through his own fault only shall anyone die: the teeth of him who eats the unripe grapes shall be set on edge.

³¹ The days are coming says the Lord, when I will make a new covenant with the house of Israel and the house of Judah.

³² It will not be like the covenant I made with their fathers, the day I took them by the hand to lead them forth from the land of Egypt; for they broke my covenant, and I had to show myself their master, says the Lord.

³³ But this is the covenant which I will make with the house of Israel after those days, says the Lord. I will place my law within them, and write it upon their hearts; I will be their God, and they shall be my people.

³⁴ No longer will they have need to teach their friends and kinsman how to know the Lord. All, from least to greatest, shall know me, says the Lord, for I will forgive their evil doing and remember their sin no more."

"Open your hearts to me, my people. Surrender, my children, to your Triune God, for I shall set you free. I will give you life eternal.

"Shalom, my people. I love you, my children.

"Thank you, my little one, for remaining obedient to my call."

Approved by Rev. Paul Caporali, 1998 September 23

1998 September 28
EUCHARISTIC ADORATION

Jesus said: "My beloved little one, thank you for coming to spend this time with me. Praise be to Jesus, for Jesus is Lord, Saviour, Reconciler of all nations.

"Oh, my precious daughter, you, as the rest of my children, have come under attack because of your dedication to me, but all my children must understand that in offering up all completely to me during these times, will save many souls who otherwise would have no one to pray for them.

"You, my children must always remember Satan is under my control, and has been allowed to give his venomous attacks, but you must remember, my children, he is allowed by me, and I will never give you more than you can handle. But you must always call out to me, and in calling out to me, you are surrendering to me. Offer all these attacks to me and you shall see how I will carry your burdens.

"Remember the words of "footprints in the sand." During the heaviest trials of his life, my answer was, 'I carried you through those times.' Oh, my beloved children, do not despair but come to me. I will carry you through all your heartaches, through all your trials, for I am your Jesus of mercy, who loves each one of you.

"I formed you in the womb. I know each of you by name. You are each in the palm of my hand. Do not fear for fear is not of me. Know that at the moment you cry out for me, I have already taken care of you.

"Open, my beloved one, to Psalms, Chapter 22, verse 17."

THE BOOK OF PSALMS
PSALMS 22: The Passion and the Triumph of the Messiah

¹⁷ **Indeed, many dogs surround me, a pack of evil doers closes in upon me; they have pierced my hands and my feet;**
¹⁸ **I can count all my bones. They look on and gloat over me;**
¹⁹ **they divide my garments among them, for my clothing they cast lots.**
²⁰ **But you, O Lord, be not far from me; O my help, hasten to aid me.**

²¹ **Rescue my soul from the sword, my loneliness from the grip of the dog.**

²² **Save me from the lion's mouth; from the horns of the wild bulls, my wretched life.**

²³ **I will proclaim your name to my brethren; in the midst of the assembly I will praise you:**

²⁴ **"You who fear the Lord, praise him; all you descendants of Jacob, give glory to him; revere him, all you descendants of Israel.**

²⁵ **For he has not spurned nor disdained the wretched man in his misery, nor did he turn his face away from him, but when he cried out to him, he heard him."**

"No, my children, I never turn away from any of you. On the contrary, it is *you*, my children, who close their hearts to me.

"Do not spurn me, your Jesus of mercy. Open your hearts to me when you pray for your children, for yourselves, for your neighbours, for my people. Pray not for change, but pray for all to remain in my Holy Will.

"My beloved children, when I ask for preparation, I ask for preparation of your souls to always be ready, for I have told you many times, I come as a thief in the night.

"You see these torrents of weather chaos? Many were prepared physically but how many were prepared spiritually?

"I love you, my children. Shalom, my people.

"Thank you, my beloved little one, for remaining obedient to my call."

Approved by Reverend Paul Caporali, 1998 September 28

1998 September 29
Feast of St. Michael, St. Gabriel and St. Raphael
EUCHARISTIC ADORATION

Jesus said: "My beloved little one, thank you for opening your heart to me, and for coming to spend this time with me on this holy feast day of my Archangels Michael, Gabriel, and Raphael; my holy protectors of the faithful.

"Today I have released many souls from the pangs of justice: purgatory; in honour of this holy feast day. My children have forgotten the many souls suffering their purgatory for the error of their ways while on this earth. For many of these souls, it was only my mercy given through the acclamations and petitions from those of my children who offered their prayers for these souls, many unknown to them, yet willing to pray for them. This love of my children for others opens the gates of my mercy, as the devoted love of my archangels bequeathed my mercy upon the many souls today.

"Why my children, do you not realize the magnitude of my mercy and my love? Is it because you are too consumed with the materialistic enticements of this world, creating your own downfall by thinking only of yourself and not of others!.

"Why, my children do you continue to close your hearts and minds to my truths, which will set you free? I ask you, my children, today, open your hearts to my request of total surrender, through prayer, sacrifice, the Holy Sacraments, that you may be one of my faithful to receive the mercy of my love and the protection of my great archangels during the heavy trials ahead.

"I do not create havoc in your life. I *am* peace and love. This you will see and realize as you surrender completely and totally to me. Do not be like the servant who was given coins to build on, and instead stored them, while the others increased their coins. And when the master asked his servants for an account of what they had done with the coins given them, they each had brought back more than given them, except for the one who stored his coins.

"Open, my beloved one, to Luke, Chapter 19, verse 12."

THE GOSPEL ACCORDING TO LUKE
LUKE 19: The Parable of the Sums of Money

¹² He said, "A man of noble birth went to a faraway country to become its king, and then return.

¹³ He summoned ten of his servants and gave them sums of ten units each, saying to them, 'Invest this until I get back.'

¹⁴ But his fellow citizens despised him, and they immediately sent a deputation after him with instructions to say, 'We will not have this man rule over us.'

¹⁵ He returned, however, crowned as king. Then he sent for the servants to whom he had given the money, to learn what profit each had made.

¹⁶ The first presented himself and said, 'Lord, the sum you gave me has earned you another ten.'

¹⁷ 'Good man!' he replied. 'You showed yourself capable in a small matter. For that you can take over ten villages.'

¹⁸ The second came and said, 'Your investment, my lord, has netted you five.'

¹⁹ His word to him was, 'Take over five villages.'

²⁰ The third came in and said: 'Here is your money, my lord, which I hid for safekeeping.

²¹ You see, I was afraid of you because you are a hard man. You withdraw what you never deposited. You reap what you never sowed.

²² To him the king said: 'You worthless lout! I intend to judge you on your own evidence. You knew I was a hard man, withdrawing what I never deposited, reaping what I never sowed!

²³ Why, then, did you not put my money out on loan, so that on my return I could get it back with interest?'

²⁴ He said to those standing around, 'Take from him what he has, and give it to the man with the ten.'

²⁵ 'Yes, but he already has ten,' they said.

²⁶ He responded with, 'The moral is: whoever has will be given more, but the one who has not will lose the little he has.

²⁷ Now about those enemies of mine who do not want me to be king, bring them in and slay them in my presence.'"

"For you see, my children, I, your Jesus of mercy, will allow the graces to flow amongst you who have opened your hearts to me, surrendering in total abandonment to me. But for those of you who turn away from me, you relinquish all my mercy to those willing to remain in me, with me, and for me.

"Shalom, my people. I love you, my beloved little one. Thank you for remaining obedient to my call."

Approved by Reverend Paul Caporali

1998 September 30
Feast of St. Jerome
EUCHARISTIC ADORATION

Jesus said: "Praise be to Jesus, for Jesus is Lord, Saviour, Redeemer and Reconciler of all nations. My beloved children, today we celebrate another feast day of one of my beloved, Jerome, who showed dedication, love and total surrender. For you see, my children, total surrender immolates in submission, humility, piety and love. This, my beloved children, is needed, that you may reach sanctity, which I desire for all my children.

"Yes, it may sound impossible, but my children, with me, all is possible. You must not be satisfied at less, for your goal must always be to strive for sanctity. I give you the means and the way, but you must first surrender to my holy will in order to attain all from me, with me, through me and for me. This will bring you salvation, not only for yourselves through my mercy, but for all my children, willing to open their hearts in total surrender to me, your Jesus of mercy.

"You must remember, my children, your time is not my time, and though you hear messages of distress, you must always pray and discern the context of these messages. My children who remain obedient to my will should never fear, for as I have told you many times, fear is not of me. Words that are given must always be prayed over, discerned, and then release yourselves to my holy will. The message should never preoccupy your minds to take away the precious moments of your lives with misery or mistrust, but should draw you closer to me in total faith, trust and surrender.

"Occupy your time with me in prayer, supplication, the Holy Sacraments, love and mercy to your families and to all my children, not in needless worry, which causes confusion and disturbance. No, my children, focus on me, on my love and my mercy through prayer. I *am* light, not darkness and misery. I am peace and love, but you must seek my way through surrender.

"Open, my beloved, to 1 Corinthians, Chapter 13, verse 8."

THE FIRST EPISTLE OF PAUL TO THE CORINTHIANS
1 CORINTHIANS 13: Excellence of the Gift of Love

⁸ Love never fails. Prophecies will cease, tongues will be silent, knowledge will pass away.

⁹ Our knowledge is imperfect and our prophesying is imperfect.

¹⁰ When the perfect comes, the imperfect will pass away.

¹¹ When I was a child, I used to talk like a child, think like a child, reason like a child. When I became a man I put childish ways aside.

¹² Now we see indistinctly, as in a mirror; then we shall see face to face. My knowledge is imperfect now; then I shall know even as I am known. There are in the end three things that last: faith, hope, and love and the greatest of these is love.

1 CORINTHIANS 14: The Gift of Prophecy

¹ Seek eagerly after love. Set your hearts on spiritual gifts — above all, the gift of prophecy.

² A man who speaks in a tongue is talking not to men but to God. No one understands him, because he utters mysteries in the Spirit.

³ The prophet, on the other hand, speaks to men for their upbuilding, their encouragement, their consolation.

"My beloved children, pray for all my vessels. Their road is hard and necessary. Can you walk this road of my beloved vessels? Do not judge, my children. Pray, my children.

"Shalom, my people.

"Thank you, my beloved little one, for remaining obedient to my call."

Approved by Reverend Paul Caporali

1998 October 01, Thursday
Feast of St. Therese the Little Flower
EUCHARISTIC ADORATION

Jesus said: "Praise be to Jesus, for Jesus is Lord, Saviour and Sanctifier, my beloved little one. I am Reconciler of all nations. As we celebrate today another great feast, my little way, St. Therese, a true spouse of surrendering love. Her little way, not one of great speaking accomplishment or distinguished nobility, but a simple way of pure love, brought this child to sanctity. Why, my children, do you not see the simplicity and purity of my love. Therese knew the way in offering herself completely through love. Is this such a difficulty for you, my children?

"Open, my beloved, to Psalm 26."

THE BOOK OF PSALMS
PSALM 26: The Prayer Of An Innocent Man

¹ **Grant me justice Lord! I have walked without blame. In the Lord I trusted; I have not faltered.**
² **Test me, Lord and try me; search my heart and mind.**
³ **Your love is before my eyes. I walk guided by your faithfulness.**

Jesus said: "My beloved Therese knew that by putting all trust in me, I would lead her way through perfect conformity to my way. Her 'little way' proved the right path to sanctity."

Psalm 26 cont'd:

⁴ **I do not sit with deceivers, nor with the hypocrites do I mingle.**
⁵ **I hate the company of evil doers, with the wicked I do not sit.**

Jesus said: "How many times, my children, I have spoken to you of focusing on me, not the self-centered ways of the world, which deceive you into scandalous ways; the evil trickery permeating from the enticements of the worldly ways, confusing our minds and deadening the life of your soul, closing your hearts to my truths? All this from the manipulative enticements and ways of the world. Do not stay in the company of the wicked, my beloved children, but choose the 'little way' of my beloved Therese, simple love."

Psalm 26 cont'd:

⁶ **I will wash my hands in innocence and walk round your altar, Lord,**
⁷ **lifting my voice in thanks, recounting all your wondrous deeds.**
⁸ **Lord, I love the home where you dwell, the tenting place of your glory.**

Jesus said: "The simplicity of your love is what I ask of you, my children; that I may reign in the temple of my glory, your soul purified in my splendour and grace, through your willingness of surrender, as my beloved Therese's 'little way,' the path of sanctity, the road to eternal life with me, through me, for me.

"Shalom, my beloved children. Thank you, my gentle one, for remaining obedient to my call."

Approved by Reverend Paul Caporali

1998 October 20, Tuesday
TEACHING FROM OUR LOVING MOTHER

Our Loving Mother said: "My beloved children, praise be to Jesus, for Jesus is Lord, Saviour, Redeemer and Reconciler of all nations. I come, my beloved children, to thank you in the Almighty Names of the Father, Son and Holy Spirit, for the offerings of prayers, praise and worship which you bestowed with such love. This love offered the much needed sacrifice which appeased the hearts of your most loving, crucified Saviour and mine, your loving Mother of the Redeemer.

"Oh, my children, this call to you was a call given through the love and mercy of your Triune God, for the merciless corruption and deception your world is in. This call to you, my beloved children, was a necessity, not for your Triune God, but for each of you, my beloved children; because you have seen for yourselves the destructive path this world has taken upon itself through the venomous corruption of sin and malice. But your Triune God is a God of mercy, a God of love and a God of justice. And, as you have been told, many times it is only prayer, sacrifice, and the holy Sacraments that can mitigate and, yes, even stop the pangs of justice you decree upon yourselves.

"My beloved children, do not stop this prayer, sacrifice and coming to my Son in the most Holy Sacraments, because this day of reparation called for has 'passed.' On the contrary, continue in this manner of seeking to appease your Triune God, not only yesterday or today or tomorrow, but rather make a commitment to continue this desire to appease your Triune God until you have been called to stand before your Triune God in judgement.

"You have been told many times through my Son's loving vessels how it only took one man, Martin Luther, to destroy through conflict and division to the holy Magisterium, the church. Remember, my children, as it only took one to destroy, it can take the dedication, love and surrendering of one child to build back up the holy mother church. This, through the love and mercy of your Triune God. Nothing is an impossibility with your Triune God.

"So, I come to you as the Mother of all nations, asking for your unity amongst you, my children, in prayer, sacrifice, and obedience. Yes, my children, obedience to the holy mother church. Had my Son not been obedient to the Holy Will of the Father in allowing himself to be the holy sacrificial Lamb in dying on the holy cross for each of you, you would not have the gift of life eternal.

Open you hearts in surrender, my children. Surrender and obedience will bring unity; and with unity in the one, true, holy, catholic and apostolic church. But this can only happen through prayer, sacrifice, obedience and the holy Sacraments.

"Open, my beloved little one, to Sirach, Chapter 23, verse 13."

THE BOOK OF SIRACH
SIRACH 32: The Providence of God

[14] **He who would find God must accept discipline; he who seeks him obtains his request.**

¹⁵ He who studies the law masters it, but the hypocrite finds it a trap.

¹⁶ His judgement is sound who fears the Lord; out of obscurity he draws forth a clear plan.

¹⁷ The sinner turns aside reproof and distorts the law to suit his purpose.

¹⁸ The thoughtful man will not neglect direction; the proud and insolent man is deterred by nothing.

¹⁹ Do nothing without counsel, and then you need have no regrets.

²⁰ Go not on a way that is set with snares, and let not the same thing trip you twice.

²¹ Be not too sure of smooth roads,

²² be careful on all your paths.

²³ Whatever you do, be on your guard, for in this way you will keep the commandments.

²⁴ He who keeps the law preserves himself; and he who trusts in the Lord shall not be put to shame.

Approved by Rev. Paul Caporli

1998 October 26, Monday
Mary's Mediterranean Pilgrim's Cruise
EUCHARISTIC ADORATION

Jesus said: "My beloved daughter, praise be to Jesus, for Jesus is Lord, Saviour and Redeemer. I am your Jesus of mercy, reconciler of all nations.

"Yes, my children, I, your Jesus of mercy, welcome you on this voyage. You my children, each called by name, to be here as my latter day apostles and saints, to go forth in my name. To be here as examples of my truths, to teach others through examples of words and deeds. I know of the many trials and sometimes even hardships that it took for you to be here. But you were called as you were chosen and through your willingness and your love for me; you came, my beloved chosen vessels.

"I ask you, my beloved children, to offer all to me. Trials will come. Even now many of you have obstacles and trials trying to dissuade you from my peace, and my love. But I ask you to offer these inconveniences to me, out of your love to me, in reparation for the many sins being committed against my most wounded Sacred Heart, and that of my most Holy Mother's Wounded Immaculate Heart. As my Holy Mother spoke to my little one this morning, I will bring many manifestations of my love and my mercy upon each of you, as you so lovingly and willingly have opened your hearts to me. Come in total surrender to me, my children, and you will see a new way to live in this world of confusion and corruption. You will see and live a life of happiness with me, through me and for me.

"Come to me as the instruments of my love, as you were chosen. That you may go forth as instruments of my love and my mercy. Proclaim in my name the truths of my love and mercy to all, and you shall see the essence of my love showered not only on yourselves, but your families, and all those willing to surrender in love to me.

"Open, my beloved, to Deuteronomy, ch. 26, v1."

THE BOOK OF DEUTERONOMY
DEUTERONOMY 26: Thanksgiving for the Harvest

1. **When you have come into the land which the Lord, your God, is giving you as a heritage, and have occupied it and have settled in it,**

2. **you shall take some first fruits of the various products of the soil, which you harvest from the land, which the Lord, your God, gives you, and putting them in a basket, you shall go to the place which the Lord, your God, chooses for the dwelling place of His Name.**

3. **There you shall go to the priest in office at that time and say to him, "Today, I acknowledge the Lord, my God, that we have indeed come into the land which he swore to our fathers that he would give us.**

4. **The priest shall receive the basket from you and shall set it in front of the altar of the Lord, your God.**

5. **Then you shall declare before the Lord, your God, "My father was a wandering Aramean, who went down to Egypt with a small household and lived there as an alien. But there he became a nation great, strong and numerous.**

6. **When the Egyptians maltreated and oppressed us, imposing hard labour upon us,**

7 we cried to the Lord, the God of Our Fathers, and he heard our cry and saw our affliction, our toil and our oppression.

8 He brought us out of Egypt with his strong and outstretched arm, with terrifying power, with signs and wonders;

9 and bringing us into this country, he gave us this land flowing with milk and honey.

10 Therefore, I have now brought you the first fruits of the products for the soil which you, O Lord, have given me. And having set them before the Lord, your God, you shall bow down in his presence.

11 Then you and your family, together with the Levite and the aliens who live among you, shall make merry over all these good things, which the Lord your God has given you.

Approved by Reverend Karempelis
& Reverend Paul Caporali

1998 October 27, Tuesday
Mary's Mediterranean Pilgrim's Cruise
EUCHARISTIC ADORATION

Jesus said: "My beloved children, I, your Jesus of mercy, call each of you to the font of my mercy, that you may refresh yourselves with my pearls of everlasting grace I so willingly desire to shower upon each of you. 'How,' you ask? Through my most perfect offering of love; the most perfect prayer; the Sacrament of the Holy Mass; the Holy Sacrament of the Eucharist, where I call each of you daily. Have you responded to my call, that you may receive these precious pearls of my love?

"If you have not responded to my call, then ask yourselves, "Why not?" What is it that draws you away from me; from the precious gifts I wish to bestow upon each of you? What is it in this materialistic world of yours which draws you away from me, from the realization of my true presence in the Holy Sacrament of the Eucharist?

"Oh, my precious children, in order that your spiritual life does not stagnate, you must seek me in all, that I may be the main focus of your life, in order that your spiritual growth matures and is nurtured daily. Now is the time for you to surrender completely and totally to me, for you do not know the hour. I come as a thief in the night!

"Will you be ready? Are you prepared? Or will your lamps be empty, as were those in my scripture teaching?

"I have invited you, the bridegroom beckoning the bride, before the wedding feast. Do not shun your bridegroom, my beloved children. Open your hearts completely to me.

"Open, my beloved little one, to Luke, Chapter 21, verse 34."

THE GOSPEL ACCORDING TO LUKE
LUKE 21:

³⁴ Be on your guard lest your spirits become bloated with indulgence and drunkenness and worldly cares. The great day will suddenly close in on you like a trap.

³⁵ The day I speak of will come upon all who dwell on the face of the earth.

³⁶ So be on the watch. Pray constantly for the strength to escape whatever is in prospect, and to stand secure before the Son of Man.

THE GOSPEL ACCORDING TO MATTHEW
MATTHEW 25:

⁶ At midnight, there was a cry, "Behold, the bridegroom! Come out to meet him!"

⁷ Then all those virgins got up and trimmed their lamps.

⁸ The foolish ones said to the wise, "Give us some of your oil, for our lamps are going out."

⁹ But the wise ones replied, "No, for there may not be enough for us and you. Go instead to merchants and buy some for yourselves."

¹⁰ While they went off to buy it, the bridegroom came and those who were ready went into the wedding feast with him. Then the door was locked.

¹¹ Afterwards the other virgins came and said, "Lord, Lord, open the door for us!"

¹² But he said in reply, "I tell you, I do not know you!"

¹³ Therefore stay awake, for you know neither the day nor the hour.

Jesus said: "I love you, my children. Shalom, my people. "Thank you, my little one, for remaining obedient to my call."

Approved by Reverend Karempelis
& Reverend Paul Caporali

1998 October 29, Thursday
Mary's Pilgrim's Cruise
EUCHARISTIC ADORATION

Jesus said: "Praise be to Jesus for Jesus is Lord, Saviour, Redeemer, Reconciler of all nations.

"My beloved children, as you come to me in Eucharistic Adoration, make this commitment to me of total surrender. I have told you many times, this release of your will to my Holy Will removes the boundaries of your spiritual life, and is the beginning of total surrender.

"Throughout these years, as my Holy Mother continues to plead to your Triune God for my mercy upon you, my children, her tears open the gates to my mercy, but it seems as if her pleas to her children go unheard.

"Oh, my precious children, I do not come to chastise you, for I see the desires of each of your hearts. I see the love of you, my children, here on this voyage, where you so willingly and lovingly opened your hearts to my will. But I come to ask you to surrender this will to me, not only now but as you return to your homes, to your everyday way of life. Do not allow yourselves to return to your old ways, your old life, but continue on this journey you have begun here with me and with my holy Mother. For you see, it was through the intercession of my holy Mother for you my children, that the outpouring of the many graces are being released upon you. And as you return to your homes, remember these moments that you spent with me in Eucharistic Adoration, that you continue to seek to spend this time with me, where you have Eucharistic Adoration, so that I may continue to shower these graces of my mercy upon you and your families.

"I have opened the doors to you, my children, to all my children who will seek me and spend time with me in Eucharistic Adoration. Now it is completely up to you whether you desire to continue on this journey with me, through me, and for me.

"Open, my beloved one to Psalm 138."

THE BOOK OF PSALMS
PSALM 138: Hymn of a Grateful Heart

[1] **I thank you, Lord, with all my heart; before the Gods to you I sing. I bow low toward your Holy Temple. I praise your name for your fidelity and love. For you have exalted over all your name and your promise. When I cried out you answered. You strengthened my spirit.**

Jesus said: "Oh my children, do you not see the magnitude of the mercy and love, I, your Triune God so willingly want to give you?

"Shalom, my people. I love you, my little one. Thank you, for remaining obedient to my call."

Approved by Reverend Karempelis
and Reverend Paul Caporali

1998 November 16, Monday
Feast of St. Margaret of Scotland
EUCHARISTIC ADORATION

Jesus said: "Thank you for opening your heart for my teaching, my little one. These teachings are given to you, my children, out of my love and mercy, to show you my way; to teach you my way. But are you willing? For it is a difficult road, my road; but if you surrender to me and open your hearts to me, I will carry you through this road. It is in trusting in me, following my way, through prayer, sacrifice, and the Holy Sacraments. But you each have a free will. So many times you have heard these words.

"To those of you who have listened, you are on this journey with me. At times you feel this closeness with me; then you come to a path which seems a bit rockier and my presence you cannot feel. But do not become discouraged, for I am always with you. It is a road you must cross, but not alone; I am always with you, and though you feel alone, it is trust you must learn.

"As a child taking its first steps alone, the parents, ever watchful, allowing the child to manoeuvre itself in order to learn the steps it must take in order to walk alone, but never the parents far behind, in order to make sure they are near enough when the child takes a fall, ever ready to pick the child up and help the child to start over again, until the child can walk alone. The difference being I never leave you alone. I am always with you.

"But you have a free will and I will never force you, my children, nor will I take your free will away from you. It is entirely up to you, if you wish to continue this journey with me, for me and through me! The reward at the end of this journey with me? Eternal life, my children.

"As on any journey, you must be prepared for the many obstacles you will encounter and again as I have spoken to you; preparation is always prayer, sacrifice, and the Holy Sacraments. This is the preparation I speak of to you over and over.

"Are you ready, my children? Are you prepared?

"This journey continues on through me, with me and for me, and I am always with you, for I carry you, in the palm of my hand.

"Open, my beloved little one, to Luke, Chapter 18, verse 1."

THE GOSPEL ACCORDING TO LUKE
LUKE 18:

1 **He told them a parable about the necessity of praying always and not losing heart.**
2 **"Once there was a judge in a certain town who neither feared God nor man.**
3 **A widow in that city kept coming to him saying, 'Give me my rights against my opponent.'**
4 **For a time he refused, but finally he thought, 'I care little for God or man,**
5 **but this widow is wearing me out. I am going to settle in her favour or she will end by doing me violence.'"**
6 **The Lord said, "Listen to what the corrupt judge has to say.**
7 **Will not God then do justice to his chosen who call out to him day and night? Will he delay long over them, do you suppose?**
8 **I tell you, he will give them swift justice. But when the Son of Man comes, will he find any faith on earth?"**

Jesus said: "My beloved children, will you continue on this journey with me that when I, the Son of man comes, will take you with me as the faithful of the earth?

"I love you, my people. Shalom, my children.

"Thank you, my beloved little one, for remaining obedient to my call."

Approved by Rev. Paul Caporali

1998 November 19, Thursday
EUCHARISTIC ADORATION

Jesus said: "My beloved little one, as the days grow closer to the day of Thanksgiving, how many truly invite me into their homes in thanksgiving for the many blessings they have received throughout the year? Thanksgiving day is now where families get together with family, friends, laughter, and complacency. Their thinking is surrounded by their materialistic values. Do they start off their day with me? I invited them to my Holy Mass to feast with me.

"Do they invite me into their hearts, surrendering to my holy will? Am I one of their invited guests into their home; into their hearts? Have they prepared my home, my temple, their souls, for my stay within them?

"Oh, my children, do not remain in the complacency of taking all you have been given for granted, for you must remember it is I, who has bestowed the many graces you have received.

"The land you live in was created by my Father for you, my children; the sun, the stars, given to you by my Father to give you light and warmth for your bodies. But most important, my Father, the Creator, gave you his only begotten Son to die on a cross that you may have life eternal. How many of you remember in thanksgiving this gift which your Triune God has so willingly, so lovingly, bestowed to all of humanity?

"This day of Thanksgiving comes only once a year, but daily you are bestowed many blessings, many graces, from your Triune God, who never tires of showing you love. Can you not spend a moment daily to remember your Triune God with love?

"Open, my beloved little one, to Wisdom, Chapter 11, verse 2."

THE BOOK OF WISDOM
WISDOM 11:

² They journeyed through the uninhabited desert, and in solitude they pitched their tents;
³ they withstood enemies and took vengeance on their foes.
⁴ When they thirsted, they called upon you, and water was given them from the sheer rock, assuagement for their thirst, from the hard stone.
⁵ For by the things through which their foes punished, they, in their need, were benefited."

Jesus said: "Why is it, my children, I continue to plead and my words go unheard?

"Shalom, my people. I love you, my little one. Thank you for responding to my call."

Approved by Reverend Paul Caporali

1998 December 05, Saturday
EUCHARISTIC ADORATION
St. Francis Retreat Center, Las Cruces, New Mexico

Jesus said: "Praise be to Jesus for Jesus is Lord, Saviour, Reconciler of all nations.

"My beloved daughter, how my children have pleased me in coming to be here, in this holy place of sacrifice. For I know it has been a sacrifice for my children to spend these days away from home, but I open the gates of my mercy and my love upon each child present here and there families, for surrendering to my Holy Will and coming to spend this time with me. These graces showered upon them and their families are unboundless, as I desire to show this my love for any child willing to come to me.

"As my beloved son [priest], has spoken of Advent being a time of beginning, my children, surrendering to me, is a beginning. A beginning for my latter-day saints and apostles.

"Yes, my children, I understand the words apostles and saints seem incomprehensible in these times, but you must understand it has always been the goal each child has been given. For you, my children, were and are always created in the image and likeness of your Triune God. And as this gift of life has been bestowed upon each of you out of the love and mercy of your Triune God, why would you think less would be expected from you in order that you may attain the gift of life eternal? This being the case and understanding, that each of you must strive to attain sanctity, not only a desire on your part, but a *goal,* always first and foremost.

"My beloved children, you were given an invitation to join me not only here this weekend, but wherever there is Eucharistic Adoration or the Holy Sacrifice of the Mass. Not only this weekend, but everyday of your existence, I invite you to seek me in all and to surrender to me completely.

"Oh my beloved children, do you not realize the magnitude of my love for each and everyone of you. You are created in the image and likeness of your Triune God. It is unfathomable the amount of love and mercy I wish to give each of you. But I do not force this upon you, as each of you has been given a free will to accept or deny this my love and mercy. It is a willingness, an acceptance and surrender on your part to make this journey with me, and which allows the gates of my mercy and love to flow.

"My beloved son, my holy priest with the consecrated hands, spoke to you of steps to be taken in order to make this journey with me. It is an invitation I give you, to take the steps, to make this journey with me, through me and for me. A journey that ends with life eternal and begins with surrender of your will to my Holy Will. Are you willing, my beloved children?

"Open, my little one, to Isaiah Ch 33."

THE BOOK OF ISAIAH
ISAIAH 33: Restoration of Zion

17 Your eyes will see a king in his splendour, they will look upon a vast land.

18 Your mind will dwell on the terror. "Where is he who counted, where is he who weighed? Where is he who counted the towers?"

19 To the people of alien tongue you will look no more. The people of obscure speech, stammering in a language not understood.

²⁰ Look to Zion, the city of our festivals; let your eyes see Jerusalem as a quiet abode, a tent not to be struck, whose pegs will never be pulled up, nor any of its ropes severed.

²¹ Indeed the Lord will be there with us, majestic; yes the Lord our judge, the Lord our lawgiver, the Lord our king, he it is who will save us.

²² In a place of rivers and wide streams on which no boat is rowed, where no majestic ship passes,

²³ The rigging hangs slack; it cannot hold the mast in place, nor keep the sail spread out. Then the blind will divide great spoils and the lame will carry off the loot.

²⁴ No one who dwells there will say, "I am sick"; the people who live there will be forgiven their guilt.

Jesus said: "My beloved children, I have spoken to you of a beginning, and now as this era of my holy Mother's appearances on this earth comes to an end, a new beginning of the reign of the Holy Spirit and your Jesus crucified begins. You only need to seek through surrender and love, through the holy Sacraments, and through sacrifice, your Triune God; and then you will have entered upon this journey with me."

Approved by Reverend Paul Caporali

1998 December 11, Friday
MESSAGE FROM OUR LOVING MOTHER

Our Loving Mother said: "My beloved daughter, thank you for remaining obedient to our call. As I have promised you, my beloved Josyp saw within his heart the icon which I have requested. This Icon to be done as my gift to the world on these final days of my apparitions on this earth.

"This icon which I have requested will have a special grace placed on each copy that is placed within my children's homes: a grace of fortitude and protection upon each who come before this icon in complete love and surrender to the Holy Will of the Blessed Trinity.

"As I have told you, my little one, it is my desire that through this icon many will come to know the presence of my Son within their hearts, and will return to their Triune God with a love and desire to surrender to the Holy Will of their Triune God.

"It is also my desire that through this icon, the house of prayer that my Son has requested will come to fulfilment.

"I ask you, my children, who have been given many graces in this land of the United States, to open your hearts to see that his house of prayer is completed.

"I bless each of you in the Almighty Name of the Father, Son and Holy Spirit. I love you my children."

Approved by Rev. Paul Caporali

1998 December 14, Monday
EUCHARISTIC ADORATION

Jesus said: "Praise be to Jesus, for Jesus is Lord, Saviour, Redeemer, Reconciler of all nations.

"Welcome, my beloved little one. I ask you to listen with your heart, for I know how difficult the trials have been for you, and this makes it difficult to listen with your heart. Focus only on me. What have I told you, my beloved little one, these your driest and darkest moments are when I am closest to you. These are the times that as you continually seek me in all, focus only on me. I will turn the darkness into light, for I am light, love, and mercy.

"My precious child, if only my children would seek me, as you have done, not only during the many trials, but seeking me at all times. All those seeking me would have my love fulfilling within the very depths of their being. They would have the peace which this world cannot give, for my peace is not of this world.

"As this time draws nearer to the celebration of my birth, my death, my resurrection; bringing life to all mankind; for that is what the day of my birth was: a gift to all humanity: life eternal.

"So, my precious beloved children, as this day of celebrations grows closer, do not celebrate this day as the world celebrates this day; but celebrate it with me, for me and through me. Prepare yourselves for this day through the Sacraments: the Sacrament of Reconciliation, which cleanses your soul from all error of sin, in order that your soul, my temple, be ready, to receive the greatest of all gifts given to humanity. I came to you as the Christ Child and died for you as your Jesus crucified, in order that you would be able to receive me, alive, body, blood, soul and divinity in the Sacrament of the Holy Eucharist. And what do all my gifts lead to? Life eternal for your souls, my children.

"How did this all begin my children? As a babe in the manger in a stable, I willingly came to you out of my love. I willingly come to you in the Sacrament of the Holy Eucharist out of my love. I willingly died for each of you out of my love. Do you willingly come to me out of your love?

"Open, my beloved one, to Exodus Ch 40, v31."

THE BOOK OF EXODUS
EXODUS 40: Erection of the Dwelling

[31] Moses and Aaron and his sons used to wash their hands and feet there,

[32] for they washed themselves whenever they went into the meeting tent or approached the altar, as the Lord had commanded Moses.

THE GOSPEL ACCORDING TO JOHN
JOHN 1:

[1] In the beginning was the Word; the Word was in God's presence, and the Word was God.

[2] He was present to God in the beginning.

[3] Through him all things came into being, and apart from him nothing came to be.

[4] Whatever came to be in him, found life, life for the light of men.

[5] The light shines on in darkness, a darkness that did not overcome it.

JOHN 6:

[33] For the bread of God is that which comes down from heaven and gives life to the world.

John 6 cont'd:

⁶² **"What if you were to see the Son of man ascending to where he was before?**
⁶³ **It is the spirit that gives life; the flesh is useless. The words I spoke to you are spirit and life.**
⁶⁴ **Yet among you there are some who do not believe." [Jesus knew from the start, of course, the ones who refused to believe, and the ones who would hand him over].**

Jesus said: "Which of these children are you, my beloved ones? Those that are to follow or those that are to betray me?

"Shalom, my people. I love you, my little one. Thank you for remaining obedient to my call."

Approved by Reverend Paul Caporali

1998 December 16, Wednesday
EUCHARISTIC ADORATION

Jesus said: "Praise be to Jesus for Jesus is Lord, Saviour, Redeemer.

"Thank you, my beloved one, for coming to spend this time with me in Eucharistic Adoration. My children who willingly open their hearts in surrender to me, coming to be with me in Eucharistic Adoration, I shower with the graces of perseverance, fortitude and strength.

"My beloved children, these days, where chaos runs rampant in a society of evil doers, unless they come to me in contrition for the error of their ways, they will see the evil they have brought upon themselves and all those around them.

"I have told you, my children, I am a loving God; a merciful God; but I am also a God of justice, and I have warned you many times, not only through the words of my Holy Mother, but also many times I have pleaded with you, my children, to change your ways and return to me. But to my dismay my words go to deaf ears.

"Now the deaf will not only hear my justice, they will see my justice!

"This message has taken much of your strength, my beloved little one, for you feel the weight of the world upon your shoulders. I have allowed this, my daughter, that you may offer to me all this suffering in reparation for the sins of this world. But soon the world will have to suffer the pangs of my justice if they are not willing to change the error of their ways.

"My beloved ones, my mercy and protection will be upon those of my children who have come to me in total submission and love; and, as I have promised, I will protect those and their families who, as they have known me, I know them.

"Open, my beloved one, to Deuteronomy Chapter 7, verse 9."

THE BOOK OF DEUTERONOMY
DEUTERONOMY 7: *Destruction of Pagans*

⁹ Understand then that the Lord your God is God indeed, the faithful God who keeps his merciful covenant down to the thousandth generation towards those who love him and keep his commandments,

¹⁰ but who repays with destruction the person who hates him; he does not dally with such a one, but makes him personally pay for it.

Jesus said: "I have warned you, my children. It is I who is in control and has always been in control.

"You see the barren desert ahead, a wasteland of empty promises and worldly possessions. Will these possessions care for you now? In this barren desert, who will give you drink to refresh yourselves? For your worldly ways have poisoned the land you live in. You have followed the god of lies. Will he now save you and give you life eternal? No, my children, the god of lies brings destruction upon destruction. But you have a free will.

"Come to me now, my beloved ones. Come to the springs of everlasting grace, that your souls be ready and my grace refresh you with life eternal.

"I love you, my children. Thank you, my beloved one, for remaining obedient to my call."

Approved by Reverend Paul Caporali

January 1, 1999

"My beloved son, Father Bishop Danylak, how your love and dedication to my service has pleased me. You, my son, set an exemplary example of how the holy Sacrifice of the Mass should be offered and loved by all my sons,' realizing my real presence, the holy Sacrament of the Eucharist. I bless you, my son! I love you, my son! I thank you also for the obedience shown me, in arranging the meeting with my beloved John Paul and my daughter Patricia, and for aquiring the relics for my house of prayer. At this time, my son, I once again ask your assistance in making the introduction of this child to the Bishop of Las Vegas, also making him aware of My desire for this house of prayer to be built on the land now occupied by the Carmelite Sisters, which they will soon be leaving for their new site. I ask that this land be allowed to be purchased by the Ministry of His Teachings for this my house of prayer. My son, as you pray and discern over this message you will be given the confirmation needed to know that this is my desire. I also ask that as you read the teachings given to my little one, Patricia, that you look within your heart to write the words needed as a forward for this book, which I have requested to be put together by my beloved John. I am with you, my son! I love you, my son! I bless you, my son!

"Your Jesus of mercy."

Approved by Rev. Paul Caporali

January 2, 1999

Praise be to Jesus for Jesus is Lord, Redeemer, Reconciler of All Nations.

Jesus said: "My beloved daughter, open your heart for my teaching.

"My children, have you not heard my pleas? Oh, my children, lost in this world of materialism and social injustice! I have come, my beloved ones, that through my teachings, hearts will be opened! my pleas, ears will hear! That I, your Jesus crucified, does not turn away from you, has never abandoned you! On the contrary, I have opened the gates of my mercy as never before in the history of mankind! For had I not, this world's existence would have been gone from the error of sin! More souls have been lost to the evil one's snares than the souls of Sodom and Gomorrah, and yet my mercy has outweighed my justice! Through your prayers, sacrifice, pleaded for by my Holy Mother, has brought this reprieve, for her tears shed for all our children touch the depth of the Heart of your Triune God!

"Won't you listen, my children, when I say it only took one man, Martin Luther, to create schism, bringing dissension and destruction into the church! It can take just one to bring unification and restoration! You, my children, are asked for prayer, sacrifice, the Holy Sacraments and surrender!

"Do not let these words go unheard, my children! My mercy, My love surrounds each of you! Wrap yourself in this mercy, this love, through me, with me, and for me!

"Remember the words in Genesis, Chapter 3, Verse 14:"

14 Then the Lord God said to the serpent, "Because you have done this, you shall be banned from all the animals and from all the wild creatures; on your belly shall you crawl, and dirt shall you eat all the days of your life!

15 I will put enmity between you and the woman, and between your offspring and hers. He will strike at your head, while you strike at his heel."

My children, do not concern yourselves with words, dates, and chastisements, but go forward with me, your Jesus crucified! Has another laid down his life for your life?

Genesis, Chapter 3, Verse 22:

22 Then the Lord God said, 'See, the man has become like one of us, knowing what is good and what is bad! Therefore he must not be allowed to put out his hand to take fruit from the tree of life also, and thus eat of it and live forever.'

23 The Lord God therefore banished him from the Garden of Eden, to till the ground from which he had been taken.

24 When he expelled the man, he settled him east of the Garden of Eden; and he stationed the cherubim and the fiery revolving sword, to guard the way to the tree of life.

"I am the way, the light and the life, my children! Why do you continue to live in darkness?

I love you, my beloved little one. Thank you for remaining obedient to our call."

Approved by Reverend Paul Caporali

January 11, 1999
Eucharistic Adoration

Praise be to Jesus for Jesus is Lord, Saviour, Redeemer, Reconciler of All Nations

Jesus said: "Welcome, my beloved daughter, thank you for coming to visit with me and for remaining obedient to my call. I come as your Jesus of mercy, bringing you once again, my teaching.

"My children, do not remain complacent in your spiritual journey with me. It is in continually seeking me in all, inviting me continually into your hearts, that you can progress along this journey, with me, through me and for me! This, I have told you, is the beginning of surrender! Ask me for the grace to presevere in this journey. For the grace of faith to trust in me! For the grace to desire to surrender completely and totally to my Holy Will! For you see, my children, it is necessary to seek my graces in all the concerns in your daily life. Know that I give these graces freely as you ask me, as a father giving with love to his children.

"Focus on me, my children, in all that you do, and you will see a difference in your lives, because you then begin to realize that I am always with you, even if you don't invite me, you don't realize that I am your Triune God! I see and know all! I even know the deepest secrets of your heart, but you seem to forget these things!

"Remember, my children, I knew you before you were born! I hold you in the palm of my hand! But if you become complacent in your journey with me, you become more worldly in your thoughts, in your lives, and soon, you forget that I, your Triune God, am always with you.

"The lifestyles and ways of the world become your main concern and your spiritual journey with me is stifled. You forget you and this world were created by your Triune God, in the Image and likeness of your Triune God, instead of focusing on me and your spiritual growth with me! You become worldly, and the materialistic values draw you away from truth, godliness, and then the life of your soul is deadened from the error of sin.

"Open your hearts, minds, with the graces I am so willingly to give though the Holy Sacraments! Through prayer! Through sacrifice! Through me, my children! For me, my children! With me, my children!

"Remember this, my children, if you can't invite me to be with you, then you don't belong there! I love you, my children.

"Open, my beloved little one, to Hebrews, Chapter 3, Verse 1."

¹ **Therefore holy 'brothers' sharing in a heavenly calling, reflect on Jesus, the apostle and high priest of our confession**

² **Who was faithful to the one who appointed him, just as Moses was faithful in (all) his house**

³ **But he is worthy of more glory than Moses, as the founder of a house has more honor than the house itself**

⁴ **Every house is founded by someone, but the founder of all is God**

⁵ **Moses was 'faithful in all his house' as a servant to testify to what would be spoken**

⁶ **but Christ was faithful as a son placed over his house. We are his house, if only we hold fast to our confidence and pride in our hope.**

"I am always with you, my children! Invite me into my temple, your soul!

"I love you, my little one."

Approved by Reverend Paul Caporali

January 12, 1999, Tuesday

"My beloved son, Father Bishop Danylak,

"It has been placed in my son Josyp and daughter Patricia's heart a retreat pilgrimage, during the time of the beatification of my beloved Pio.

"As in the past I have asked your assistance in seeing to my requests, I once again ask that you make it possible for the blessing of the icon requested by my Holy Mother, by my beloved John Paul. I also ask that the icon of my beloved Pio also be blessed at this time which my son Josyp will take at the time of my beloved Pio's beatification. It is my desire that a day of reparation be done during this pilgrimage with you celebrating the Holy Sacrifice of the Mass and speaking of the importance of the Holy Sacrament of the Eucharist as well as Eucharistic Adoration.

"My son, these times have been spoken of in many prophetic writings, and much prayer, sacrifice and supplication is needed to appease my most wounded Sacred Heart and that of my Holy Mother's Immaculate Heart. This is why when my children are willing to appease my heart through prayer and the desire to please me, I open the gates of my mercy upon all my children.

"My son, please open your heart for my direction and I will give you the strength to go forward with me, through me and for me. This retreat pilgrimage is a means of reparation and many hearts will be opened as they see the dedication and love given in the painting of these icons, I ask that these children making this retreat pilgrimage along with you have the special opportunity to witness the blessing of these icons by my beloved John Paul during the offering of the Holy Sacrifice of the Mass. For many will then know of the love given by my Holy Mother in the request of this icon, her desired token of love to her children through this icon.

"I leave you with a very special blessing, my son, as you go forward in my name to see this holy work is accomplished for me, with me, and through me.

"Your Jesus of mercy."

January 15, 1999, Friday
Eucharistic Adoration

Praise be to Jesus for Jesus is Lord

Jesus said: "My beloved little one, I am your Jesus of mercy wanting to make my residence within my temple, your soul, my children! You have a free will to surrender completely to me, to focus completely on me! I have asked you for preparedness of your soul for my occupancy, through the Sacrament of Reconciliation. It is more necessary to prepare your souls more often in these times where the evil is so prevalent, ready to extinguish my light within your soul, trying to bring you into his realm of evil and decay, closing hearts and minds to my truths, to my light in this world of darkness and corruption. This is why I plead with you, my children, to come to the sacraments more often, not only to seek my forgiveness but to receive the grace I so willingly want to give you! For these graces will fill your hearts with my love, my strength. These graces are given as the sacramentals are given, as aid, consolation and armor! They are tokens of my love and mercy for you, my children, and your weapons against the evil attacks and attrocities being committed. They are not tokens of superstition but tokens of my love. I have asked you to protect yourself, your family, Through me, with me, for me, with the Holy Sacraments, prayer, sacrifice and sacramentals. Put my armor on daily by reading Ephesians 6, Psalm 91 and Read my word daily! Consecrate yourselves and your family, my children, for you see the outright mercilous attacks, the venom loosed in this world. Know that I am always with you! You only need call out to me! I have never left you! Focus on me, my children, and you will be led by my light within you! How do you recieve this light? Keep this light? By what I have told you, through me, with me and for me! I am the light in this darkness! Open your hearts to me through the Holy Sacraments, prayer, sacrifice, Eucharistic Sdoration, I am always there waiting for you! I have the answers! I love you, my children.

"Open, my beloved one, to Ephesians Ch. 6."

10 **Battle against Evil — Finally draw your strength from the Lord and from his mighty power.**

11 **Put on the armor of God so that you may be able to stand firm against the tactics of the devil.**

12 **For our struggle is not with flesh and blood but with the Principalities, with the Powers, with the world rulers of this present darkness, with the evil spirits in the heavens;**

13 **Therefore, put on the armor of God, that you may be able to resist on the evil day and having done everything, to hold your ground**

14 **So standfast with your loins girded in truth, clothed with righteousness as a breastplate.**

15 **and your feet shod in readiness for the gospel of peace.**

¹⁶ In all circumstances, hold faith as a shield, to quench all the flaming arrows of the evil one.

¹⁷ And take the helmet of salvation and the sword of the Spirit which is the Word of God.

Jesus said: "Open now, my little one, to Psalm 91."

¹ You who dwell in the shelter of the Most High - who abide in the shadow of the Almighty.

Jesus said: "My children, listen with your hearts, I am the shelter of the most high. Your soul is my temple! Is your soul ready for the most high?"

² Say to the Lord "My refuge and fortress, My god in whom I trust"

Jesus said: "If you trust in me, I shall never forsake you, my children!"

³ God will rescue you from the fowler's snare, from the destroying plague.

Jesus said: "I will never abandon you, my children! You must always remember Satan has no power over you but the power you give him from the error of sin!"

⁴ Will shelter you with pinons, spread wings that you may take refuge; God's faithfulness is a protecting shield

Jesus said: "Your armor, my children, is the Holy Sacraments, this grace I so willingly shower upon each of you in the Holy Sacraments, but unless you come to the Sacraments of Reconciliation, the Holy Sacrifice of the Mass, the Holy Sacrament of the Eucharist, How can you recieve my grace, your armor?"

⁵ You shall not fear the Terror of the Night nor the arrow that flies by day

Jesus said: "Remember, my children, fear is not of me! Trust me! Surrender to me!"

⁶ Nor the pestilence that roams in darkness, nor the plague that ravages at noon.

Jesus said: "I am peace, my children. Seek my peace! Seek my mercy and you will have light within, the light this world cannot give!"

⁷ Though a thousand fall at your side, ten thousand at your right hand, near you it shall not come

Jesus said: "Near you it shall not come because I am your Triune God!"

⁸ You need simply watch; the punishment of the wicked you will see
⁹ You have the Lord for your refuge; you have made the Most High your stronghold
¹⁰ No evil shall befall you, no affliction come near your tent
¹¹ For God commands the angels to guard you in all your ways
¹² With their hands they shall support you let you strike your foot against a stone
¹³ You shall tread upon the asp and the viper, trample the lion and the dragon
¹⁴ whoever clings to me I will deliver; whoever knows my name I will set on high
¹⁵ All who call upon me I will answer, I will be with them in distress; I will deliver them and give them honor
¹⁶ With length of days I will satisfy them; and show them my saving power

Jesus said: "Do not treat my words lightly, my children, you can see for yourselves the chaos this world is in! Violence begets violence! But come to me, I will give you shelter, love and peace! I love you, my children. Thank you, my little one for remaining obedient to my call, I am with you."

January 21, 1999, Feast of St. Agnes

Jesus said: "My beloved daughter, thank you for coming to spend this time with me. Many times you have asked the question why I give messages regarding 'dire consequences.' My little one, it is always my desire that my children pray and discern all messages and teachings. They must always remember I am a God of mercy and of justice. You should know, as your loving Jesus of mercy, my children, through your prayers, you can bring mitigation, and that which comes through my justice is done in my time.

"As I have told you many times — your time is not my time!

"The ways of the world are not my ways and your understanding or perception of what will be or 'can' be are only that! The possibilities of your understanding or comprehension will come according to your willingness to prayer and acknowledging that all is done according to my Holy Will.

"You must always be prepared, for as I have spoken of to you many times, you know not the hour I come as a thief in the night!

"Today is the feast day of my beloved Agnes, whose trials and tribulations were tremendous, but in her desire to please me, she surrendered early in her life her will to my Holy Will. She suffered greatly for this, but was given much more in return! For her place here with me is eternal life, eternal peace and eternal joy incomprehensible. Ask for her intercession in prayer, that you will be willing to surrender your will to me as she did, and through her willingness to surrender, even in the time of her suffering, she had peace and love and strength! My peace, my love and my strength, which brought her forth into the presence of my glory — life everlasting.

"You must remember, my children, you are in this world, not of this world. You are not yet able to comprehend my truths if you are not willing to surrender and trust solely in me! Do not look ahead, for that time is not here! Do not look behind, for that time is past! Be with me now! Focus on me now! For I am the truth, the light and the way! I will be your strength if you only come to me! pray, surrender, sacrifice! Come to me in the holy Sacraments! Come to me in Eucharistic Adoration for your answers! I will give you all you need, but it is up to you!

"Open, my beloved one, to Amos, Chapter 9, verse 9."

⁹ **But I will not destroy the house of Jacob completely, says the Lord, for see I have given the command to sift the house of Israel among all the nations, as one sifts with a sieve, leaving no pebble fall to the ground.**

¹⁰ **By the sword shall all sinners among my people die, those who say, 'evil will not reach or overtake us.'**

¹¹ **On that day I will raise up the fallen hut of David. I will wall up its breaches, raise up its ruins and rebuild it as in the days of old.**

"My beloved children, focus on me! I am your answer to all that disturbs! The peace and love which I so willingly want to give you, why will you not accept?

"I am your Jesus of mercy! Shalom, my people; I love you, my little one.

"Thank you for remaining obedient to my call."

February 3, 1999, Eucharistic Adoration

Jesus said: "My beloved daughter, praise be to Jesus, for Jesus is Lord, Saviour, reconciler of all nations.

"I come to you, my children, as your Jesus of mercy, wanting to fill you with my grace. The grace of fortitude, which is my strength within you to go forward with me, through me, for me. Yes, my children, it is an uphill battle, this road I ask you to walk with me, and though this path is rocky and winding, I ask you to take my hand which has always been reaching out to you, but it is up to you to take my hand.

"So many times you think you are walking alone but I have never left you. Others of you think that you must walk this road alone. What you don't understand because of your human thinking, is unless you take my hand and walk with me, you will never reach the end of this road. It is a road walked with me, for me and through me! A spiritual journey which began with each of you at birth, yes, my children, for each of you are created in the image and likeness of your Triune God.

"You have questioned, then, why do so many not know of God? Because the world in its evil and pernicious ways through the error of sin beginning with Adam and Eve, turned away from the grace given them, turned away because of the error of sin. But God the Almighty Father gave the human race another chance, He gave His only begotten Son, to die on a cross. I, your Jesus crucified, died for each one of you, in order that you would have the gift of life eternal. But many refused this gift, and through the ages this continuous error of sin closes the minds to truths, thus closing the minds of their children and children's children to truth, therefore taking away the many gifts of graces your Triune God so willingly wants to give all His children.

"Open your hearts to me, my children! Do not take these gifts away from your children or your children's children! On the contrary seek these gifts, through me, for you and your children. Many times I have told you how! The Holy Sacraments, prayer, sacrifice, surrrender!

"Open, my beloved one, to Genesis, Chapter 4, Verse 6."

⁶ So the Lord said to Cain; "Why are you so resentful and crestfallen?

⁷ If you do well, you can hold up your head, but if not — sin is a demon lurking at the door, his urge is toward you, yet you can be his master"

"My beloved children, you see the evil all around you! Evil ways encompassing and ready to snare! I give you my hand to walk away with me! For me and through me! You only need to come to me! Surrender to me!

"Open, my beloved, to Genesis, Chapter 9, Verse 6."

⁶ If anyone sheds the blood of man, by man shall his blood be shed; For in the Image of God has man been made.

"Remember it is because of the love of the Father you are each created in the image and likeness of your Triune God! Walk with me, my children. I shall never leave you! I love you! That you, my children, and your children's children may receive the many gifts I want to give you! Open your heart to me! Follow me, I am the way, the light and the truth!

"Shalom, my people. I love you, my little one.

"Thank you for remaining obedient to my call."

Approved by Reverend Paul Caporali

February 13, 1999
Eucharistic Adoration

Jesus said: "My beloved little one, thank you for coming to spend this time with me. Praise be to Jesus for Jesus is Lord, Saviour, Redeemer, Reconciler of all nations.

"If my children could see the grace I shower upon them if they willingly, lovingly come to spend time with me, seeking me in all they do, putting their Triune God first in their life — this would not only change their lives, but bring graces upon all my children. As my son, my beloved priest spoke in his homily — when one sins, this sin is not personal, it affects all of my Mystical Body! Sin is error and this error causes more unrest and decay in this already erroneous, sinful world. But I am your Jesus of mercy, and when a child, as yourself, my beloved little one, comes to me in love, surrendering your will to my Holy Will, this brings much needed graces unto my children and it is these graces that bring conversion and change. But it is very few opening their hearts to these graces and so few willing to surrender to my Holy Will! So few, wanting to put me, your Jesus of mercy, first in their lives. They do not see with the eyes of their soul, but with the eyes of this materialistic world which blinds them to my truths, blinds them to their Triune God! This because of sin — the corruption of their souls! Sin, the corruption of their children's souls.

"As I have told you many times, my beloved little one — the focus of my children is not on me but on the materialistic values they set before them, a sad misconception of 'happiness' and they will find that this erroneous, sadistic world of materialism will be their downfall! It is a paganistic world that you, my children, have chosen — chosen over your Triune God, and you will be lost in this world of deception and evil! Sadly, as you lose your souls to the evil one, your examples will also show your children this pernicious path of evil. Is this what you have chosen for yourselves and your children or will you open your eyes, your hearts to me, your Triune God, before it is to late? Where will this free will of yours take you, my children? Life eternal? Or death to your soul for all eternity! Pray, surrender, sacrifice, the Holy Sacraments, life eternal!

"Open, my beloved one, to Leviticus, Chapter 27, Verse 21."

²¹ If then you become defiant in your unwillingness to obey me, I will multiply my blows another sevenfold, as your sins deserve.

²² I will unleash the wild beasts against you, to rob you of your children and wipe out your livestock, till your population dwindles away and your roads become deserted.

"I offer you my love, my children, to you and your children! To your children and your children's children! It is your choice to accept or deny!

"Shalom, my people. Thank you, my beloved one, for remaining obedient to my call."

"God the Father said: "My beloved daughter, will you open your heart to me to listen for the words I wish to give to My children, words from your Father Almighty? I created you, my children, will you not listen?

"My beloved Sons' words, why do they go to deaf ears? Do not let these words spoken by me go unheard, for they are not spoken lightly:

"You have created a den of evil; truth you no longer comprehend. You have created havoc and turmoil where you know not peace in your hearts but malice and paganistic values unknown even to Sodom and Gomorrah. You look around to the trees, the stars, the land and it is as if you have put blinders not only to your eyes, but to your mind as well! You know not what truth, peace, beauty and love is! Just as robots, you walk this earth clinging to the false promises of happiness by the one banished from everlasting joy, peace and happiness.

"I have given you the word made flesh, given unto death, so that you, my children, would have life eternal, after he who crawls on his belly brought sin into the world through humans searching to be greater than the Almighty. Yet in my love and mercy, I gave my only begotten Son to die on a cross, that original sin would be removed and once again eternal life with me, your option.

"Throughout history man has been given truth in the word and the word testifying to the supreme being, who created all and can destroy all! Yet throughout time, the snares of the evil one continues to encompass, entangle egotistic minds into believing there is no God, there is no hell, and there is no soul! As Satan led the fallen angels to the pits of hell, ask yourselves, where do your erroneous ways lead you?

"Open, my beloved one, to Genesis, Chapter 3, Verse 1."

¹ The Fall of Man - Now the serpent was the most cunning of all the Animals that the Lord God had made.

"Open your hearts, listen to the words, defiant ones! Are you so foolish as to not realize I created you and you will each stand before me?

¹ The serpent asked the woman, "Did God really tell you not to eat from any of the trees in the garden?"
² "We may eat of the fruit of the trees of the garden
³ It is only about the fruit of the tree of the middle of the garden that God said, 'You shall not eat or even touch it, lest you die.'"

"The woman and the serpent's snare, through its cunning ways, began its deception to my words!"

⁴ But the serpent said to the woman: "You certainly will not die!
⁵ No, God knows well that the moment you eat of it your eyes will be opened and you will be like gods who know what is good and what is bad."

"And throughout time man has seen he was created for only a certain amount of time, man will never conquer death to the body, But to live in my Holy Will gives life eternal to the soul! Why, then do you remain blinded to truth by the evil deceptions from the master deceiver of all truths? I, your Father, gave you truth undeniable, I gave my Son to die on a cross, that all could have life eternal. This is truth unchangeable!"

> ⁶ **The woman saw that the tree was good for food, pleasing to the eyes, and desirable for gaining wisdom. So she took some of its fruit and ate it; and she also gave some to her husband, who was with her and he ate it.**

"My children, the master of lies comes in many disguises in order to win over his prey! Do not follow the ways of the world! No, you must follow truth undeniable, He that gave His life for each one of you, in order that you may have life eternal!

"I, Yaweh, your Father Almighty, your Creator, await your decision! You will come before me! You will stand in judgment! You will have made the choice!

"Thank you, my daughter, for opening your heart and remaining obedient to my call."

Approved by Reverend Paul Caporali

February 17, 1999
Ash Wednesday at Eucharistic Adoration

Jesus said: "My beloved daughter, praise be to Jesus, for Jesus is Lord, Saviour, Redeemer, Reconciler of All Nations. Open your heart to me, my daughter, do not let all the distractions of this world sway you from your purpose of spending this time with me.

"Today, my children, I ask you to remember the cross; the cross which I carried for each of you; the cross which is your path to eternal glory. Are you willing, my children? Ask yourselves this! Are you willing to carry my cross? It will take not only sacrifice, but a willingness to surrender!

"Today is a beginning! For this is what the Lenten season is, a beginning! As I spent forty days and forty night in prayers, the beginning to the path of Calvary — my preparation! And this is what I offer you, a preparation to walk with me, the path of Calvary, carrying the cross you have each been given, in order to alleviate the cross I carry for each of you. But are you willing, my children? sacrifice, surrender; the Holy Sacraments, surrender; supplication, surrender. Each step you take to get closer to me there is surrender! And as you begin to get closer to me, surrendering totally and completely to me becomes a constant desire of relinquishing your will to mine. Focus on me, today my children, and you will begin this path of Calvary with me, for me, and through me, and you will have begun the preparation to the foot of the cross!

"Open, my beloved one, to Luke, Chapter 8, Verse 11."

[11] The Parable of the Sower Explained — This is the meaning of the parable. The seed is the word of God.

[12] Those on the path are the ones who have heard, but the devil comes and takes away the word from their hearts, that they may not believe and be saved.

[13] Those on rocky ground are the ones who, when they hear, receive the word with joy, but they have no root; they believe only for a time and fall away in time of trial.

[14] As for the seed that fell among thorns, they are the ones who have heard, but as they go along, they are choked by the anxieties and riches and pleasures of life, and they fail to produce mature fruit.

[15] But as for the seed that fell on rich soil, they are the ones who, when they have heard the word, embrace it with a generous and good heart, and bear fruit through perseverance."

Approved by Reverend Paul Caporali

February 20, 1999
Eucharistic Adoration Saturday
Franciscan Center Retreat House, Andover, Mass.

Praise be to Jesus, for Jesus is Lord, Saviour, Redeemer, Reconciler of all nations

Jesus said: "My beloved daughter, I bring peace and joy to my beloved children, who have come to spend this time with me, here on this holy ground. My children have gladdened my heart and lifted the sorrow given me, from the many who have turned away from me! Because of this love and supplication they have brought to me, here in Eucharistic Adoration, I have released from the pangs of purgatory, all their relatives, friends and aquaintances! They are here with me now, singing praises of joy and love to their Triune God.

"My beloved children, this act of my love and mercy, given to you, as my beloved son [priest] spoke of this morning, "A grace to erase," the sins, which my new saints, who have been brought to me, suffered for in the pangs of purgatory. I love you, my children. Thank you each for responding to my call.

"Open, my beloved one, to Psalm 23 & 24"

Psalm 23: The Lord, Shepherd and Host

1 A Psalm of David — The Lord is my shepherd there is nothing I lack.
2 In green pastures you let me graze: to safe waters you lead me.
3 You restore my strength. You guide me along the right path for the sake of your name.
4 Even when I walk through a dark valley, I fear no harm for you are at my side; your rod and staff give me courage.
5 You set a table before me as my enemies watch you anoint my head with oil; my cup overflows.
6 Only goodness and love will pursue me all the days of my life; I will dwell in the house of the Lord for years to come.

Psalm 24: The Glory of God in Procession to Zion

1 A Psalm of David - The earth is the Lord's and all it holds, the world and those who live there.
2 For God founded it on the seas, established it over the rivers.
3 Who may go up the mountain of the Lord? Who can stand in his holy place?
4 The clean of hand and pure of heart, who are not devoted to idols, who have not sworn falsely.
5 They will receive blessings from the Lord, and justice from their saving God.

⁶ Such are the people that love the Lord, that seek the face of the God of Jacob.

⁷ Lift up your heads, O gates; rise up, you ancient portals, that the king of glory may enter.

⁸ Who is this king of glory? The Lord, a mighty warrior, the Lord, mighty in battle.

⁹ Lift up your heads, O gates; rise up, you ancient portals, that the king of glory may enter.

¹⁰ Who is this King of Glory? The Lord of hosts is the King of Glory.

Approved by Reverend John C. Hughes, M.S.

February 21, 1999, Sunday
Eucharistic Adoration

Praise be to Jesus, for Jesus is Lord Savior, Redeemer, Reconciler of all nations.

Jesus said: "Thank you, my beloved daughter, for remaining obedient to my call. I know how difficult this trip was for you to make, but your willingness and obedience brought great happiness to my most wounded Sacred Heart.

"If my children would only realize that I am your Jesus of mercy, that I will never be outdone in my love and mercy. If they would only realize this, they would have true peace and true happiness. But this can only be given from me.

"My children, this world created by my Father to be a place of beauty, love, peace and joy, is far from what my Father had planned for his children. Why? Because of man's ingratitude and selfish ways.

"When Moses was given the tablets of God's laws, it was so that man could understand what was to be displeasing and forbidden, as when Adam and Eve were told not to eat of a certain tree in the Garden of Eden. But as with Eve, the children wouldn't obey, so they were punished and left to wander alone in the desert for forty years. And so it has been throughout time, man's disobedience to the laws of your Triune God and as my Father's words continue to deaf egotistical ears, again man will be shown through punishment, that my Father, the Creator Almighty, will not be disobeyed.

"Oh, my children you do not understand the consequences you can bring down upon yourselves and your children. But as I have promised, those of you, my children, who have remained obedient to the laws of your Triune God, who are so willingly and lovingly trying to live as God the Father has asked, need not fear, for you will be under the protection of your Triune God.

"Surrender is what I ask, my children. Are you willing?

"Open, my beloved, to 1 Corinthians, Ch 3."

¹⁰ According to the grace of God given to me, like a wise master builder, I laid a foundation and another is building upon it. But each one must be careful how he builds upon it.
¹¹ For no one can lay a foundation other than one that is there, namely, Jesus Christ.

1 Corinthians, Ch 10:

⁸ Let us not indulge in immorality as some of them did and twenty-three thousand fell within a single day.
⁹ Let us not test Christ as some of them did, and suffered death by serpents.
¹⁰ Do not grumble as some of them did, and suffered death by the destroyer.

1 John, Ch 3:

⁴ Everyone who commits sin commits lawlessness, for sin is lawlessness.

⁸ Whoever sins belongs to the devil, because the devil has sinned from the beginning, indeed the Son of God was revealed to destroy the works of the devil.

¹² Unlike Cain who belonged to the evil one and slaughtered his brother. Why did he slaughter him? Because his own works were evil, and those of his brother righteous.

²³ And his commandment is this; we should believe in the name of his Son, Jesus Christ, and love one another just as he commanded us.

²⁴ Those who keep his commandments remain in him and he in them, and the way we know that he remains in us is from the spirit the he gave us.

"Shalom, my people. Thank you, my little one, for remaining obedient to my call."

Approved by Reverend Paul Caporali

February 22, 1999
Divine Mercy Shrine
Monday

Praise be to Jesus, for Jesus is Lord! I am your Jesus of Mercy!

Jesus said: "Welcome, my beloved children, thank you for opening your hearts for my direction. Nothing, my children is a coincidence, follow my way, open your hearts, I have called you each by name. Oh, my precious children, how my love eminates forth from the rays of my mercy. You come to be here in this holy place, on this holy ground, out of your love for me you opened your hearts and were led here to my shrine — my holy ground. How you have pleased me — soothed my most Wounded Sacred Heart, by surrendering to my Holy Will. If my children would only listen to my words! Surrender! This is what I ask and this is why you have been called here, to be with me and soothe my Wounded Heart, to say the words "my Jesus I trust in you" — do you not realize, that had not my beloved Faustina opened her heart to my will, to my words, this holy place would not be here, this holy ground where my children can come to be here, with me. Do you see, my beloved little one, how in surrendering humbly, in opening your hearts to me, my children, how my graces are poured forth — the soothing balm of my love! So willingly I want to give you, my graces, my children. So many do not see how these graces of my love can flow, nor do they see what possibilities will come from these graces. Oh, my children I am your Jesus of mercy. Your Jesus who calls out to each of you, to refrain from the worldly enticements and errors of this world! To return to me who loves you with a pure love, which is not of this world. It is a love that can fill your entire being. A love that can never nor will ever be of this world! How do you receive this Love, my children — come to me, I will show you the way.

"Open, my beloved little one, to 1 John, Ch 5."

⁴ **For whoever is begotten by God conquers the world, and the victory that conquers the world is our faith .**

⁵ **Who (indeed) is the victor over the world but the one who believes that Jesus is the Son of God.**

⁶ **This is the one who came through water and blood, Jesus Christ, not by water alone, but by water and blood. The spirit is the one that testifies and the Spirit is Truth.**

⁷ **So there are three that testify.**

⁸ **The spirit, the water, and the Blood, and the three are of one accord.**

⁹ **If we accept human testimony, the testimony of God is surely greater. Now the testimony of God is this, that he has testified on behalf of his Son.**

¹⁰ **Whoever believes in the Son of God has this testimony within himself. Whoever does not believe, God has made him a liar by not believing the testimony God has given about his Son.**

¹¹ **And this is testimony: God gave us eternal life, and this life is in his Son.**

¹² **Whoever possesses the Son has life; whoever does not possess the Son of God does not have life.**

Jesus said: "My beloved children, do you not see that dying unto yourselves and receiving my life within you that you can have life Eternal. As you receive me alive, body, blood, soul and divinity you receive life. The evil one wants you to believe the Holy Eucharist is only bread and not my true Presence!"

2 John:

⁷ **Many deceivers have gone out into the world, those who do not acknowledge Jesus Christ as coming in the flesh; such is the deceitful one and the antichrist.**

Jesus said: "These times you are in, my children, where the true presence is denied, I come to give you manifestations of my love and mercy, as you, my children, witnessed in Eucharistic Adoration this past holy retreat weekend, and as you will begin to see, those of you who will open your hearts to my desire of inviting me to be with you on a spiritual journey retreat presentation with Eucharistic Adoration, will testify to these manifestations of my love! Open your hearts to my desires, my beloved children, that you may see the love and mercy of your Jesus of mercy!"

Third Letter of John

³ I rejoiced greatly when some of the brothers came and testified to how truly you walk in the truth.

⁴ Nothing gives me greater joy than to hear that my children are walking in the truth.

⁵ Beloved, you are faithful in all you do for the brothers, especially for strangers;

⁶ they have testified to your love before the church. Please help them in a way worthy of God to continue their journey.

⁷ "For they have set out for the sake of the Name and are accepting nothing from the pagans.

⁸ Therefore, we ought to support such persons, so that we may be co-workers in the truth.

Jesus said: "My beloved children, this my ministry of my teachings, is to go forth in this journey I wish you to share with me! But it is necessary for you to open your hearts! I will lead the way! As my gifts were given this past retreat, so shall they be given each time you invite my beloved little one to bring this retreat presentation to your area. For I wish that you will have the opportunity to spend this journey with me! That many may spend this journey with me! Are you willing, my beloved children, and if not, then ask yourselves what distracts you from spending this time with me!

"Open, beloved one, to Ephesians 6."

¹⁸ With prayer and supplication, pray at every opportunity in the spirit, to that end, be watchful with all perseverance and supplication for all the holy ones.

¹⁹ And also for me, that speech may be given me to open my mouth, to make known with boldness the mystery of the gospel,

²⁰ For which I am an ambassador in chains, so that I may have the courage to speak as I must.

Jesus said: "My children, read my teaching given on the retreat [February 20, 1999]. Do you not see the generosity of my heart, I will never be outdone, my love, my mercy, I so willingly want to give to you, but it is all up to you, for you have a free will!"

Ephesians 6

²¹ So that you also may have news of me and of what I am doing, Tychicus, my beloved brother and trustworthy minister in the Lord, will tell you everything:

²² I am sending him to you for this very purpose, so that you may know about us and that he may encourage your hearts.

²³ Peace be to the brothers, and love with faith, from God the Father and the Lord Jesus Christ.

²⁴ Grace be with all who love our Lord Jesus Christ in immortality.

Jesus said: I am your Jesus of mercy. Thank you, my beloved little one, for remaining obedient to my call.

Approved by Reverend Paul Caporali

February 26, 1999, Friday
Eucharistic Adoration

Praise be to Jesus for Jesus is Lord, Saviour, Redeemer

Jesus said: "I am your Jesus of mercy, my beloved children, coming to thank you; thanking you for the love in which you gathered in your prayer groups, a continous act of supplication for your fellowman, for the errors they are committing against my most wounded sacred heart. As you understood the words given to you, my beloved little one, from the story told, yes, my children have carried their fellowman on their backs, as the youngster carried his friend on his back, and when asked, wasn't the friend heavy, he answered, no sir, he's my brother! You, my children, have given of yourselves out of love for your brother — this dialog of love, between yourselves and your Triune God! For as your words of supplication were lifted for the errors of your brothers, graces as the stars in the heavens poured forth! Now it is up to each child to open their hearts to receive these graces! Listen with your heart, my daughter. Prayer is victory and Eucharistic adoration is the epitome of all prayers and all love! So, my beloved children, you who have offered to me the epitome of all love through your act of love, have opened the gates of my love and mercy! Graces unmeasureable upon you and your families! For my love is never outdone! This is what I desire of my children, that they be the instruments of my love, true examples of my love, servants of my love! Vessels propagating my love! In this way my children, man's hearts of stone will be opened! Thank you each, for responding to my call!

"Now open, my beloved one, to 1 Timothy, Ch 1."

12 I am grateful to Him who has strengthened me, Christ Jesus Our Lord, because he considered me trustworthy in appointing me to the ministry.

13 I was once a blasphemer and a persecutor and an arrogant man, but I have been mercifully treated because I acted out of ignorance in my unbelief.

14 Indeed, the grace of Our Lord has been abundant, along with the faith and love that are in Christ Jesus.

15 This saying is trustworthy and deserves full acceptance: Christ Jesus came into the world to save sinners. Of these I am the foremost.

16 But for that reason I was mercifully treated, so that in me, as the foremost, Christ Jesus might display all his patience as an example for those who would come to believe in him for everlasting life.

17 To the King of Ages, incorruptable, invisible, the only God, Honor and Glory forever and ever. Amen.

1 Timothy Ch 2

¹ First of all, then, I ask that supplications, prayers, petitions, and thanksgivings be offered for everyone;
² For Kings and for all in authority, that we may lead a quiet and tranquil life in all devotion and diginity.
³ This is good and pleasing to God Our Savior;
⁴ Who wills everyone to be saved and to come to knowledge of the truth.
⁵ For there is one God. There is also one mediator between God and the human race, Christ Jesus, himself human,
⁶ Who gave himself as ransom for all.

"Peace to you, my beloved children. Shalom, my people. Thank you, my beloved daughter for remaining obedient to my call."

Approved by Reverend Paul Caporali

March 4, 1999, Thursday
Eucharsitic Adoration

Praise be to Jesus, for Jesus is Lord, Saviour, Redeemer, Reconcilar of All Nations

Jesus said: "My beloved little one, I come, your Jesus of mercy, to open the hearts of my children, to release the world from the bondage of sin and error which this world is plagued with. Eucharistic Adoration opens the gates of my mercy upon the world! Why child, because children will realize my true presence, body, blood, soul and divinity! Truth undeniable! The flames of my mercy, my justice, in the hearts of mankind, given to open the hardened of hearts! All through witnessing my true presence! Realizing I come to each person, alive, body, blood, soul and divinity, the Sacrament of the Holy Eucharist.

"Never before in the history of mankind, has the diaboloical forces been as apparent as now in these times. Never before in the history of mankind has man's opposition to his Triune God, been so merciless and ostentatious, denying the existence of God, denying my true presence in the Holy Sacrament of the Eucharist. As I have said before, man lives the existence of robots, seeking only to live for materialism, in materialism and with materialism. This, my beloved one, is why the Father Almighty has allowed this gift to mankind, in these present times, the manifestations of my love. Opening the hearts of many through the realization of my true presence in the Holy Sacrament of the Eucharist.

"Man has always sought signs, manifestations, in order to believe! Signs and manifestations are given because of a surrender of love, surrendering of the will to your Triune God; seeking not only to believe, but seeking to love and surrender to your Triune God. In your willingness to surrender to my Holy Will, my beloved little one, as you take my teachings, where you are invited, this is what I desire; open with the holy sacrifice of the Mass, Benediction, and then the teachings. Children's hearts will be opened; manifestations of my love will be given; truth undeniable, shown in the flames of my love, will be placed in the hearts of the hardened and testimony upon testimony will fill this land, so that in this hour of conquest, all who surrender will see and know that evil will never triumph. I am your Jesus of mercy.

"Open, my beloved one, to Tobit, Ch 13."

1. **Blessed be God who lives forever, because his kingdom lasts for all ages.**
2. **For he scourges and then has mercy; he casts down to the depths of the nether world and he brings up from the great abyss. No one can escape his hand.**

6. **When you turn back to him with all your heart, to do what is right before him, then he will turn back to you, and no longer hide his face from you.**

10. **Praise the Lord for his goodness, and goodness of the king of the ages, so that his tent maybe built in you with joy.**
11. **A bright light will shine to all parts of the earth; Many nations shall come to you from afar.**

Jesus said: "I am the light, the life of the world, my children, open our hearts that my eternal flame will burn within the hearts of all mankind. Shalom, my people. I love you, my little one, thank you for remaining obedient to my call."

Approved by Rev. Paul Caporali

March 11, 1999

Jesus said: "Peace, my beloved children, during this holy Lenten season. I welcome you each as you make this daily journey with Me. I understand the reluctance to carry the cross, my children, for you must remember, I also came as man, that I may remain obedient to the holy Will of the Father. And in essence, this is my desire of you, that you each take your cross according to my Holy will, knowing that as you remain in total surrender and humility before Me, your Jesus of mercy; surrendering your will to my Holy Will, as I surrendered mine to God the Father Almighty and carried the cross down the Via Dolorosa in total surrender.

"As Simon was chosen to help carry my cross, so I have been chosen to help you carry each of your crosses. Abandonment to my holy Will lessens the weight of your crosses, for you see, my children, I have never left you alone nor do I ever leave you alone, unless you close your hearts to my truths, then this is done through your own free will.

"Do not close your hearts and minds to me! Do not shut me out, for I love you each, and I know you each by name, for I carry you in the palm of my crucified hand!

"During this Lenten season, do not worry your minds with what is to be! Many times I have told you, that time is not here! Do not look behind you, for that time is gone! But focus on me, on your journey with me! Through me and for me!

"Dwell in me, my children, not in materialism and in proving or un-proving the messengers or messages! How many times, I have told you, if you do not pray and discern the messages, you will be led astray, contemplating your future instead of contemplating your journey with me, through me, for me!

"I give you the manifestations of my love, but how many of you are willing to open your hearts to my desires?

"Remember, my children, your time is not my time! Your comprehension of my words, is only that, for only the Father knows the hour!

"Shalom, my people. Thank you, my beloved little one, for remaining obedient to my call.

"Open, my beloved one, to Tobit, Chapter 14, Verse 4."

⁴ and flee into Medea, for I believe God's Word, which was spoken by Nabum against Nineveh. It shall all happen, and shall overtake Assyria and Nineveh, indeed, whatever was said by Israel's prophets, whom God commissioned, shall occur. Not one of all the oracles shall remain unfulfilled, but everything shall take place in the time appointed for it.

Daniel 2, Chapter 2, Verse 2:

² So he ordered that the magicians, enchanters sorcerers and Chaldeans be summoned to interpret the dream for him. When they came and presented themselves to the King

³ He said to them, "I had a dream which will allow my spirit no rest until I know what it means."

¹⁰ The Chaldeans answered the king. "There is not a man on earth who can do what you ask, O king; never has any king, however great and mighty, asked such a thing of any magician, enchanter, or Chaldean.

¹¹ What you demand, O king, is too difficult there is no one who can tell it to the king except the gods who do not dwell among men."

²⁷ In the king's presence Daniel made this reply. "The Mystery about which the king has inquired of the wise men, enchanters, magicians and astrologers, could not explain to the king.

²⁸ But there is a God in heaven who reveals mysteries, and he has shown King Nebuchadnezzar what is to happen in days to come."

1 Corinthians, Chapter 2, Verse 5:

⁵ So that your faith might rest not on human wisdom but on the power of God.

7 **Rather we speak God's wisdom, mysterious, hidden, which God predetermined before the ages for our glory**

8 **and which none of the rulers of this age knew, for if they had known it, they would not have crucified the Lord of Glory.**

9 **But as it is written, "What eye has not seen, and ear has not heard, and what has not entered the human heart, what God has prepared for those who love him."**

13 **And we speak about them not with words taught by human wisdom, but with words taught by the Spirit, describing spiritual realities in spiritual terms.**

Approved by Reverend Paul Caporali

March 29, 1999

Jesus said: "I come to you, my beloved, these final days of this holy week. Ask yourselves, my children, have you walked these holy days in reparation and preparation for the walk down the Via Dolorosa with me? Or have you been occupied with what is happening in your world today? Then ask yourselves, my children, how can you change what is happening in this egotistical, self-decaying world of error and destruction!

"Would it not be for the few of you who have opened your hearts to my truths, in surrender, this world of yours would have cast itself into total destruction!

"Had it not been but for the merciful love of the Father, the shedding of many tears by my Holy Mother, your loving guardian, the merciless, venomous manipulations of the evil one would have led you into oblivion! And the amount of souls lost, incomprehensible! This ploy of the evil one, to take as many souls with him to the pits of Gehenna, has been told to you many times over. Yet the mercy of the Father begets the venomous attacks of the conspirator of death to souls.

"Oh, my beloved children how many times I have repeated to you over and over how it took only one person to separate the church! It can take but one to rebuild the hearts of many, to set example before the others, that of surrender, prayer, sacrifice and love! Would it not be that for the love and mercy of the Almighty Father, man's desecration and corruption to truth would have brought the wrath of destruction upon this world! See the mercy of the Father, the sacrifice of your Jesus crucified, the redemptive love of the Holy Spirit!

"Open, my beloved, to Psalm 93, Verse 1."

1 **The Lord is King robed with majesty, the Lord is robed, girded with might, the world will surely stand in place, never to be moved.**

2 **Your throne stands firm from of old, you are from everlasting, Lord.**

3 **The flood has raised up, Lord; the flood has raised up its roar; the flood has raised its pounding waves.**

4 **More powerful than the roar of many waters, more powerful than the breakers of the sea, powerful in the heaven is the Lord.**

5 **Your decrees are firmly established, holiness belongs to your house, Lord, for all the length of days.**

"My people, Satan reigns only with one which is manipulated by evil. He is allowed, my children, remember the word, 'allowed,' to roam the earth, he has no power over man, only that which is released to him. So why do you focus on what may happen, what does this gain you?

"Why do you focus on where you will go for protection, when I have shown you the way?

"Why do you needlessly worry over the fears of catastrophes when I have shown you my mercy?

"You have the power of choice, for you have a free will! Focus not on what is to be or where you are to go, but focus on me, and you will have my peace, my love, my mercy.

"I have never left you, my children; I am not anxiety, I am peace, the peace this world does not know!

"Follow me, my children, I am the way!

"Shalom, my people, I love you.

"Thank you, my beloved little one, for remaining obedient to my call."

Approved by Reverend Paul Caporali

April 1, 1999

Jesus said: "My beloved little one, praise be to Jesus, for Jesus is Lord, Saviour, Reconciler of All Nations — open your hearts to me, my children, I will give you rest.

"Rest from the anxiousness and worries of this world. Come to the shelter of my most wounded sacred heart, for I am your Jesus of mercy.

"As we walk the path of the Via Dolorosa, look to the faces on the side of the road, the contempt, anger and hate in their eyes, not understanding or realizing truth — that I am the Son of the Father Almighty! So ready and willing to crucify this man they see, who claims to be the Son of God!

"When you, my children, encounter a homeless person, one who has nothing but the clothes on his back, dirty, and sweaty, with no place to go, do you offer a loving glance, a kind word, or do you turn your face as those that mocked and turned away from me? Ask yourselves, my children, what if this man in the streets, a homeless beggar, were you ? Remember children, it is only by the grace of your Triune God that it is not you walking in their place!

"Oh, my children, in this world, plagued with disaster upon disaster, wars in many of your countries, when killing and violence is the only thing these children see, do you still not realize how your prayers, sacrifices, Holy Sacraments and your love is needed? When will you open your eyes? What will open your eyes?

"I your, Jesus of mercy, love you each, with an unconditional love! Do you love your fellow man unconditionally? Never judge anyone, my children, this is not your right, but pray for your fellow man, my children!

"Open, my beloved daughter, to Matthew, Chapter 13, Verse 18."

[18] Hear this the parable of the sower:

[19] The seed sown on the path is the one who hears the word of the kingdom without understanding it, and the evil one comes and steals away what was sown in his heart.

[20] The seed sown on rocky ground is the one who hears the word and receives it at once with joy,

²¹ **But he has not root and lasts only for a time. When some tribulation or persecution comes because of the word, he immediately falls away.**

²² **The seed sown among thorns is the one who hears the word, but then worldly anxiety and the lure of riches chokes the word and it bears no fruit.**

²³ **But the seed sown on rich soil is the one who hears the word and understands it, who indeed bears and yields a hundred, or sixty or thirty-fold.**

"Shalom, my people. I love you, my children.

"Thank you for remaining obedient to my call, my little one."

Approved by Reverend Paul Caporali

April 15, 1999

Jesus said: "I, your Jesus of mercy, say this to you:

"Beloved children of My most wounded, sacred heart, how you appease my wounded heart when, in these days of turmoil in the world, the world rejects me. Yet you, most willing, beloved ones of my heart, soothe my heart when you dedicate yourselves to me through prayer!

"Many confirmations have been given to you, showing you how this my ministry is led by me, with me, and through me. This little one, precious of my Heart, has opened her heart for my directives, which will guide you in this most important work, caring for the beloved ones of my Heart — my precious sons, my priests, and in doing so, carry forth his holy work in the focus of me, your Jesus of mercy, the one you come to love and honor in Eucharistic Adoration!

"You will see this ministry flourish as no other, as my Father also directs this what is so close to His Heart! This land in Nevada shall have built on it a retirement home for my priests. It will have a House of Prayer retreat center. It will have in front of the mountain my temple, my house built that my children will come to honor me there. This land will always be protected by my great angelic choirs of the north, the south, the west and the east. You will place a residence for my third order passionists, which will care for my priests and offer themselves to me for my work, through prayer, penance and sacrifice! my children will gather here on this holy land where many will bring homage to me. You will see great signs attesting to my presence and that of my holy Mother's presence on this holy land!

"My beloved children, know that always you must remain obedient to the holy Magisterium of my church! Then, and only then, do you do honor to my holy will! All who are with me, shall know me! Those who come against me in this holy work shall be stripped of all, that they will know they have not only offended me, but the Father Almighty. Pray, my beloved children! Remain always in my presence and you will always know my security, my love and my mercy!

"Now, my beloved little one, open to Job, Chapters 38, 39, 40 and 42.

THE LORD'S SPEECH
CHAPTER 38

¹ **Then the Lord addressed Job out of the storm and said:**

² **Who is this that obscures divine plans with words of ignorance?**

³ **Gird up your loins now, like a man; I will question you, and you tell me the answers!**

⁴ **Where were you when I founded the earth? Tell me, if you have understanding.**

⁵ **Who determined its size; do you know? Who stretched out the measuring line for it?**

⁶ **Into what were its pedestals sunk, and who laid the cornerstone,**

⁷ **while the morning stars sang in chorus and all the sons of God shouted for joy?**

⁸ **And who shut within doors the sea, when it burst forth from the womb,**

⁹ **when I made the clouds its garment and thick darkness its swaddling bands?**

¹⁰ **When I set limits for it and fastened the bar of its door?**

¹¹ **And said: Thus far shall you come but no farther, and here shall your proud waves be stilled!**

¹² Have you ever in your lifetime commanded the morning and shown the dawn its place

¹³ for taking hold of the ends of the earth, till the wicked are shaken from its surface?

¹⁴ The earth is changed as is clay by the seal, and dyed as though it were a garment;

¹⁵ But from the wicked the light is withheld, and the arm of pride is shattered.

¹⁶ Have you entered into the sources of the sea, or walked about in the depths of the abyss?

¹⁷ Have the gates of death been shown to you, or have you seen the gates of darkness?

¹⁸ Have you comprehended the breadth of the earth? Tell me, if you know all:

¹⁹ Which is the way to the dwelling place of light, and where is the abode of darkness,

²⁰ that you may take them to their boundaries and set them on their homeward paths?

²¹ You know, because you were born before them, and the number of your years is great!

²² Have you entered the storehouse of the snow, and seen the treasury of the hail

²³ which I have reserved for times of stress, for the days of war and of battle?

²⁴ Which way to the parting of the winds, whence the east wind spreads over the earth?

²⁵ Who has laid out a channel for the downpour and for the thunderstorm a path

²⁶ to bring rain to no man's land, the unpeopled wilderness;

²⁷ to enrich the waste and desolate ground till the desert blooms with verdure?

²⁸ Has the rain a father; or who has begotten the drops of dew?

²⁹ Out of whose womb comes the ice, and who gives the hoarfrost its birth in the skies,

³⁰ when the waters lie covered as though with stone that holds captive the surface of the deep?

³¹ Have you fitted a curb to the Pleiades, or loosened the bonds of Orion?

³² Can you bring forth the Mazzaroth in their season, or guide the Bear with its train?

³³ Do you know the ordinances of the heavens; can you put into effect their plan on the earth?

³⁴ Can you raise your voice among the clouds, or veil yourself in the waters of the storm?

³⁵ Can you send forth the lightnings on their way, or will they say to you, "Here we are"?

³⁷ Who counts the clouds in his wisdom? Or who tilts the water jars of heaven

³⁸ so that the dust of earth is fused into a mass and its clods made solid?

³⁹ Do you hunt the prey for the lioness or appease the hunger of her cubs,

⁴⁰ while they crouch in their dens, or lie in wait in the thicket?

³⁶ Who puts wisdom in the heart, and gives the cock its understanding?

⁴¹ Who provides nourishment for the ravens when their young ones cry out to God, and they rove abroad without food?

CHAPTER 39

¹ Do you know about the birth of the mountain goats, watch for the birth pangs of the hinds,

² number the months that they must fulfill, and fix the time of their bringing forth?

³ They crouch down and bear their young; they deliver their progeny in the desert.

⁴ When their offspring thrive and grow, they leave and do not return.

⁵ Who has given the wild ass his freedom, and who has loosed him from bonds?

⁶ I have made the wilderness his home and the salt flats his dwelling.

⁷ He scoffs at the uproar of the city, and hears no shouts of a driver.

⁸ He ranges the mountains for pasture, and seeks out every patch of green.

9 Will the wild ox consent to serve you, and to pass the nights by your manger?

10 Will a rope bind him in the furrow, and will he harrow the valleys after you?

11 Will you trust him for his great strength and leave to him the fruits of your toil?

12 Can you rely on him to thresh out your grain and gather in the yield of your threshing floor?

13 The wings of the ostrich beat idly; her plumage is lacking in pinions.

14 When she leaves her eggs on the ground and deposits them in the sand,

15 Unmindful that a foot may crush them, that the wild beasts may trample them,

16 she cruelly disowns her young and ruthlessly makes nought of her brood;

17 For God has withheld wisdom from her and has given her no share in understanding.

18 Yet in her swiftness of foot she makes sport of the horse and his rider.

19 Do you give the horse his strength, and endow his neck with splendor?

20 Do you make the steed to quiver while his thunderous snorting spreads terror?

21 He jubilantly paws the plain and rushes in his might against the weapons.

22 He laughs at fear and cannot be deterred; he turns not back from the sword.

23 Around him rattles the quiver, flashes the spear and the javelin.

24 Frenzied and trembling he devours the ground; he holds not back at the sound of the trumpet,

25 but at each blast he cries, "Aha!" Even from afar he scents the battle, the roar of the chiefs and the shouting.

26 Is it by your discernment that the hawk soars, that he spreads his wings toward the south?

27 Does the eagle fly up at your command to build his nest aloft?

²⁸ On the cliff he dwells and spends the night, on the spur of the cliff or the fortress.

²⁹ From thence he watches for his prey; his eyes behold it afar off.

³⁰ His young ones greedily drink blood; where the slain are, there is he.

CHAPTER 40

¹ The Lord then said to Job:

² Will we have arguing with the Almighty by the critic? Let him who would correct God give answer!

³ Then Job answered the Lord and said:

⁴ Behold, I am of little account; what can I answer you? I put My hand over My mouth.

⁵ Though I have spoken once, I will not do so again; though twice, I will do so no more.

⁶ Then the Lord addressed Job out of the storm and said:

⁷ Gird up your loins now, like a man. I will question you, and you tell me the answers!

⁸ Would you refuse to acknowledge My right? Would you condemn me that you may be justified?

⁹ Have you an arm like that of God, or can you thunder with a voice like his?

¹⁰ Adorn yourself with grandeur and majesty, and array yourself with glory and splendor?

¹¹ Let loose the fury of your wrath,

¹² tear down the wicked and shatter them? Bring down the haughty with a glance,

¹³ bury them in the dust together; in the hidden world imprison them?

¹⁴ Then will I, too, acknowledge that your own right hand can save you.

¹⁵ See, besides you I made Behemoth, that feeds on grass like an ox.

¹⁶ Behold the strength in his loins, and his vigor in the sinews of his belly.

¹⁷ He carries his tail like a cedar; the sinews of his thighs are like cables.

¹⁸ His bones are like tubes of bronze; his frame is like iron rods.

¹⁹ He came at the beginning of God's ways, and was made the taskmaster of his fellows;

²⁰ For the produce of the mountains is brought to him, and of all wild animals he makes sport.

²¹ Under the lotus trees he lies, in coverts of the reedy swamp.

²² The lotus trees cover him with their shade; all about him are the poplars on the bank.

²³ If the river grows violent, he is not disturbed; he is tranquil though the torrent surges about his mouth.

²⁴ Who can capture him by his eyes, or pierce his nose with a trap?

²⁵ Can you lead about Leviathan with a hook, or curb his tongue with a bit?

²⁶ Can you put a rope into his nose, or pierce through his cheek with a gaff?

²⁷ Will he then plead with you, time after time, or address you with tender words?

²⁸ Will he make an agreement with you that you may have him as a slave forever?

²⁹ Can you play with him, as with a bird? Can you put him in leash for your maidens?

³⁰ Will the traders bargain for him? Will the merchants divide him up?

³¹ Can you fill his hide with barbs, or his head with fish spears?

³² Once you but lay a hand upon him, no need to recall any other conflict!

CHAPTER 42

¹ Then Job answered the Lord and said:

² I know that you can do all things, and that no purpose of yours can be hindered.

³ I have dealt with great things that I do not understand; things too wonderful for me, which I cannot know.

⁵ I had heard of you by word of mouth, but now My eye has seen you.

⁶ **Therefore I disown what I have said, and repent in dust and ashes."**

Approved by Reverend Jose Vettiyankal

May 12, 1999, Wednesday
Garabandal, Spain

Praise be to Jesus for Jesus is Lord, Redeemer, All Merciful.
Jesus said: "My child, innocent of my heart, open your heart to my words. You have been brought to this holy ground that you may surrender totally and completely to me. Your will unto mine! How, My daughter, by faith — I am your Jesus of mercy, teacher, consoler, holy redeemer and protector of the faithful!

"Come to me, my children, surrendering your will completely and totally to me! Reaffirming your love to me, renouncing the ways of the world. Remembering each one of you were created in the image and likeness of the Almighty and are not of this world! Do not extinguish the flame of my love within your heart by allowing yourselves to continue in the worldly ways. No, my beloved children of my heart, focus only on me and I shall renew in your hearts a love and strength which is not of this world. Become as Little children, denying yourselves the worldly existence and trusting only in me! Through me and for me!

"As you come before me in total surrender, I will shelter you in my heart, protecting you as a father protects his children! And you will know it is my armor, my strength, my love, my mercy encompassing each one of you!

"I am your Jesus of mercy, teacher, consoler, holy redeemer and protector of the faithful! I have given you my weapons, my children, the Holy Sacraments, sacrifice, prayer! Come before me, in Eucharistic Adoration, where I await you, alive, body, blood, soul and divinity! I await you, my children, I love you, my children! Thank you, daughter, for remaining obedient to my call.

"Open to Exodus 15:"

¹¹ **Who is like to you among the Gods, O Lord? Who is like to you, magnificent in holiness? O terrible in renown, worker of workers**

¹² When you stretched out your right hand, the earth swallowed them!

¹³ In your mercy you led the people you redeemed, in your strength, you guided them to your holy dwelling.

June 1, 1999, Tuesday
Feast of St. Justin, St. Thomas Aquinas
Reno, Nevada

Praise be to Jesus for Jesus is Lord, Saviour, Redeemer, Reconciler of all nations

Jesus said: "Open your heart, daughter of my heart, that these words reach those of deaf ears. For you, my children, have continued with deaf ears! Clinging to the manipulations of the evil one, through the materialistic values set before you as your gods! The First Commandment of the Almighty — do not put strange gods before you for there is only one God, the one who created the world, created man! In my mercy, my justice, I have withheld my hand of justice! Open your hearts to my words! A chance to return to your Triune God! But as you have been told many times, you have a free will which will never be taken away from you!

"You question the laws of the church, continuously making accusations, becoming disobedient to the Holy Magisterium of the church! You question the holiness of the clergy, yet you Sanhedrins disobedient with your judgements! By whose authority do you have the right to judge? Only your Triune God has full authority of judgement, for you were created only in the image and likeness of the Almighty, you were not created to become your own gods!

"How many times, I have spoken of obedience, through prayer, sacrifice, the Holy Sacraments and instead you allow the decay of the evil one to set foot in lamb's clothing, the manipulation, confusion and disobedience to my truths! You speak of Canon Law, misrepresentation according to your dictates, and wants of understanding, to your judgements! My church is still the holy Magisterium and has my true Pope, its leader, and you now have opened the doors of confusion through your own misguided, misrepresentation of my truths! When I stood before the Sanhedrians, and they called for my crucifixion, in total obedience to the Almighty, I laid down my life for each one of you! My church was not yet headed by the apostles, and on the evening of Holy Thursday, when I spoke to each the words, "This bread is my body, this wine my blood," the first holy sacrifice of the Mass, as priest, prophet, messiah I lead my church on earth, making Peter it's head, "On this rock I shall build my church," the cornerstone of truth, obedience, holy apostolic! You now dare to infiltrate your judgements upon my church! Beware that your righteousness does not become your downfall!

"Where does trust in the Lord, rationalize this your behavior? Pray, discern, sacrifice, obedience, trustful surrender are the teachings I leave you with, my children!

"Open, daughter, to Judges, Ch 2:"

¹³ Because they had thus abandoned him and served Baal and the Ashtaroth.
¹⁴ The anger of the Lord flared up against Israel, and he delivered them over to plunderers who despoiled them. He allowed them to fall into the power of their enemies round about whom they were no longer able to withstand.
¹⁵ Whatever they undertook, the Lord turned into disasters for them, as in his warning he had sworn he would do till they were in great distress.
¹⁶ Even when the Lord raised up judges to deliver them from the power of their despoilers.
¹⁷ They did not listen to their judges, but abandoned themselves to the worship of other gods. They were quick to stray from the way their fathers had taken, and did not follow their example of obedience to the commandments of the Lord.

Approved by Rev. Fr. Paul Caporali
and Rev. Fr. Jose Vettiyankal

June 9, 1999, Wednesday

Praise be to Jesus for Jesus is Lord, Redeemer, Reconciler of All Nations.

Jesus said: "Thank you for opening your heart , my little one, for many have been called but refuse the mercy of my Love! The gifts which I your Jesus of mercy wish to bestow to all of my children.

"Have I not shown you my mercy, my children, in the many manifestations of my love, given to all that through opening your hearts, surrendering to my Holy Will, you will not lose your souls to the evil one.

"Here where all mercy, love and truth flow from my most wounded Sacred Heart, is your shelter, your protection! Freely given, but it is up to each one of you. Now is the time for you to realize that my mercy, my love is unconditional! Given to all! You only need to open your hearts to me! Surrender to me, your love in return. Why is this so difficult for you, my children?

"Listen, my children, to the following promise I make each of you! Do not close your hearts. For many this will be the last of your chances to renounce the path you are following, for your hearts are becoming hardened from the worldly enticements you continue to wallow in, which deprive and corrupt, which will only take you to the eternal fires of Gehenna engulfing you into the deepest crevices of the pits of everlasting flames which you yourselves have released yourselves to! No, my children, return to me, your Jesus of mercy, who comes before you, beckoning the bride to the bridegroom. Realize this may be your only and last chance for salvation. My children, I have spoken to you of asking the intercession of my great warrior, protector of the faith, St. Michael. Call out in prayer, for his intercession is mighty! I have made this promise to each of you who make this pilgrimage to the Shrine of St. Michael, asking his intercession especially in these corrupt times, a special grace of protection will be placed around your children who are losing their souls are on this road to perdition through violence, drugs, sexual misconduct! There are many of your youth out in this world, runaways!

"For each of you who will make this pilgrimage that I have requested to the Shrine of St. Michael, 7 x 777 of these children souls will be saved, that is for each one of you, my children, making this pilgrimage, not just your children, my beloved one, but many others' children!

"Open, my little one, to Exodus, 17:"

¹ From the desert of Sin the whole Israelite community journeyed by stages, as the Lord directed, and encamped at Rephidim. Here there was no water for the people to drink.

² They quarreled, therefore, with Moses and said, "Give us water to drink." Moses replied, "Why do you quarrel with me? Why do you put the Lord to a test?"

³ Here, then, in their thirst for water, the people grumbled against Moses saying, "Why did you ever make us leave Egypt? Was it just to have us die here of thirst with our children and our livestock?"

⁴ So Moses cried out to the Lord, "What shall I do with these people? A little more and they will stone me!"

⁵ The Lord answered Moses, "Go over there in front of the people, along with some of the elders of Israel, holding in your hand, as you go, the staff with which you struck the river.

⁶ I will be standing there in front of you on the rock in Horeb. Strike the rock, and the water will flow from it for the people to drink." This Moses did, in the presence of the elders of Israel.

⁷ The place was called Massah and Meribah, because the Israelites quarreled there and tested the Lord saying, "Is the Lord in our midst or not?"

Approved by Reverend Jose Vettiyankal

June 27, 1999
Eucharistic Adoration
Saturday, St. Francis Roman Catholic Church, Riverside, CA

Praise be to Jesus for Jesus is Lord, Saviour, Redeemer, Reconciler of all nations.

Jesus said: "My beloved children, how you soothe my most wounded Sacred Heart by coming to spend this time here with me in this my little Chapel of Peace. I thank you, my beloved children and I welcome you each time you take this special time out of the busy-ness of the world, take this time in order to refresh your spiritual life with me, for me and through me, for in this world of

confusion where so many of my children do not realize the importance of coming to spend time with me, they remain complacent and
continue to live in the world, with the worldly desires, materialistic
values their gods! A world of darkness which they have allowed
themselves to remain in! Whereas you, my beloved ones, have
chosen the better part, redemption for your souls through coming to
spend time with me!

"You see, my children, the conditions of this world, the direction the children are taking in this world, confusion, chaos, immorality, killing, vengeance, sexual misconduct, drugs, the tools of the
evil one, the examples of the adults! What chance do the youth have,
this is "normal" daily living! How can the youth not lose their souls
to the evil one?

"Man's egotistical and corruptible desires have created a world
of darkness, not only within themselves but around themselves!
They know not truth, nor love, nor mercy for one another and this
is the example they have set for the youth! Look at what you
yourselves have created, my children! A world without peace,
without love, without mercy, blinded to truth, and the price you have
paid with not only your souls but with the souls of your children for
all eternity! When will you open your eyes, my children? When will
you open your hearts, your minds? You have a free will and look
where this free will has gotten you!

"Open, my little one, to 1 Corinthians, Ch 5:"

6 **Your boasting is not appropriate. Do you not know that a
little yeast leavens all the dough**
7 **Clear out the old yeast, so that you may become a fresh
batch of dough, inasmuch as you are unleavened. For our
Paschal Lamb, Christ has been sacrificed.**
8 **Therefore let us celebrate the feast, not with the old yeast,
the yeast of malice and wickedness, but with the unleavened
bread of sincerity and truth.**

Jesus said: "I love you my children. Thank you, my little one,
for remaining obedient to my call."

Approved by Reverend Jose Vettiyankal

Sunday, July 25, 1999
Eucharistic Adoration

Praise be to Jesus! For Jesus is Saviour, Redeemer, and Reconciler of all nations.

Jesus said: "Thank you, my beloved little one, for coming with your son to spend this time with me. If more parents would take this time bringing their children to me in Eucharistic Adoration, teaching their children of their Triune God, through example, the chaos this world is in would not be. I have pleaded over and over with my children to set the example of prayer to their children. This is where change would come, where so many souls would not be lost. But my words go to deaf ears. The youth of this world continue in the error of perdition. The youth no longer seek peace for they do not know what true peace is. They continue to lavish in the immoral decay of this generation's conception, of seeking to please themselves, making their own rules through the pleasures, enticements of this world that Satan fills this world with. Enticements which decay the souls into complacency of a dark and corrupt world and the parents, the "adults" wonder why this world is in such decay and corruption. Look at the examples being shown, violence, sexuality, drugs. How many times I have begged my children to return to prayer, the Sacraments. How many times the tears of my Mother shed for all of our children. How many have listened? How many have complied with our pleadings? When I asked my children to open their hearts for the pilgrimages to the Shrine of St. Michael, I had promised 7 x 777 souls of the youth would be saved. One child responded. All the others questioned why such a message be given and yet they don't give a second thought, the enticements of the world.

"Oh, my children, where is your faith and trust in your Jesus of mercy. Am I not a God of mercy? Am I not a God of love? Question yourselves why it is so incomprehensible that I would not offer more than what the worldly enticements offered by the deceiver, master of lies, offers. See how the evil one manipulates, closes your minds to my truths? Seek not to undermine my truths, but seek to trust in my truths and to surrender to me your Triune God.

"Open My beloved one to James, Ch 1."

¹⁶ Do not be deceived, My beloved brothers.
¹⁷ All good giving and every perfect gift is from above, coming down from the Father of Lights, with whom there is no alteration or shadow caused by change.
¹⁸ He willed to give us birth by the Words of Truth, that we may be a kind of first fruits of His Creatures.

"Know this."

Saturday, August 14, 1999
Our Lady of Grace Catholic Church

Praise be to Jesus! For Jesus is Saviour, Redeemer, and Reconciler of all nations.

Jesus said: "My beloved children, in these closing days of summer and you start to become anxious as you see the seasons changing briskly, the fall ending shortly and the winter approaching rapidly, you anticipate this 'new millennium' with a serious anxiousness to impending disasters.

"Has my Mother not come to you for years, preparing you, pleading with you for change? For those few who have listened, though at times you may have lapsed, you understood the importance and necessity of those pleas. Had you not, the disasters, earthquakes, tornadoes, hurricanes, flooding, torrential rains and fires would have been more serious. Do you not yet realize, my children, the seriousness of the consequences your world has degraded itself to? Do you not see my Justice or are you just unwilling to see my Justice?

"What is it left that you do not understand? Have I not told you more than once "evil begets evil?" You should now pray for My intervention.

"Oh, my children, I as your Jesus of mercy, wants only to give you my love. Why do you deny this, my love, for worldly enticements? Was it not I who shed my blood for each one of you? This is how much I love you! How much do you love me? How much do your children love me? Do your children even know of me? And, if not, why is that, my children?

"Open, beloved one of my heart, to Daniel 2, Chapter 2, V 1 through 49."

1 In the second year of his reign, King Nebuchadnezzar had a dream which left his spirit no rest and robbed him of his sleep.

2 So he ordered the magicians, enchanters, sorcerers, and Chaldeans be summoned to interpret the dream for him. When they cam and presented themselves to the king.

3 he said to them, "I had a dream which will allow my spirit no rest until I know what it means."

4 The Chaldeans answered to king (Aramaic): "O king, live forever! Tell your servants the dream and we will give its meaning."

5 The king answered the Chaldeans, "This is what I have decided: unless you tell me the dream and its meaning, you shall be cut to pieces and your houses destroyed.

6 But if you tell me the dream and its meaning, you shall receive from me gifts and presents and great honors. Now tell me the dream and its meaning."

7 Again they answered, "Let the king tell his servants the dream and we will give its meaning."

8 But the king replied: "I know for certain that you are bargaining for time, since you know what I have decided.

9 If you do not tell me the dream, there can be but one decree for you. You have framed a false and deceitful interpretation to present me with till the crisis is past. Tell me the dream, therefore, that I may be sure that you can also give its correct interpretation."

10 The Chaldeans answered the king: "There is not a man on earth who can do what you ask, O king; never has any king, however great and mighty, asked such a thing of any magician, enchanter, or Chaldean.

11 What you demand, O king, is too difficult, there is no one who can tell it to the king except the gods who do not dwell among men."

12 At this the king became violently angry and ordered all the wise men of Babylon to be put to death.

¹³ When the decree was issued that the wise men should be slain, Daniel and his companions were also sought out.

¹⁴ Then Daniel prudently took counsel with Arioch, the captain of the king's guard, who had set out to kill the wise men of Babylon:

¹⁵ "O officer of the king," he asked, "what is the reason for this harsh order from the king?" When Arioch told him,

¹⁶ Daniel went and asked for time from the king, that he might give him the interpretation.

¹⁷ Daniel went home and informed his companions Hananiah, Mishael, and Azariah,

¹⁸ that they might implore the mercy of the God of heaven in regard to this mystery, so that Daniel and his companions might not perish with the rest of the wise men of Babylon.

¹⁹ During the night the mystery was revealed to Daniel in a vision, and he blessed the God of heaven:

²⁰ *"Blessed be the name of God forever and ever, for wisdom and power are his.*

²¹ *He causes the changes of the times and seasons, makes kings and unmakes them. He gives wisdom to the wise and knowledge to those who understand.*

²² *He reveals deep and hidden things and knows what is in the darkness, for the light dwells with him.*

²³ *To you, O God of my fathers, I give thanks and praise, because you have given me wisdom and power. Now you have shown me wisdom and power. Now you have shown me what we asked of you, you have made known to us the king's dream."*

²⁴ So Daniel went to Arioch, whom the king had appointed to destroy the wise men of Babylon, and said to him, "Do not put the wise men of Babylon to death. Bring me before the king, and I will tell him the interpretation of the dream." Arioch quickly brought Daniel to the king and said,

²⁵ "I have found a man among the Judean captives who can give the interpretation to the king."

²⁶ The king asked Daniel, whose name was Belteshazzar, "Can you tell me the dream that I had, and its meaning?"

²⁷ In the king's presence Daniel made this reply: "The mystery about which the king has inquired, the wise men,

enchanter's, magicians and astrologers could not explain to the king.

²⁸ But there is a God in heaven who reveals mysterys and he has shown King Nebuchadnezzar what is to happen in days to come; this was the dream you saw as you lay in bed.

²⁹ To you in your bed came thoughts about what is to be;

³⁰ To me also this mystery has been revealed; not that I am wiser than any other living person, but in order that its meaning may be made known to the king, that you may understand the thoughts in your own mind.

³¹ "In your vision, O king, you saw a statue, very large and exceedingly bright, terrifying in appearance as it stood before you.

³² The head of the statue was pure gold, its chest and arms were silver, its belly and thighs bronze,

³³ the legs iron, its feet partly iron and partly tile.

³⁴ While you looked at the statue, a stone which was hewn from a mountain without a hand being put to it, struck its iron and tile feet, breaking them in pieces.

³⁵ The iron, tile, bronze, silver, and gold all crumbled at once, fine as the chaff on the threshing floor in summer, and the wind blew them away without leaving a trace. But the stone that struck the statue became a great mountain and filled the whole earth.

³⁶ "This was the dream; the interpretation we shall also give in the king's presence.

³⁷ You, O king, are the king of kings; to you the God of heaven has given dominion and strength, power and glory;

³⁸ men, wild beasts, and birds of the air, wherever they may dwell, he has handed over to you making you ruler over them all; you are the head of gold.

³⁹ Another kingdom shall take your place, inferior to yours, then a third kingdom, of bronze, which shall rule over the whole earth.

⁴⁰ There shall be a fourth kingdom, strong as iron; it shall break in pieces and subdue all these others, just as iron breaks in pieces and crushes everything else.

⁴¹ The feet and toes you saw, partly of potter's tile and partly of iron, mean that it shall be a divided kingdom, but yet have

some of the hardness of iron. As you saw the iron mixed with clay tile,

[42] and the toes partly iron and partly tile, the kingdom shall be partly strong and partly fragile.

[43] The iron mixed with clay tile means that they shall seal their alliances by intermarriage, but they shall not stay united, any more than iron mixes with clay.

[44] In the lifetime of those kings the God of heaven will set up a kingdom that shall never be destroyed or delivered up to another people; rather, it shall break in pieces all these kingdoms and put an end to them, and it shall stand forever.

[45] That is the meaning of the stone you saw hewn from the mountain without a hand being put to it, which broke in pieces the tile, iron, bronze, silver, and gold. The great God has revealed to the king what shall be in the future; this is exactly what you dreamed, and its meaning is sure."

[46] Then King Nebuchadnezzar fell down and worshiped Daniel and ordered sacrifice and incense offered to him.

[47] To Daniel the king said, "Truly your God is the God of gods and Lord of kings and a revealer of mysteries; that is why you were able to reveal this mystery."

[48] He advances Daniel to a high post, gave him many generous presents, made him ruler of the whole province of Babylon and chief prefect over all the wise men of Babylon.

[49] At Daniel's request the king made Shadrach, Meshach, and Abednego administrators of the province of Babylon, while Daniel himself remained at the king's court.

Friday, August 29, 1999
Eucharistic Adoration, Feast of St. Monica
Immaculate Conception Catholic Church
Albuquerque, New Mexico

Praise be to Jesus! For Jesus is Lord, Saviour, Redeemer, and Reconciler of all nations.

Jesus said: "Welcome, my beloved ones, daughters of my Heart, on this special feast day of another close to my Heart, who devotedly and consistently prayed for her family. Not only became a great saint, but her son as well, a doctor of the church. This, her story, should give hope to all parents. As my beloved Father has spoken to you, know that no parent's prayers go unheard. The evil one would love all to think this, but it is another of the evil ones tactics, using the love of the parents for their children, encouraging the parents' despair over their children's souls. This is not from the Triune God, my beloved ones, *never* despair over the souls of your loved ones, on the contrary, *Pray* for them, and then release them with faith, trust and total surrender to your Triune God. For as I have stated many times, no parent's prayers ever go unheard.

"As you release your loved ones in prayer to your Triune God, then pray for all others and their children and especially for all those children who have no one praying for them. As you do this, you will begin to see the mercy and love of your Triune God. Because then you will focus, not on despair, but on trustful surrender, which is what all must do in order to stay in the presence of your Triune God. This, my children, will take you onto the path of sanctity, which all my children must strive for. In order to obtain the spiritual life of sanctity, you must all desire to be a saint, for it is only possible that as saints you will reside here in heaven with your Triune God. Focus on me, my children, focus only on me, then your desires for sanctity will become constant in your life and through your love and example, you will not only draw your loved ones to me and to eternal glory, but will also draw all you come in contact with. All my beloved children, focus on me and you focus on love and life eternal. Not only for yourselves, but for your children and for all others around you. I love you, my children.

"Open, my beloved one, to 2 Corinthians, Chapter 1, V 3."

³ **Blessed be the God and Father of our Lord Jesus Christ, the Father of compassion and God of all encouragement**
⁴ **Who encourages us in our every affliction, so that we may be able to encourage those who are in any affliction with the encouragement with which we ourselves are encouraged by God.**
⁵ **For as Christ's sufferings overflow to us, so through Christ does our encouragement also overflow.**
⁶ **If we are afflicted, it is for your encouragement and salvation; if we are encouraged, it is for your encourage-**

ment, which enables you to endure the same sufferings that we suffer.

⁷ Our hope for you is firm, for we know that as you share in the sufferings, you also share in the encouragement.

⁸ We do not want you to be unaware, brothers, of the affliction that came to us in the province of Asia; we were utterly weighed down beyond our strength, so that we despaired eve on life.

⁹ Indeed, we had accepted within ourselves the sentence of death, that we might trust not in ourselves but in God who raises the dead.

¹⁰ He rescued us from such great danger of death, and he will continue to rescue us; in Him we have put our hope (that) He will also rescue us again.

¹¹ as you help us with prayer, so that thanks may be given by many on our behalf for the gift granted us through the prayers of many.

Approved by Reverend Paul Caporali

Monday, September 20, 1999
Eucharistic Adoration
Mary, Star of the Sea

Praise be to Jesus! For Jesus is Lord, Saviour, Redeemer of all nations.

Jesus said: "Welcome, my beloved little one, daughter of my heart. Thank you for coming to receive my teachings. How my children desire materialism, they do not see the spiritual realm I so wish to fill them with, on the contrary they have become numb to the calling, the pleading, I your Jesus of mercy have so willingly given to man. Instead they seek the riches of the world the materialism, security of their jobs, homes, finances. And yet the security of prayer, the Holy Sacraments, holiness, these do not enter into their minds. The children of the world do not seek security for their souls. As you see the pictures of hurricanes, tornadoes, earthquakes, fires, these torrents shown on the daily news, the ugliness and destruction that is deteriorating the world. This is what their souls look like to me, my beloved one. The corruption and destruction of their souls, leading them to straight to the eternal fire, but do they listen to the many warnings I have given? Do they open their hearts to the many words I have spoken? To the many words my holy Mother has given?"

(Patsy: But Jesus, many say the words you speak are just inspiration that we have in our hearts, that most of these teachings and messages are just repetition in different ways. Why can't you give them a sign that they can believe?)

"All my little ones, the words given so many times go to deaf ears, are the signs given they do not want to hear."

(Patsy: but maybe they don't understand the signs, Jesus, sometimes it is very hard for me to understand.)

"My little one, beloved one of my heart, that is why I ask you for more prayer time. Why I ask all my children to spend more time with me in prayer. The evil one has blinded so many with the materialistic ways of the world. My children rush to work, rush for sports events, rush to theatres, shopping centers, rush to sit in front of the television. They make time to sit in coffeehouses, to relax with music. The vacations, outings that they plan. How many include me in any of that? How many make plans which include me, your Jesus, who died on the cross for you? How many include thanksgiving to the Almighty Father who created this world? Who created man himself. How evil my children have chosen to forget their Triune God. You see my beloved one, it's mans "free will" that has made the choice to put the Triune God out of their minds, out of their daily lives. This all through their free will.

"Open, my beloved one of my heart, to Ezekiel, Ch. 11 and 21."

Approved by Reverend Paul Caporali

October 14, 1999
Eucharistic Adoration, Thursday 11:00 AM

Praise be to Jesus for Jesus is Lord, Saviour, Redeemer, Reconciler of all nations.

Jesus said: "I am your Jesus of mercy, my beloved little one, as I am your Jesus of justice! My heart cries out to mankind! As we spoke earlier, many teachings I have given, many messengers I have sent and yet the evil continues to stagnate the heart of mankind. Many continue to stay in the error of sin.

"You, beloved daughter of my heart, I have allowed to feel the perilousness and hopelessness of which man had brought upon themselves through their evil desecrations and manipulations with which they continue. Not only do they desecrate the love and purity of my holy Mother, but also the eternal and perfect love of your Triune God, who allowed the death of your Jesus crucified for all humanity! This is truth undeniable! Yet decay of the souls of mankind through the continuous error of sin brings forth destruction through lies instead of truths! Hate instead of love! Maliciousness instead of kindness! Unrest of peace! Yet all question why the world is in the condition it is in!

"As my son [Protestant minister speaking at the hospital], spoke of 'Cause and Effect,' the 'cause' of destruction due to the 'effect' of sin — 'cause' of suffering in the world to 'effect' of sin — which I your Triune God allows! For all is done through the Holy Will of the Father!

"My children, through their free will, deny my truths and continue in the error of sin! In order that they may see the error of sin, I may allow, as the perfect Will of the Father who knows best, may allow suffering! For nothing is done without the Will of the Father! If my children so allow, through their own free will to 'surrender' to the holy and perfect Will of the Father, then as the Father's perfect plan was to create all in the image and likeness of your Triune God and live in His perfect Will which would 'cause' through the surrender to the Holy Will of the Father the 'effect' which would then have been, the 'perfect' peace, love and truths in this world. But as you see, my beloved one, humanity chooses not the 'perfect Will' of your Triune God but the imperfect free will of man, which is bringing suffering, destruction to the soul of man, upheaval and chaos to the world.

"What are the 'causes' and 'effect' of the choices you have made, my children, through your own 'free will' which your Triune God has allowed?

"Yes, my beloved little one, I am love! I am mercy, but I am also justice!

"Now, beloved one of my heart, open to Daniel, Ch 3:"

²⁶ "Blessed are you, and praise worthy, O Lord, the God of our fathers, and glorious forever is your name.

²⁷ For you are just in all you have done; all your deeds are faultless, all your ways always right, and all your judgments proper.

²⁸ You have executed proper judgments in all that you have brought upon us and upon Jerusalem, the holy city of our fathers. By a proper judgment you have done all this because of our sins;

²⁹ For we have sinned and transgressed by departing from you, and we hade done every kind of evil.

³⁰ Your commandments we have not heeded or observed, nor have we done as you ordered us for your good.

³¹ Therefore all you have brought upon us, all you have done to us, you have done by a proper judgment.

³² You have handed us over to our enemies, lawless and hateful rebels; to an unjust king, the worst in all the world.

³³ Now we cannot open our mouths; we your servants, who revere you, have become a shame and a reproach.

³⁴ For your name's sake, do not deliver us up forever, or make void your covenant.

Approved by Reverend Paul Caporali

October 21, 1999
Eucharistic Adoration

Praise be to Jesus for Jesus is Lord, Saviour, Reconciler of all nations.

Jesus said: "Peace, my beloved one, daughter of my heart. Thank you for coming to spend this time with me. How I yearn for all my children to return to me, their saviour, their redeemer. I want to give them the graces so necessary for their souls. That they may see with the eyes of their soul! hear with the ears of their soul! But they remain blinded by the error of sin which prevents their reasoning to what is truth.

"Oh beloved little one, daughter of my heart, as you see the spiritual nourishment through the grace given as you come to seek me daily in attending the holy sacrifice of the Mass, you realize the

313

importance of these graces given as the trials sometimes become overwhelming. But as you open your heart surrendering your will to my Holy Will, knowing that I am the only answer. I am truth. This you have seen for yourself, as when you are feeling the heaviness of the weight of the world and you think it is just too heavy, the evil one preys upon this weakness but you call out to me and I draw you ever so close to me!

"How many times my beloved Fr. Luke spoke to you of not going by feelings! Yes, my child he taught you well, for one needs to learn that in this world of corruption, myths, sin and error, it will only be by the graces given through the Holy Sacraments, prayer, surrender, faith in the mercy and justice of your Triune God, that mans existence will survive. Had it not been for the many prayers and pleadings of my holy mother the hand of justice would have already consummated the force of destruction and most of the world's population been lost to the evil one!

"Open to Acts, Ch 10."

[34] Then Peter proceeded to speak and said, "In Truth I see that God shows no partiality.

[35] Rather, in every nation whoever fears Him and acts uprightly is acceptable to Him.

[36] You know the word that He send to the Israelites as he proclaimed peace through Jesus Christ Who is Lord of All.

Baruch Ch 2:

[15] Justice is the Lord, our God, and we today are flushed with shame, we men of Judah and citizens of Jerusalem

[16] That we, with our kings and rulers, and priests and prophets, and with our fathers

[17] Have sinned in the Lord's sight

[18] And disobeyed Him. We have neither heeded the voice of the Lord, our God, not followed the precepts which the Lord set before us

[19] from the time the Lord led our fathers out of the land of Egypt until the present day, we have been disobedient to the Lord, our God, and only too ready to disregard his voice.

²⁰ And the evils and the curse which the Lord enjoined upon Moses, his servant, at the time he led our fathers forth from the land of Egypt to give us the land flowing with milk and honey, cling to us even today

²¹ for we did not heed the voice of the Lord, our God, in all the words of the prophets whom he sent us

²² But each one of us went off after the devices of our own wicked hearts, served other gods, and did evil in the sight of the Lord, or God.

Approved by Reverend Paul Caporali

Friday, November 5, 1999
Eucharistic Adoration

The icon spoken of below is the one requested by Mama Mary in the December 11, 1998 message. The icon arrived from Josyp Terelya on November 4, 1999, the feast day of St. Charles Borromeo. It was also blessed on November 4, 1999 by the Most Reverend Bishop Joseph Sartoris, auxiliary bishop of Los Angeles, San Pedro Region at Little Company of Mary Hospital Chapel.

Jesus said: "Peace, beloved daughter of my Heart. Praise be to Jesus for Jesus is Lord, Saviour, Redeemer, Reconciler of all nations. Thank you child, for coming to spend this time with me."

(Thank you Jesus, for having the Bishop Bless the icon.)

Jesus said: "My little one, my beloved son Josyp has pleased me in this image he has drawn with his love to honor me. As I have spoken to you, this icon requested by my beloved mother has been given special blessings as I have promised. Those of my children who place this icon in their homes will not only have the grace of fortitude and perseverance but also as the come with love to Me before this icon will receive all the promises given to my beloved St. Margaret Mary who was given special promises to those who would honor the beloved image of my Sacred Heart!

Josyp has painted this icon with my most wounded Sacred Heart and the crown of thorns piercing my heart showing the rays extending forth. Josyp has captured the beauty of the many graces represented in these rays extending forth from my Heart which I desire to give to all who come to me with love, sincerity and a surrender of their will to my Holy Will! Oh, my beloved children of my most wounded Sacred Heart, please accept this gift of my love through this image requested from the love of my Holy Mother to each of you! Are you willing my children? I love you, your Jesus of mercy.

"Open, my little one, to Psalm 57."

Twelve promises to St. Margaret Mary Alacoque

1. All graces necessary in their state of life.
2. Peace in their homes.
3. Comfort in all their sufferings
4. Safe refuge against all snares of their enemies in life, and above all, in death.
5. Bestow abundant blessings upon all their undertakings.
6. Sinners shall find in my heart the source of aninfinite ocean of mercy.
7. Fervent souls shall mount to high perfection.
8. Bless every home in which the image of Sacred Heart is honored.
9. Tepid souls shall become fervent.
10. Will give to priests the gift of ouching the most hardened hearts.
11. Those sho promote this devotion shall have their names written in my heart, never to be effaced.
12. To all who receive the Sacrament of Communion on the first Friday of the month for nine consecutive months, the grace of final repentance.

May the peace and love of the Holy Family be wit you and you always in the hearts of Jesus and Mama Mary.

Approved by Reverend Paul Caporali

Friday, November 12, 1999
Eucharistic Adoration

Praise be to Jesus for Jesus is Lord, Saviour, Redeemer of all nations.

Jesus said: "Beloved children of My heart, you have been in prayer over this request I have made through "His Teachings Ministry." My beloved little one has known in her heart this desire of my house of prayer. A retreat center and retirement center to care for my beloved priests. Many times after they are not able to continue their duties on a constant basis, or are restricted due to health or age, they find themselves alone with no one to care for them, after so many years of service to you, my children. Now is the time I come before you asking as is said in my word, to those of you who have been given much, much is expected. Will you now answer my call? I know all that you have returned to me with love and continue to return to me with love. Yes, this is one of many times I have requested my house of prayer and how many have responded with a willingness? As your Jesus had nowhere but a stable to come into this world, I came anyway just for you! As I had only straw and not a king's pillow to lay my head, I came anyway because I love you. And when it came time to die on a cross for you, I did not refuse but extended my arms and allowed the nail to pierce each hand because I love you. Now I see my beloved sons who have given of themselves for me, that you would have the opportunity of receiving me alive, body, blood, soul and divinity in the most holy sacrament of the Eucharist, for you because I love you. The passage given to you in scripture to prepare this place for my priests, are you willing? How many more times shall I seek shelter, as my holy parents sought shelter on the day of my birth? Are you willing, my beloved children of my heart? Will you build my house of prayer?

"Open, beloved one of my heart, to Ezekiel, Ch. 44:"

²⁸ They shall have no inheritance. I am their inheritance; you shall give them no property in Israel, for I am theirproperty

²⁹ They shall eat the cereal offering, the sin offering, and the guilt offering, whatever is under the ban in Israel shall be theirs.

30 All the choicest first fruits of every king, shall belong to the priests; likewise the best of your dough shall give to the priest to bring a blessing down upon your house.

Ezekiel, Ch. 45

1 When you apportion the land into inheritances, you shall set apart a sacred tract of land for the Lord, twenty-five thousand cubits, surrounded by a free space of fifty cubits, shall be assigned to the sanctuary.

Jesus Said: "This, my beloved, shall be my resting place, the holy of holies, are you willing, or will I seek another place to rest as my holy parents had to?"

4 This shall be the Sacred part of the land belonging to the Priests, the ministers of the Sanctuary, who draw near to minister to the Lord; It shall be a place for their homes and pasture land for their cattle.

Jesus said: "Which of you hear these words in their hearts and close your door to he who seeks shelter?

"I love you, my children. Thank you for responding to my call."

Approved by Reverend Paul Caporali

Sunday, November 28, 1999

Praise be to Jesus for Jesus is Lord, Almighty, King, Saviour, Redeemer.

Jesus said: "Oh, beloved one of my heart, many the graces I have bestowed upon my children! Graces which so many have refused! Did I not offer the grace to those who would but open their hearts to my words, so simple a request I beseeched from my children. To spend one hour with me in Eucharistic Adoration, the holy Sacrifice of the Mass on the same day with my presentation, where they would then not only hear the words of my beloved mother but spend this time in meditation with me! These three requests for a release of their family, friends, acquaintances, souls on the same day they responded with love to these of my requests! Why did they not respond? Did you not realize, my children, how the prayers of the souls, the saints in heaven would exclaim with praise and glory their intercession for you, my children, who remain in this earthly abyss which draws you away from me! Do you not realize this immense gift of my love, which I desired to give to those of your family whose souls suffer in purgatory? What blinds you, my children, to these gifts? Is it your lack of faith in my love for you? What draws you away from me, your Jesus of mercy who died on the cross for you? Oh, beloved one of my heart, because you have pleaded with me for another chance for my children to respond to these gifts I desire to bring forth, I will not yet take away this gift. I will await the response of my children. They have a free will! I love you, my children. Thank you, my beloved daughter, for responding to my call.

"Now open to Job, Ch. 15 V. 2 through 35."

Job, Chapter 15 Verses 2 - 35

² **Should a wise man answer with airy opinions, or puff himself up with wind?**

³ **Should he argue in speech which does not avail, and in words which are to no profit?**

⁴ **You in fact do away with piety, and you lessen devotion toward God,**

⁵ **Because your wickedness instructs your mouth, and you choose to speak like the crafty.**

⁶ **Your own mouth condemns you, not I; you own lips refute you.**

⁷ **Are you indeed the first-born of mankind, or were you brought forth before the hills?**

⁸ **Are you privy to the counsels of God, and do you restrict wisdom to yourself?**

⁹ **What do you know that we do not know? What intelligence have you which we have not?**

¹⁰ **There are gray-haired old men among us more advanced in years than your father.**

¹¹ **Are the consolations of God not enough for you, and speech that deals gently with you?**

¹² Why do your notions carry you away, and why do your eyes blink,

¹³ So that you turn your anger against God and let such words escape your mouth!

¹⁴ What is a man that he should be blameless, one born of woman that he should be righteous?

¹⁵ If in his holy ones God places no confidence, and if the heavens are not clean in his sight,

¹⁶ How much less so is the abominable, the corrupt man, who drinks in iniquity like water!

¹⁷ I will show you, if you listen to me; what I have seen I will tell—

¹⁸ What wise men relate and have not contradicted since the days of their fathers,

¹⁹ To whom alone the land was given, when no foreigner moved among them.

²⁰ The wicked man is in torment all his days, and limited years are in store for the tyrant;

²¹ The sound of terrors is in his ears; when all is prosperous, the spoiler comes upon him.

²² He despairs of escaping the darkness, and looks ever for the sword;

²³ A wanderer, food for the vultures, he knows that his destruction is imminent.

²⁴ By day the darkness fills him with dread; distress and anguish overpower him.

²⁵ Because he has stretched out his hand against God and bade defiance to the Almighty,

²⁶ One shall rush sternly upon him with the stout bosses of his shield, like a king prepared for thecharge.

²⁷ Because he has blinded himself with his crassness, padding his loins with fat,

²⁸ He shall dwell in ruinous cities, in houses that are deserted, That are crumbling into clay

²⁹ with no shadow to lengthen over the ground. He shall not be rich, and his possessions shall not endure;

³⁰ A flame shall wither him up in his early growth, and with the wind his blossoms shall disappear.

³¹ for vain shall be his bartering.

³² His stalk shall wither before its time, and his branches shall be green no more.

³³ He shall be like a vine that sheds its grapes unripened, and like an olive tree casting off itsbloom.

³⁴ For the breed of the impious shall be sterile, and fire shall consume the tents of extortioners.

³⁵ They conceive malice and bring forth emptiness; they give birth to failure.

It was this morning that Jesus came to me asking me to open my heart in prayer for His children. He told me Hewas taking away the grace of the release of the souls in purgatory because His children have not responded to the graces He was so willing to give. I asked Him to give us another chance but He did not answer. It wasn't until He came again requesting that I take this teaching that I knew He was going to give us another chance.

Note: The three requests that Jesus refers to includes having a presentation, Mass and Eucharistic Adoration all on the same day.

May the love and mercy be with you always,

Patsy Soto

Approved by Reverend Paul Caporali

Message on 1-6-2000
Feast of Blessed Andre Bissette

The little Brother who worked many, many miracles, who Patsy has been devoted to for many years, on the special day Mama Mary came to Patsy with a message from her Son Jesus to tell her and her husband that this ministry was going on a "new journey." A journey not only that Mama Mary would lead them through, but also, "carry" them through.

Little did Patsy know, that it was also in preparation for what was going to come.

For the past almost fourteen years, Patsy has been writing the messages given to her "for the world," but as of yesterday, 1-7 of the year 2000, Jesus has told Patsy that there will no longer be given to Patsy, messages to the world.

Jesus said: "I have given messages to my children, but they have not listened, so the messages to the world at this time will stop" (through Patsy).

Patsy then asked Jesus, "Does this mean they will stop through every one else or just me?"

Jesus said: "Do not focus on other ministries, focus on me. I will continue to give you messages privately, and for certain of my children. I will continue to make my presence known during the presentations."

Patsy then asked: "Does this mean you're taking away the grace of the release of the souls from purgatory?"

Jesus then said: "At this moment, I am only taking away the messages to the world. I will give you a final message that you will place behind the image of the icon of my Holy Mother painted by my beloved Josyp Terelya. This image I requested of my beloved Mother."

Approved by Fr. John C. Hughes

January 7, 2000
Icon of Mary Message

Praise be to Jesus, for Jesus is Lord, Saviour, Redeemer and Reconciler of all nations.

Jesus said: "Thank you, beloved daughter of my heart, for opening your heart for my words. You are having difficulty writing because of the injury to your hand. Thank you, my daughter for trying.

"I have given yet another gift to my children. This icon which my beloved Josyp has painted with love. A gift to the world.

"Look into our eyes, my children. See the love and mercy I and my Holy Mother desire to give you.

Our hearts, your sanctuary, your protection. Do not refuse.

Approved by Fr. John C. Hughes

Jesus had requested Josyp to paint these icons showing His "Sacred Heart," and Our Lady's "Immaculate Heart." They are a pair now, which in these times, Jesus has promised a "special protection" to all who place them in their homes and venerate them and pray before them. As He said, "look into the eyes" and see the love and mercy waiting for us.

*These Icons are copyrighted to "His Teachings Ministry."

To purchase go to the web site:

http://www.post1.com/home/avemaria

or write to:

His Teachings Ministry
873 West 24th #1
San Pedro, CA 90731

Telephone: (310) 519-1507